CLEANING AUGEAN STABLES

Examining Drama's Strategies

Leon Katz

Cleaning Augean Stables: Examining Drama's Strategies
by Leon Katz

ISBN-13: 978-1479297092 – Create Space Edition

Leon Katz
18050 Calvert Street
Encino, CA 91316
leonk1919@yahoo.com

Contents

Preface
Cleaning Augean Stables

A greatly revered Professor of Philosophy at CCNY was known for his love of his students and his annihilating skepticism. Teaching the history of Western philosophy, he reduced all the major systems to flawed syllogisms, and so hobbled and eventually destroyed their efficacy that he left students with nothing to hold on to but pristine intellectual rigor and universal doubt. For this benefaction, he was habitually brought up short and asked, "Professor Cohen" – he was Morris Raphael Cohen of the razor-sharp intellect and the healing smile – "if you destroy every system in philosophic tradition, what positive values or creed do you offer in their place?" to which he invariably replied, "When Hercules cleaned out the Augean stables, it was a day's work."

Several generations of his graduates were left with a sort of guilt-driven life-vow. When confronted by any set of words, any at all, they were bound to belabor them, even if silently, with cauterizing scrutiny like his own. If they were words, they were in stables, and needed to be cleaned. Just as Socrates' sacred task was to belabor the unexamined life, so he, and now we, were sworn to belabor unexamined thought. Depending on the thickets of unreason through which we tracked in later professional years, the habit of sneering in advance at what was said, either diminished or flourished. In the hard or respectable sciences like nuclear physics, it tended to wait on evidence before pouncing. In the soft or TV sciences like psychology, it flourished.

For myself, having wandered into the fields of dramatic theory on the one hand and practical playwriting on the other, it flourished considerably. Feeding that original guilt-propelled vow

1

were mounds of unexamined thought lying overripe in the stables of Playwriting *Principles*, and, almost of their own accord, the weapons for their cauterizing came to hand. How it fell out:

I once had the daunting task of curating a collection of five thousand plays produced in the American theater from roughly 1800 to 1950 ranging from the stillborn to the celebrated hits of their day. Leafing through that mountain of scripts, it became obvious that every couple of decades or so, there was a subtle shift in the pious verities that controlled the psychology, the morality, and the very structure of acceptable, not to speak of hugely successful, plays. The movement from one set of verities to another was glacial, but over the course of a century and a half, it was, to say the least, glaringly detectable. What was equally glaring was that the critical shibboleths of any period, while meaning to answer to the basic values of the drama, have in fact little to do with drama itself, but answer to another need: to see reflected in popular plays the wisdom of the moment as it solidifies in the cliché marketplace. The "craft" that is imposed on playwrights in any period, including our own, is sometimes little more than a translation into critical jargon of the moral, social and psychological pieties of the moment. But they become templates, and any practicing playwright will tell you that – crude or irrelevant or worn thin as they may be – putting together a play that's said to "work" means essentially squeezing the play's shape and thought into one of those templates.

And vestigial memory shapes those templates too – vestiges of those Ancients – essentially Aristotle's *Poetics* sloppily understood but reverenced. They too warp and chain playwriting models and add grossly to their banality. The most harmful "guiding principles" are also the most validated. To enumerate: (1) that conflict is the drama's universal principle, in fact, its very essence; (2) that the structural unity of a play must be an action; (3) that Aristotle's Poetics remains, with a couple of minor updates, the functional arbiter of the drama's "rules;" (4) that characters, to win real embrace, must be empathetic; (5) that characters are on a journey, and should, after learning something, change; (6) that characters are "believable" if they're (heeding Aristotle) "consistent;" (7) that plots are best if they're "character-driven;" (8) that meaning (i.e. message) is more endearing if it's positive.

There are more shibboleths to be dealt with in the chapters that follow, but these are now the most pervasive, the most persistent, and the most constricting for playwrights who have learned their lessons too well. In themselves, none of them are false; that's not their harm. It's that none of them are universally applicable, nor remotely so, and none banish their opposites or contradictories. They are strategies among multiple strategies, on occasion useful, and often not. What's essentially wrong with them is that they answer questions before they're asked. They settle the question of appropriate strategies before they're approached or examined. They exclude the particularity of insights into the nature of character itself, structure itself, meaning itself, and encourage every play to become inherently the same play, and every consequence of meaning the same consequence with the same repetition of affect.

What audiences – or to put it more broadly, what cultures – assent to in their fictions is governed by what they truly, though sometimes secretly and sometimes unconsciously, assent to in belief. Those profound, unspoken beliefs are finally the only compelling source for the shaping of their compositions. But though they may be profoundly fixed in time, they are also and equally profoundly alterable. And since they are currently, in our own time, not one, and from period to period are certainly not one, there develop many implicit models for shaping plays. The history of playwriting is in part the history of the preservation, but at the same time the history of the subversion, of its successive models. And because of the radical alterations of belief structures and assumptions about the nature and even efficacy of existence itself, overall models that have lasted in some measure since the Renaissance, and those revived from classical times, have been subjected many times to studied overhaul.

But since vestigial belief can be a comfort and novel belief a chore, to separate the still useful from the forgettable, we'll examine the anomalies of the familiar "playwriting principles" by looking carefully at the traditions that still overwhelmingly linger, asking the obvious questions about their logic, their common sense, their continuing relevance and continuing value. That done, we'll look at the many alternative strategies that have developed within those familiar templates, and especially at examples of contemporary playwriting and screenwriting that have not only creatively but sometimes brilliantly escaped those parameters altogether. We won't, then, be recommending another "model" template, but instead, examining loads of alternative playwriting strategies with this implicit suggestion to playwrights: those that seem particularly congenial to you are likely to prove right.

Let's go back now to the very beginning, back, so to speak, to kindergarten, to look at the way plays conventionally progress from one moment to the next, how in their simplest form – plays with a single action and a single protagonist – move most familiarly from their beginning to their end. We'll describe that model with careful sobriety, and then review its inherent assumptions, examining what's missing, what's right and what's wrong with it, and cleanse if possible the more cluttered stables of that standard plot pattern: the "Action" model.

⁎

CHAPTER 1

PLOT STRUCTURE: THE "ACTION" MODEL

Dramatic narrative has two functions: to establish a logical progression for its action, and at the same time to incorporate a predicated design for the emotional response of its audience to that narrative. The basic structure of the "action" model – the single protagonist engaged in a single action – will be looked at both for its structure and for the traditional assumptions that lie behind it. Side by side with its plot, there is the second structure, as important, and in some eras more important, than the plot itself. We'll look at how its strategy is calculated to heighten the spectator's emotional receptivity

THE FORMAL UNIT

Compare: The complete formal unit of an argument is a *syllogism*. The complete formal unit of a statement is a *sentence*. The complete formal unit of a conventional drama is traditionally an *action*. The first has three parts – a major premise, a minor premise, and a conclusion. The sentence has two: a subject and a predicate. An action, like a syllogism, has three – a beginning, middle, and end. Just as arguments are made up of a string of syllogisms, one leading – hopefully, inevitably – to the next, so a play is made up of a string of actions, the one – hopefully, inevitably – leading to the next. It's the basic language, the discourse, of conventional drama.

The key moment in an action – its middle term – is the moment of change. We ask – the first thing a child or anyone asks – concerning any story or any event is: What happened? Or to put it another way: What changed? Change, the going from one state of affairs to another and the moment of change, its defining moment, is the essence of an action. If we imagine a state of affairs in which everything is static, its pictorial interest might be very high; its dramatic interest is non-existent. Conventionally, that a thing *is*, is of no dramatic interest; that a thing changes, is everything.

Of the three terms in an action, the beginning constitutes a particular state of affairs, the middle a change, or reversal, that alters that state, often to its opposite, the end is that new state which becomes the beginning, or the first term, of the succeeding action. It is the stringing together of such units of action that produces most – not all – the progressions in a play.

REVERSALS

Traditionally, then, an action has three parts – (1) an initial situation; (2) a reversal; (3) a consequence. By far, the most significant is the middle term: the reversal. It is one of the central concepts of structure in Aristotle's *Poetics* in which it is characterized not, as we're using the term here, as a rapid moment-to-moment device used continuously throughout the drama, but as the climactic moment of the entire tragedy, when the reversal (the *peripeteia*) of the protagonist's fortune is brought about by a recognition (*anagnorisis*,) [1] a discovery, of an unknown fact of so radical a nature as to bring about the tragedy's catastrophe. Best, says Aristotle, is the recognition of a family relation, that being the most affecting, he imagines, for the spectator. His prime example is particularly convincing: Oedipus' discovery, on the utterance of the messenger's final word, which confirms for him his inadvertent double guilt of parricide and incest: "The criminal you are seeking,[2] my lord, is you," which causes Oedipus' instantaneous, total recognition of his reversal-of-fortune, perhaps the most powerful dramatic reversal in the canon of Western drama.

STRUCTURING "PROGRESSIVE" ACTION[3]

Classically, Action is structured in one of two ways: as Progressive Action, or as Retrogressive Action. Let's focus first on the most uncluttered, the simplest kind: progressive action which features a single leading protagonist, in which the action is tightly structured, the progression is headlong, and there is little room for divergence from its course – the kind of play ideally envisioned by Aristotle's dictum that "plot is the soul of tragedy,"[4] and in which "character," most especially the leading character, is entirely secondary to the plot's action, and in fact is wholly there to serve it.   Character so defined can be comprehended as wholly recapitulating the overall action structure of the play – is, in fact, its instance, its exemplification.   Character so understood fits comfortably and precisely into the design, the parts, and the terms, of the action itself.   Let's distinguish its parts, and spell out the sense in which character mirrors the plot, *is* the plot.

Overall pattern: The play as a whole, as it concerns its central character, is a tale with one major reversal: The protagonist begins in a particular frame of mind, condition or situation. He ends in exactly the opposite frame of mind or situation, or, having gone through a complete journey to the opposite condition, returns to his initial one.

Clearly, the overall arc of the tale is ideally structured in terms of total opposites – from one state of affairs to its radical opposite – for the obvious reason that since story is fundamentally the story of change, the most complete change is the one to be, and is, most religiously emulated. But what change? Four possibilities: the protagonist's inward, psychological change (so much fancied frequently for its "inner logic";) his outward change of fortune (so much frequently denigrated for its straying from "inner logic"); his change of perception, (sadder but wiser, understanding what he never did before); and finally, no change at all in the protagonist or his situation, but only in the perception of the spectator (a paragon of sainthood is really, we finally discover, a devil, a Machiavelli.)

And so the overall arc of this story with its one major reversal has, so to speak, its subject and its predicate, and can be – and to verify its structure should be able to be – contracted into a single sentence which names (1) the protagonist; (2) his initial state of affairs; (3) the reversal; (4) the consequence (but note carefully the italicized words below).

To wit:

(1) A man *decides* to give up his entire way of life, wanders – with his wheels – on to Route 66, goes through a series of painfully cautionary adventures, only to *discover* that the hearth and home he gave up in the first place are closest to his heart's desire.

(2) The same man out of frustration with his life makes the same *decision*, undergoes similar adventures, but *discovers* that this new life so transcends the other that he will embrace it forever. [Both 1 and 2 signify inward change.]

(3) Same man, same *decision*, having nothing but his Harley to accompany his adventures, *discovers* that the land on which he's finally squatting in privation and misery, is on top of an oilfield – now his. [3, a change of outward fortune.]

(4) The same man *decides* to strike out courageously for personal freedom, undergoes the same adventures, until *we discover* that whether he is at home or on the road, he is neither Robin Hood nor Shakespeare, but a hopelessly mediocre conformist. [4, a change of audience perception]

Even for the single-protagonist model, there is room for considerable variation of this arc of the action. One variation: a *double* consequence (lending considerable irony to the play's outcome:)

(1) A man, living under the cloud of his guilt concerning a deed in his past, discovers that the crime was not his, but though he can live relieved of his fear of discovery, cannot rid himself of his sense of guilt.

(2) A man, living under the cloud of his guilt concerning a deed in his past, is discovered to be the previously unknown criminal, and is relieved to be apprehended.

(3) A man, living under the cloud of his guilt concerning a deed in his past, decides at long last to confess, and is not believed.

(4) A man, living under the cloud of his guilt concerning a deed in his past, until we discover he is hiding a guilt far greater and more sinister than his apparent guilt.

Two key verbs: *decides, discovers*. These are the hinges on which the protagonist's action – hence the play's action – turns. *Discovers*: Aristotle's *anagnorisis*, or recognition. But *anagnorisis* has come to have far wider application: recognitions or discoveries are multiple, are plotted throughout the action, and occasion a whole sequence of decisions, plans, etc. Rarely are all its stages overtly articulated in the play's action, but underlying that action, this is their implied, their logical, their classic, order:

Initial Situation: The first set of circumstances, the neutral story ground out of which the protagonist's action will subsequently be launched. It's neutral in the sense that its circumstances don't invite any particular change in the protagonist's motives or behavior. (The marriage is humming along, the job in the lead or asbestos factory seems ok, the monarch feels comfortable on his throne, the mafia-like instigator of corruption in town has been and still is immune to threat.) There may or may not be an incipient fault line in these circumstances, but whether or not, and whether the protagonist knows it or not, that placid situation is doomed by an:

Initial Intrusion, which is the precise point at which the action proper begins. Nothing, Aristotle pointed out, precedes the beginning of the plot; it is followed by the middle; the middle is preceded by the beginning and is followed by the end; and the end follows the middle but is followed in turn by nothing else. Inane as this perception may seem at first glance, there lies buried within it one of Aristotle's most profound lessons in the *Poetics*. We must consider in what sense it is possible to say of a plot that nothing precedes it. Events do, certainly; for aeons. If we were to trace back to the true beginnings of any tale, we'd find ourselves eventually – as Strindberg does in *The Road to Damascus*[5] when a similar inquiry is made into the origins of the guilt of a culprit under trial – back to the Garden of Eden. And similarly, if we were determined to put our finger on the end of the tale, we'd find ourselves reaching toward the end of time. So there's an implicit distinction that must be made: the distinction between plot and – let's call it – fable. The matter of fable, let us say, extends infinitely before and after; the matter of plot is constrained to a single, clearly demarcated beginning and a similarly demarcated end. How?

An analogy: Imagine the placid surface of a lake, and imagine its stillness lasting only until the moment a great rock is hurled into it, destroying instantly its placidity. The initial situation of a plot, whether it is as placid as the lake or riddled with strife and problems − a sleepy town in the dead of summer, or the Montagues and the Capulets[6] trying to murder each other in the streets of Verona, or loyal Macbeth fighting rebellions[7] in defense of the honor and rule of his monarch − that situation is understood to be ongoing, and could, as we've pointed out − with respect to the not-yet-engaged plot − go on forever. But like the boulder dropped into the lake, the intrusion dropped into it forces reaction, response. The absolute beginning, then, of the plot as distinct from the fable, is that first intrusion, the equivalent of the boulder, and the absolute end of the plot, like the ripples in the lake, comes about only when the final consequence of that intrusion is put to rest, when the last ripple started by the boulder's splash has disappeared from the lake. It is that relation between the beginning and the end, the initial intrusion and its final erasure, that circumscribes and defines the unity of the plot, the unity of the dramatic story told. It rigidly frames the plot's unified event.

Examples: "Children of Cadmus," Oedipus pleads, "tell me what is the sorrow that brings you here." A plague has visited Thebes, and it cannot be undone until the culprit who occasioned it is detected, punished and cast out of the city. Oedipus promises to accomplish this. When he discovers the culprit (himself) and he is so punished, the plague, it follows, is over. Plague begins, plague ends.[8]

The two families in Verona battle in the streets and are charged with banishment if they violate again the Duke's ultimatum to end their strife. With the double-suicide of the two lovers, the families vow to be at peace, and the families' strife ends.

Just as the plot begins in relative inertia, *stasis,* and is propelled into motion by some sort of intrusion, so the protagonist is set in motion by some such propellant: the plague, an enemy's deed, a friend's betrayal − or he wakes up one morning, as in Kafka's "Metamorphosis,"[9] to discover that he has turned into a bug. Or Cassius awakens Brutus's inherent moral hostility[10] to kingship or dictatorship. Or the thought of grasping for kingship is implanted by witches and by wife[11] in *Macbeth*. These propulsions, to say the least, awaken in the character, or reveal in him, a new, or heretofore dormant, propelling –

Motive: an example of which is Brutus, after Cassius' persuasion, being moved to consider: "It must be by his [Caesar's] death." [12] And immediately emerging from this initiating motive is its necessary –

Justification: in which the protagonist spells out the reasons which compelled – or are about to compel – his decision to act. In the most formal structuring of action, in Elizabethan tragedy, in French Neoclassical tragedy, it is invariably spoken aloud, profoundly considered, dwelled on at length. In drama in a hurry, almost always in film, it is merely implied, understood without words. Let's split its function in two: practical justification, and – more significantly – ethical justification. The explicit, fully articulated spelling out of both these justifications is precisely what gives the extraordinary texture to both characters and action. The character's speech of justification, then, is not merely a recitation of the practical options open, but illuminates most significantly the fundamental moral tone, the moral richness of the play as a whole, (and most particularly of the sensibility and profundity not only of the character, but of the writer.) With these two factors – motive and justification – we already have in effect more than half the richness of the character created, already alive, already functioning. His internal debate concludes with the character's decision, which is always a

Plan of action, never merely an intellectual judgment or a general moral perception. (The conspirators meet, Brutus and they hatch a practical plan.[13]   Or: Macbeth heeds Lady Macbeth's practical plan to murder their guest King Duncan.) But then the plan, once articulated, is *itself* brought into further question, debated alone or with others (Portia's remonstrance[14] and urging Brutus against his unspoken decision, Brutus's internal debate; or Macbeth's[15] "Two truths are told, as happy prologue to the swelling act of the imperial theme.... If [ethically] ill, why hath it given me earnest of [practical] success....? If [ethically] good, why do I yield to that suggestion whose horrid image doth unfix my hair...?" and, once again, debated for the plan's practical as well as moral efficacy, until the character arrives at a

Settled choice – his first in a chain of committed decisions – to venture this way or that, modifying or confirming or reversing his initial plan, and – active agent that he is – the plan is brought to its –

Execution: for whose treatment, there's been, historically, a choice of options: Is the execution of the plan to be a highly theatrical, lushly told sequence, or a severely truncated one? On the face of it, there's little question which we – theatrical gourmandizers – prefer. But not until the *consequence* of the plan's execution is accomplished, does the character – as plot agent – come again into play. Whether the Battle of Agincourt[16] is lost or won, whether the safe is successfully cracked, whether the murder of Duncan is achieved, whether the conspirators succeed in assassinating Caesar, matters, in terms of plot, not in itself but only in its outcome, since it is that that propels the next step in the *character's plot action*. It's the usual habit of neoclassical tragedy to leap over the plan's execution – omit the battle scene, the murder scene, the conspiracy's dark whispers, silent crawlings and final lungings and dagger thrusts, – and hurry to a messenger's report of the execution, in order that the plot can leap swiftly to its next significant phase. It is, contrarily, the habit of Shakespeare, Romantic drama, war films and cop melodrama to elongate not to say wallow in the excitement of the battle or the mayhem of the massacre or the luridness of the murder or the sustained cunning of the heist – a different order of pleasures from those of the aesthetically more stringent pursuit involved in focusing on the plot's key turning points alone. And the key turning point, after the plan is executed, whether fully played out or simply reported – is its –

Consequence: of which there are of course only three possibilities – the execution of the plan is successful, or it fails, or it is successful in one way but not in another. But whatever its apparent success or failure, it fails in the most important respect – the action is further from, not closer to, its ultimate goal ("To be thus is nothing," concludes Macbeth after the murder of Duncan and his succeeding him as monarch, 'but to be safely thus — Our fears in Banquo stick deep.")[17]   And so the —

New Situation: is a detour from the originally intended path to the goal. And it in turn invites new considerations, new moral and practical justifications, and a new, a substitute, plan: the detour that will hopefully set the action again on its original course and toward its original goal.

The action, then, is less a journey in a straight line than it is a broken-field run. To the extent that it follows a straight line in which, for example, the protagonist from the beginning wins, through his series of plans, all his interim goals and then his final one, to that extent it loses its effectiveness, in effect registering no change, no reversal. Ideally, then, the action courses through reversals — ups and downs, falling back, detouring, going forward, and worst of all, when it succeeds, its very success creating even greater obstacles, increasingly threatening situations.

This cycle of reversals usually occurs at least three times over — a sort of "rule of three" that operates in our conventional plot formulas. The third time round, the stakes, of course, are maximal — the protagonist is, for example, in mortal danger, not only of losing life or more than life, but of losing his initial goal as well.

Desperate Situation/Moment of Inanition/Final Plan: At this critical juncture, a moment intervenes when the action more or less stops, its momentum almost comes to a halt, as the protagonist considers ruefully or in agony that there is little hope of living on, (Macbeth's "Tomorrow and tomorrow and tomorrow Creeps in this petty pace...")[18] and that he now has only one recourse: an ultimate gesture, a mad, desperate, wild, final plan "Arm, arm, and out!"[19] he cries, and buckles on his armor to fight Burnham Wood and Macduff's avenging army. And the very gesture that signifies the suicide of hope becomes either the one that indeed produces total defeat, or miraculously, total success. Final reversal. Or — alternative plot strategy — each new plan brings the protagonist closer and closer to success, and the final reversal ends in total failure.

To summarize: there's the protagonist's *initial situation*; then, disturbing it, an unwelcome or possibly unendurable *intrusion*; this intrusion generates the protagonist's initial *motive*; this new motive induces him to come to a *decision* to do something; but before he acts, he deliberates, debating with himself his *justification for his decision* (working out both its moral and its practical implications); having debated alternatives, he makes his choice of *a plan of action*; and then once again deliberates on the *justification of his plan* (again debating both its moral and practical justification); at last, he's ready for the *execution of the plan*; and that carried out, he confronts its successful or unsuccessful *consequence*. And that consequence becomes immediately his new situation which generates a new motive, followed by a new decision, etc.

PLOT AS DREAMSCAPE

Basic plot structure, together with its built-in pattern of emotional seductions (discussed below,) has done yeoman service for Western drama since the Elizabethans used it fulsomely, the French Seventeenth Century Neoclassicists less flamboyantly, and later drama till our own time habitually. It served the greatest of Western dramas reliably; it served as well its most mediocre dramas, leading us sensibly to conclude that in itself it guarantees nothing but the ease of following in logical steps the development of a story from its beginning to its end. But it serves another purpose as well, a more significant one. That conventional plot format is also a "dreamscape" in which fundamental human anxieties are assuaged. The format clings to assumptions that, though reinforced by beliefs that had been taken for granted in the past, may now be more hindrance than help to contemporary playwrights struggling to find a voice of their own. The format is wedded to old assumptions that are hard to silence. But:

"Only aesthetically," wrote Nietzsche, "can life be eternally justified." Supposition that life is chaotic and meaningless, that one's destiny can go off track in any direction with no discernible purpose, is one of the more disorienting nightmares of human fantasy. Nietzsche's encouragement: Aesthetic imagination counters those fears. He argues his case metaphorically, using the structure of Greek tragedy in performance as in itself demonstrating – and providing redemption. Argued differently, the drama's traditional structure offers another metaphor for redemptive solace: the reassuring "dreamscape" of its organization, a solidly compensatory formula picturing human experience as intelligible, rational, and beyond the grip of the chaotic and the meaningless. Human destiny is reassured, blessed with the tightest possible relation between acts and goals, morally gauged behavior, and its morally meaningful outcomes. These essential factors. One impinges on the other, giving meaning to the other. Dreaming this performance, the dreamer is reassured; walking, out of the theatre, he may have doubts:

1) *that characters are defined by morally-determined decisions alone*:

"Character" is attributed by Aristotle to *moral habit*, determined by the accumulation of decisions and acts that have become more and more congenial for our person, and so are happily repeated. Neither in the *Poetics* nor in the basic plot format above, is there any other *dynamic* to explain character's acts and choices. "Character" functioning in this way is not known, and is essentially not interesting, for its internality but for its instructional value alone. But if we define the chief protagonist the way the plot-format invites us to, we'll know him not as a person, but as a parable. Given Aristotle's considerable influence on the reading of characters, and his seeing them as acting on ethical decisions alone, characters become illustrations of conduct codes, and drama becomes essentially a sermon.

2) *that they are judged and known by a uniform, culturally determined judgmental grid*:

But "character" seen in this way, not essentially interesting for its internality but for its instruction, becomes something else as well: the bearer of cultural tidings. Each choice, each justification and each act carries with it a very large, a very complex, structure of values that constitutes the essential bridge between play and spectator. Icon Rambo must climb onto a plane in a hurry so that he won't be killed, and his buddy is lying on the ground wounded. Rambo may not have time to get his buddy onto the plane before he himself is shot, but he nevertheless stops and grabs his buddy and pulls him onto the plane. In that instant, a mountain of values sits on his shoulders along with his wounded buddy, and at the same time, a corroborating mountain of values sits on the shoulders of the spectator whose delight in Rambo's choice is registered in silent applause or voluble cheers or, for the really deeply value-burdened, even tears. Those who know where the buttons are pushed have recognized long ago that such moments in dramatic performance are by far the most powerful reinforcements of a culture's values. Imbedded in conventional drama's action as manifested in its characters' behavior, is the almost-religion of the moral beliefs which never need explication or underscoring, the ones in fact so internalized that they are no longer thought, but only felt.

But culturally shared judgments don't question internal dynamics; they merely share opinion with a uniform grid of appraisal for human acts. What the social polity "learns" in observing drama, what it "infers" in that process, is the imputation, the certainty, of fixed moral values. And if that is so, then the very values by which we, the culture, appraise and define the character and his acts in drama, are being inferred and internalized by us from the very matter to which we are presumably bringing judgment to bear. In our very act of questioning, the matter in question – which is Rambo's act itself – teaches us our answer.

3) *that the causative pattern underlying the plot, logically sequenced as it is, aspires not only to demonstrate likelihood, but inevitability – in a word, a providential design.*

Causality, through tightly structured plot controlling sequences of action-reversal-consequence, gives certain proof in the "journey" of the dramatic character, from his first decision to his end, that his progress demonstrates the inevitable, and so emulates, and serves as a model for, the way things are. But what is it, in the course of this protagonist's journey that *certifies* that his first decision beginning his "journey," leads, in fact governs, that final consequence? What keeps the logic of his journey, for all its detours and reversals, on course? The reality of a providentially secure design, known by many names, is still universally assumed to be the controlling key to dramatic structure. With its watchful eye, it polices the unity of that beginning and that end, and the coursing of all the choices and the events between the two. The belief is thoroughly shared by both the skeptic's secularization of causal links and the believer's confidence in the just hand of God. Both subscribe, willy-nilly, to the governance in Greek Tragedy of the injunctions of Zeus, the curses of Poseidon, the revenges of Athena, or more overwhelmingly, the ultimate legislation of the Fates. It clearly and unavoidably controls the destiny of the human journey from act to act, accomplishing the predicated design of the God. And if, as Aristotle legislates for most effective tragedy, the end outrages our sense of proportion, our sense of fit, between the hero's initial error and his terminal catastrophe, it is that very disproportion that confirms in the most devastating way the inevitability of that design. Whether it's the Moving Finger that writes, or the God or Gods or Fate or Positivism's causal diagrams or current Psychology's certainties or more esoteric Spiritual Manifestations, traditional fictional formats have in common this interior allegiance to the Providential Design that controls the telling of tales, controls the inevitability of moral stabilities hanging over and guiding destinies to their fitting end, and that that very connection signifies, as the particular fiction has it, the way things are. Watching, or reading, we harness all those acts and consequences into a single judgmental assertion, and judge that judgment and the principle behind it as right or wrong, appropriate or inappropriate, good or bad. But never as irrelevant. We succumb automatically to the feeling that it harbors the ultimate sagacity behind story-telling. And that sagacity is? That there is connection, there is sequence, there is that reassurance. It may be all that is left of universal belief; it remains inherent, vestigial, and gives, certainty to conventional drama, the nostalgic and stabilizing comfort of the perpetual ritual of providential propriety perpetually reinvoked.

PLOTTING EMOTION

Side by side with the plot's progression, there are powerful emotional seductions structured, like the plot, into a play's progression. They're calculated to grip the spectator with a force that the logic of plot alone cannot hope to emulate. The spectator is lured – willingly – into a state of *anxiety* or *outrage* or *frustration*. And those "states" grip with a peculiarly welcome suffering of pain, irritation or bewilderment. Ideally, they begin gripping close to the play's beginning, and don't let go until close to its end. The longer they remain unresolved, the more delicious the frustration or anxiety, and when resolved, the end of frustration or anxiety is even more delicious. How do they function?

Anxiety: made up of longing, dreading, pitying, or being downright terrified – generally, a fear of what is impending or unknown to protagonist and to us (starting a journey down a river filled with crocodiles; beginning a marriage with high hopes, but with lingering suspicions; planning an escape from Guantanamo, or from kidnappers, or from a mediocre life.) *Outrage:* against injustice, unfairness, inappropriateness (the country is ruled by a despot; the sorority has been taken over by snobs; the mob is running the local nursing home; the candidate for Scoutmaster is a pedophile.) *Frustration:* about the unexplained, the unrevealed (the secret behind the door; the meaning of Rosebud; the identity of the stranger who appeared from nowhere; the explanation of the rich old lady's peculiar will; the corpse in the hallway.) All three, like the plot, are headed toward the same objective: satisfactory resolution, closure (the white explorers were saved, and the crocodiles ate only one native; the pedophile Scoutmaster almost, almost, but was unmasked in time; the Stranger from nowhere came from the future to warn us in time, but couldn't, so the world blew up.)

The first is the most arresting: it puts the spectator at once into the thralldom of personal fear. The second, somewhat less so: it puts him on his mettle to raise his uneasiness to the level of moral outrage. The third can be strong, but is the least compelling: it invites only yearning for clarification. There is a fourth that hardly figures in the emotional altitudes of these three: recognition (the story about a hometown like my own, or a parallel to my experience in the army, or about a character exactly like everybody's mother.) It offers the comfort and pleasure of recapitulating the familiar, but fairly quickly its pleasures give way, and welcome the intrusion of an anxiety, an outrage, or a puzzle.

TENSION AND RELEASE

The grip of these seductions take irresistible control by a precisely structured continuity of alternating sequences of emotional *tension* followed by intermissions of emotional *release*. The spectator's emotion is built to a level of high tension to which he becomes entirely captive, and then – ah-h! – release. The pattern is repeated incrementally, building higher and higher levels of tension, until the play's end. By the shamelessly exploitive, the pattern can reach heart stopping levels of tension before succumbing to welcome relief. But for reasonable practitioners – playwrights who have a heart – before the strategy runs amuck, their common sense tempers excess, and gains believability and even power. A notable instance of compelling tension, but perfunctorily imagined release: *Macbeth's* second act, which dramatizes the murder of King Duncan. The tension over the preparation and execution of the murder intensifies – the hush and anxiety and terror of the deed lasting for almost half the length of the play. The relief? Just after the murder is accomplished, there's a banging at the palace gates, followed by a clownish Porter delaying opening them while he entertains us with a comic soliloquy. With the entrance of the intruders, the tension resumes at once. *Macbeth*, a relatively transparent example of incrementally plotted tension-release, reaches climactic tension in its terminal battle scene in which the tyrant Macbeth is killed, and the drama ends – as all Shakespeare's tragedies and histories tend to do – with the restoration of dynastic order, which signifies, to some, relief.

"IDENTIFICATION?"

But why, in this pattern, is the spectator so thoroughly gripped? Is it his "identification" with the protagonist? His sympathetic longing for Macbeth's accomplishing his king's murder? Or is such a response only for the morally perverted? We do, in fact, "identify," as we say, with the protagonist, but not as we suppose. Watching a play has it in common with dreaming that moral inhibition gives way to morality- banked emotional fires. Is it the sociopath alone who yearns for Macbeth's successfully murdering Duncan?[20] Or the Phantom's kidnapping his beloved soprano and keeping her hostage in a backstage dungeon? The deep pleasure of the spectator's giving way to criminal longing, and the less-deep horror toward his own transgressive feeling while doing so, combine to give that peculiarly self-thrilled and simultaneously self- damning response which both "identifies" warmly and rejects violently the anticipated act in the same instant. Even in "identification" with virtuous yearning – the ideal love of Romeo and Juliet, the horrendous victimization of Clarissa Harlowe[21] or de Sade's Justine[22] – it is ideally combined, and at its most effective is always combined, with the odor of moral transgression. Plato rails and Aristotle mollifies,[23] but drama's satisfactions must run deeper than our finding solace in applauding virtue alone. Among its several temporary therapies, applauding one while succumbing to the other ranks high.

But whether our proclivities fancy the many possible virtues more or less than their many transgressions, in either case, we "identify" with – that is, are thoroughly engaged by, and anxiously attentive to – *the arrow of the action* itself as much as, or more, than the protagonist alone. That arrow – starting the action of murdering Duncan – having been launched, the tension is fixed on how and whether and when it will come to its rest. What will happen to this released action, this shot arrow? is the prime unsettling question. Our anxiety, then, *is for the action to resolve itself once it has been launched,* once provoked into being, once let out of its cage. It makes little difference whether one is morally for or against the accomplishment of the murder. The tension is still manifest. It can hang on something as great as Macbeth's progress through the elaborate procedure of Duncan's murder, or as trivial as Lady Windermere's fan[24] incriminatingly dropped in the wrong drawing room. One may or may not be anxious for the fan to be recognized and so destroy Lady Windermere's reputation; either way, we're anxious, urgently so, for the tension's resolution.

Murder over – release.   Fan found but not incriminatingly – release.   The arc of tension-release once over, we welcome the next one, which we ride once more with increasingly pleasurable anxious frustration.

MELODRAMA'S LINGERING

From the early Nineteenth Century, melodrama made explicit the anomalies at the heart of drama's form.   The more it addressed consumer satisfaction, the more its emotional plotting took over the shaping of the plot.   Together with the sham of its artifice, the sham of the period's pieties – moral, social, political – were attracted to its ways, and together they celebrated emotional rapture and intellectual mindlessness.   At its most abandoned – but also its most successful – it so eradicated any resemblance to human norms that it provoked a massive exodus from the theatre of the educated middle classes who slipped into theatre stalls only for Shakespeare and superstars.

The underlying rationale of the plot's basic format itself contributed to the delusory reassurances of full-fledged Nineteenth Century melodrama.   However muted, however qualified in mainstream theatre – then and now – the format's reassurances persisted, and offered temporary bulwark – in dream, to be sure against queasy, intrusive suspicions of the meaningless, the directionless, the possibility of nothingness.   The comfort of the form, when it was so construed, corroborated all the popular belief systems that shared similar inherent certainties and reassurances.

But already in the early decades of the century, revolutionary reflections were dissipating earlier Nineteenth Century idealisms, about which Wordsworth remembered ruefully, "Bliss was it then to be alive," during the early ardent days of the French Revolution, "and to be young was very heaven."   The two possibly greatest, certainly most profound suborners in drama of the romantic myths of that "bliss," and of those dreams of existential stabilities, were the German Büchner in his *Danton's Death* and the French equally anti-Romantic Romantic Musset in *Lorenzaccio*.   Both created protagonists of such bizarre psychological complexity as to make irrelevant drama's commitment to traditional moralisms about character, and their plots so meandered and slowed and sometimes stopped altogether as to mock the predictable causal pattern's track to closure. Unnoticed in their own moment, these two great dramas of the Eighteen Thirties anticipated many subversions to come. The propriety of conventional structure was quietly to corrode in a few instances in the later Nineteenth Century, and the corrosion itself was to lend method and matter to the *avant-garde* movements in the drama of the early Twentieth Century.

But in the deeply troubled and belabored hypocrisies of the Nineteenth Century, melodrama performed equally in the public arena outside of theatre, and was domesticated in the culture itself. The art of popular as well as political thinking learned habitually to translate the grossness of public and private motives and acts into a universally sanctioned moral loftiness. It was hardly the first time in history that this sleight-of-hand was performed, but now to a degree that made the reality of experience move so quickly into the fantasy of the unreal, that the strenuosities of melodrama became the common coin of language to a degree that matched any of the more strenuous moral and political hypocrisies of past eras. Emotional attachment to the sanctimonious followed precisely the same emotional exploitations in public life as they enjoyed in stage melodrama. The language, and the habits of feeling and even of thinking merged with the theatricalism in which it was understood that the more strenuously aggressive the emotion, the more valid the truth of its assertions. In the face of the century's unusual pleasure in these delusions, reforming its emotional and ideological habits in its drama was to be uphill work.

"REFORM"

It went slowly. We'll follow it in quick outline because it explains much of what is still lurking in our own Augean stables. A few decades into the Nineteenth Century, a new wave of interest in conventional Boulevard (or as we say, Bourgeois) theatre was somewhat reignited when melodrama underwent moderate alteration in the Well-Made Play. Its reform was bent on fostering a drama more of this world and less of melodrama's dream-theatre.   To our loss, its melodramatic habits were never abandoned, and we to a very large degree are still hostage to their banality.   The Well-Made Play was the century's first step in the direction of depicting the ordinary experience of ordinary people in their ordinary states of mind and feeling.   Though it succeeded in showing them in their ordinary settings and ways, it hardly touched on the usualness of their minds and feelings.   Those remained in melodrama's Augean stables, as they have done since in ours.

With more vigor, in the latter days of the Nineteenth Century, the Naturalists were expanding the range of causalities, positing multiple strands of unconscious and chance cause, as in Strindberg's *Miss Julie*.[25]   But unlike Strindberg's play, whether it was chance or clusters of causation or single, powerfully determining causes explored in other plays, with few adventurous exceptions, they observed religiously the formulaic patterns of melodrama.   Not too gallant a rebellion against mainstream boulevard theatre, but its very aesthetic conservatism left its mark on the "serious" theatre of the Twentieth Century and our own: the "well-constructed" plays rife with dramatic anachronism and cultural respectability.

Emile Zola's "Naturalist" drama, in 1873, not displacing but exploiting the devices of melodrama, merely nudged it in the direction of the photographically literal.   Among the prime innovations of this corrective was intended to be "character-driven" drama, the characters shaped by the "laws" of environmental and hereditary influences, which were understood by Zola to be scientifically sanctioned.   His lesson should be studied closely.   It is artifice, to be sure, but it persists in the more recent "realistic" but essentially melodramatic drama of, for example, Arthur Miller's *All My Sons* and *The Crucible*.   Zola's *Therese Racquin*[26] of 1873 is the lingering model for *The Crucible,* whose *structure* stretches neatly over Therese *Racquin's* structurally identical form.   As follows:

The play begins with Therese, who loathes her husband, plotting his murder with her lover.   The murder done, the lover is welcomed into the home of Therese and her mother-in-law, who supposes the young man was the almost-hero who tried to save rather than drown her son. After the stress of the murder – calm, plateau: Therese and her lover tend kindly to the unsuspecting old woman. Second phase: The guilt within Therese and her lover begins to eat away at their relation, and in the course of their violent mutual recriminations, the old lady hears them, learns the truth, and instantly suffers a paralytic stroke. Third phase: The old lady, paralysed, tries desperately to communicate with her weekly card-game visitors, but can do no more than move her eyes. (We're back to the extreme of melodramatic tension.) For the highest point of tension, the old lady seems able to move her arm, terrifying the two lovers as she begins to write the word, "Therese," followed by a few letters beginning the word "murderess." But since she cannot complete the word, it appears to her visitors that her message was to be, "Therese my friend." The lovers relieved by that outcome, are then increasingly subjected to the accusing stare of the old woman, the intensity of which provokes the greater intensity of their feelings of guilt and their mutual recrimination – final rising tension – which leads to their mutual suicide – resolution, release. "Character psychology" itself becomes the new template for the formulaic emotional pattern, and a step-by-step substitute for external plot events. But whether internal or external, the heart-thumping artifice of emotional lunge-and-rest remains the same.

The transfer of this pattern whole and unchanged to Twentieth Century "serious" drama is ideally demonstrated by Arthur Miller's *The Crucible,* a quintessential replica with the same tension-release sine-waves, the same heavily moralized motives and acts, the same "inevitability" in the narrative's tight causal sequence. To a considerable extent, conservative theatre practice still plays safe with close copies of Miller's model of socially-responsible drama awash with virtue but consistently compromised by its vestigial retreads of melodrama disguised as sober presentation of real problems. The model moved to film and TV, where its anomalies succeed in looking serious, lofty and new.

***

CHAPTER 2
MANIPULATING STRUCTURE

MANIPULATING REVERSALS

Subtle games are played with reversals that not only undercut their own function, but sometimes undercut the very assumptions on which dramatic action normally rests. What has been subverted of the conventional plot model? At one time or another, in stage and film practice: (1)the idea of reversal itself, (2) the idea of character logic, (3) the idea of causal continuity, (4) the idea of emotional progression, (5) the idea of closure as recovered stability. First: two familiar and traditional examples of reversals, and several variants; then examples of radical subversions of causal sequence; and then the shredding of conventional structure altogether.

The most dramatic change, as above, is obviously the one in which the action moves from one state of affairs to its opposite, most effectively with no lapse of time at all. As we'll see below, it is once again peculiarly relevant to contemporary sensibility, but as Bernard Shaw pointed out about pornography, that it has vanishing impact the more often it's exploited, such machine-gun-rapid reversals have vanishing credibility the more often they explode.

INSTANTANEOUS REVERSAL: ROSSELINI'S *OPEN CITY*[1]

Still, if exploited with some vestigial relation to reality, some of the most overwhelmingly effective scenes follow its prescription. There's a moment in Rossellini's neo-realist film *Open City* in which a pregnant Anna Magnani sees her partisan lover and soon to be husband hoisted onto a truck by German soldiers to be hauled off to a prison camp. The camera follows her running after the truck screaming No, No, No, and it is as though her whole soul is fixed on the back of the truck and the man sitting in it, and we watch her running, screaming, instinct with life and overwhelming emotion, and in an instant, a few shots and she is inert, lying in the middle of the road, dead. It could not possibly have been a more thorough change, and it could not possibly have been more irrelevant to her internal psychological momentum – a reversal, in other words, occasioned by a wholly external fact: a gunshot.

INTERNAL REVERSAL: IBSEN'S *ROSMERSHOLM*[2]

The perfect contrast to instant reversal is a play-length run of internal psychological reversals. In Ibsen's *Rosmersholm*, Rebecca undergoes a series of self-discoveries which end in her recognizing her deepest and most guilt-ridden motives, thoroughly hidden from her at the beginning of the play, thoroughly exorcised by her at the end. Each discovery, each reversal of understanding breeds a reversal of Rebecca's intent; final reversal breeds final resolution, which, like her entire journey of self-discovery, is self-engendered. It is an action model that depends to some extent on the introduction of external facts, but avoids as much as possible irrelevant external intrusion. It was the ideal of late Nineteenth Century dramatic theory and practice, the most perfect in its integrity: internal psychological journeys that lead to thoroughly moral housecleanings of the self. For purity and logic of design, it is still held as a model of dramatic structure, and for purposes of sanctification, it is visited on *Oedipus* as well, although there, it rests uneasily, since Oedipus's internal journey is not the track leading to his catastrophe.

"GAPPED" REVERSALS

Since professional psychology and popular psychobabble share much the same language, over-explicit psychologising in drama is suspect and redundant. Still, to write about human being at all, there's no doing without psychology, and so substitutions for its visible labors are resorted to. One possibility: unremarked internal reversals. Unlike the Ibsenian model in which every step toward psychological illumination is specified, here reversal is dramatized not by careful tracking, but by its opposite: *gapping* (of which there will be more to say in later contexts.) Gapping the action: in this instance, leaving out the reversal. How is this done? Suppose a protagonist fixes on a plan to rob the neighbourhood bank next morning. He's not thrilled with the plan itself, but he's determined that he must do it. He spreads the news among a limited circle of friends that he is actually going to do it in the morning, and expresses a certain pride in his determination. Everything in his story tells us he's ready to act. The next morning, he's found dead in his bed, a suicide.

What is the logical progression in the story that leads us to that final event? None. In fact on the face of it, it defies logical justification. Nor does the story backtrack subsequently to fill in the missing explanation; it remains unexplained. Nineteenth century novelists, on the other hand, found nothing so fascinating as tracking the ruminations of such a character's long night, following thought by thought his ripening for the act of suicide. Schnitzler, the great Austrian playwright, wrote a short story, "The Duel,"[3] in which the protagonist goes through just such a Proustian rumination after being insulted by a baker. He walks the Viennese streets all night contemplating suicide as his logical recourse, thought leading to debilitating thought, but finally to a thorough redemption when he discovers the baker has had a stroke during the night, and so, no necessity for suicide. Surprising result or no, every moment of the night's mental journey has been tracked; the suicide, had it come, would have been wholly reasoned, understood, anticipated. Gapping – skipping psychological progressions – leaves us to infer what reasons we please; they're now quickly summoned and easily understood. Recapitulating internal journeys is – whether specious or not – shared current wisdom.

It is also true that nothing may be left of character *texture* to be gapped. In drama and film, the sense of character may be so diminished as to be bereft of any internal complexity whatever. Diminished for whom? Oddly, for both action melodrama on the one hand, and the most esoteric drama on the other: Spiderman and Beckett. Just as there is only a rough and quickly disposed of process of "character changing" in Rambo or Terminator action films, so there is a similar lessening of focus on character in depth. Both action films and Beckett are more focused on the broadly existential (believe it or not) than on psychological portraiture – the raw fact of being alive or dead, free or bound, in danger or out of danger. Beckett's characters, extreme examples, have in that sense little or no individuality. They all share in the human plight, and since the extent to which they do is overwhelming, their claims to particularizing individuality tend to be ruefully comic, claims left over from olden times. The sense of character, both in action movies and Beckett's inaction plays have very much moved in the same direction, subjectivity very much honoured by omission, gapped.

SUBVERTED ACTION: ANTONIONI'S *L'AVVENTURA*[4]

Causal structure is subverted in another way: the overall action, normally with beginning, middle and end, concludes before it reaches its middle. A characteristic story done in this vein is Antonioni's film, L'Avventura. Two characters go off in search of the answer to a question of why an acquaintance disappeared – suicide? kidnapping? what? In the course of their search, the reason for their inquiry more or less slips from their attention, and they become otherwise occupied: the two have an affair. The premise of one story is displaced by the second, and then the second story ends as a failed action.

What concerns the narrative is not the intimate psychology of either character, but their general humanity responding to urgencies that touch on contemporary sensibility. The two who are engaged in the inquiry concerning the disappearance of their acquaintance are not committed to the task of finding the answer that will, so to speak, restore justice and order; in fact, they don't give a damn. And in the course of their inquiry, they lose interest in it altogether, and turn their attention to their own affair. Do we believe such a tale? In terms of likelihood, it holds, if not gratification, at least more credibility than the detective ferret Poirot[5] who latches on to the plot's question and munches unswervingly toward its answer.

As to the second story in which the two are presumably in love and committed to their affair, the very innocuousness of the events they experience in the course of their inquiry – which they've half-forgotten anyhow – and the innocuousness of their relation to one another, and the hopeless pointlessness of their arrival at a place where they are met by their own social set, the meaninglessness of all that leaves them in the position of not giving a damn either about their affair or about one another – and possibly even about themselves.

The momentum that carries these characters forward is exactly the opposite of the momentum that carries forward traditional characters going through the paces of an action. The essence of their character momentum is their intentionality, their urgency in moving toward a goal. But in *L'Avventura*, the goal evaporates twice over, and the characters, instead of moving strongly toward their goals, move with less and less urgency until they have none. What has happened is that the fabric of storytelling has gone through a shift in which the very idea of action is brought into question. Some of the most compelling and significant Twentieth Century works question the idea of progressive action somersaulting through its conventional loops, and betray the structural value and even the meaning of its operation.

DISTENDED AND INVISIBLE REVERSALS

Along with the pleasures of the studiedly childish dramatic genres that make no pretense of adhering to the real world, the patterning of action in the way melodrama did it and does it invites at the same time an exactly opposite response, a feeling more enervating than exhilarating: hostility. Hostility to the assumption that we're at ease with the beliefs that support these forms.

What is the occasion for uneasiness? The comfortable, the believable, point of entry into a play or film has, for certain plays and films, changed significantly. In the Nineteenth Century, the essential engagement began with the quick gripping of an audience's emotions. Though that audience would put up with gaping yawns of exposition, once that dutiful chore was done, emotion had to be gripped and stay gripped until the end.

Underlying hysteria in Nineteenth Century audiences longed for that exercise. We've added to the pleasures of this still vital and still functioning appeal, another and very different underlying emotional posture – apathy and torpor. The demand we make is verifiability. At first glance, it must be so: it's the way people look, behave, speak, the way their streets, rooms, cars, are put together – the guarantee of sufficient reality. And that guarantee is insisted on even in the patently unreal. Says Danny Pang, the producer of ghost-genre films, "When it comes to horror, Americans crave explanation. Every detail has to be logical. Why is the ghost flying? Why is the ghost walking? Why does the ghost attack that guy and not the other guy, they keep asking. But this is a ghost story," he complains, logically. "Ghosts are already illogical." Just as in the Nineteenth Century it was hard to get the audience's emotions back on track if emotional sequence was interrupted, so now if verifiability is momentarily in question, belief is hard to restore.

Apathy's skepticism buys slowly into belief. The more rapidly, the more frequently story reversals are clustered, the less they're believed. To win belief, even acknowledgement, the action line is outrageously distended. Characteristically, slow, sometimes almost nonexistent curves of action, extremely tempered, hardly punctuated, hardly expressed reversals, are what accord with spectators in some of our most powerful and distinctively contemporary plays and films. Anticipating them by a century, Chekhov exploited patterns of langorously distended and barely perceptible reversals. Take Andrey in *The Three Sisters*[6] as textbook example. In the course of the play, he undergoes devastating and total reversal, but its exhibition in the telling is consistently suppressed, so tucked into the action of the play that its echo is more in evidence than its voice.

At the beginning, he is ill at ease, embarrassed, vulnerable, but at the end of the first act, he finds himself – glowingly, passionately, ardently – confessing his love to Natasha. At the end of the play, he is cuckolded, frustrated, desperate and the image of his future and for him, the town's, are hopelessly bleak. The moments that signify in bringing about this change, are so suppressed by Chekhov that they are almost invisible, distending its duration in slow progression over the play's four acts and over the full two years of its narrative time. We never observe or experience any of the palpable moments of reversal in that progress. Instead of showing the moment when Andrey, out of increasing malaise and disappointment, determines to mortgage the family's house and take the money to the gambling table – Dickens, Balzac and Dostoevsky would not have passed up that moment of fateful decision – we hear that such a thing has happened in a scene in which his wife Natasha is complaining bitterly about his irresponsible behaviour. What do we hear from Andrey? Little, almost nothing. His plight, his pain, his decisions, are unspoken but deafeningly clear. We see the consequence of his total reversal, but no moment of that reversal itself.

In the third act, we have another glimpse of what's been happening, and has already happened, to Andrey, but only a glimpse. In a confessional moment, when he is defending his wife against the implicit hostility of his sisters, and strenuously asserting his admiration for her qualities, he suddenly bursts out: "Don't believe me, sisters, don't believe me!" It's a startling and marvellously effective reversal in his monologue, to be sure, but not at all a plot reversal, only the confirmation of an incremental change that already occurred. In the final moments of the play, Andrey's is one of six story resolutions that conclude concurrently (in itself an extraordinary feat in dramatic structure,) so that the potentially unique impact of his story's resolution is neutralized by the fact that the color of his story's resolution becomes imbued with and merges with the color of the others.

This distension and suppression of character and plot reversal is precisely what earns, slowly and incrementally, our belief. The stories told in Chekhov's plays are – as stories – identical with the quasi-sentimental, quasi-ironic melodramatic stories in the novels and tales of the latter Nineteenth Century and early Twentieth – indistinguishable, as stories, from Maupassant's or Schnitzler's.[7] But with his distanced and suppressed reversals, they approximate more the texture of the normal, the unremarkable, so that the alarming differences deliberately exploited in storytelling between the fictional world of sharp reversals and the world as it is normally known in its daily unrelentingness   are in Chekhov sufficiently suppressed to leave room for larger approximations of credibility, and considerably more invitation to our sluggish trust.

But the most radical subversion of all these strategies – strategies which considerably alter but don't altogether deny the validity of "plot" and "character"- is accomplished absolutely by Beckett, in whose two most celebrated plays neither plot nor character exist. Martin Esslin[8], states this fact, I think, exactly:

> "*Waiting for Godot*[8] and *Endgame*[8] … are dramatic statements of the human situation itself. They lack both character and plot in the conventional sense because they tackle their subject matter at a level where neither character nor plot exist. Characters presuppose that human nature, the diversity of personality and individuality, is real and matters; plot can exist only on the assumption that events in time are significant. These are precisely the assumptions that the two plays put in question. Hamm and Clov, Pozzo and Lucky… are not characters but embodiments of basic human attitudes…. And what passes in these plays are not *events* with a definite beginning and a definite end, but types of *situation* that will forever repeat themselves."

Here is the strategy, almost unique to Beckett, that makes possible dramatic structure without its essential givens: a circling, distended, repeated and again repeated delineation of the fixity of situation. The plays are still canvases gradually accruing definition – the "action" is the close to motionless accretion of suggestions and hints of certainties that might or might not add up finally to a coherent landscape. *Landscape* is the appropriate word: it's the one used by Stein[9] to describe drama with no forward motion. Troubled by what she called the "syncopated" relation between stage presentation and audience's cognitive and emotional receptivity, she projected the notion of eliminating the dimension of time altogether so that plays might move at will over the whole "field" of its representations. Beckett is at one with the ideal of a fixity of "landscape" in which progression from moment to moment is made only to the landscape's particularity. His refusal to "journey" but to begin and end in *stasis,* suggests a perception of reality as not so much in headlong lunges toward the future, but as possibly in the more familiar likelihood of its going nowhere at all.

SUBVERTING CAUSALITY

The subversions of outlandish comedy have for a long time played havoc with the very idea of regular causal sequence. Part of the joke is in leaping over sense, sequence, continuity, for the hell of it. Arlecchino's account of his trip to the moon,[10] Grabbe's[11] gate-crashing his own play to finish it off with the actors, Buster Keaton's[12] running into a movie theatre and onto the screen, are intended as parenthetical aberrations from the solemnity of right causal thinking, not as its challenge. But at the turn of the century, in the 1890's and early 1900's, the challenge subtly, gently, began to insinuate itself into conventional dramatic structure with easy mockery at first, and then with a revisionism that made causality's grip on dramatic action legitimately questionable.

The Importance of Being Earnest[13] is a brilliant instance in which conventional closure trying hard to fit the causal basics is gently nudged. *The Importance of Being Earnest* inherited the comic-serious but also potentially tragic theme of the abandoned baby who discovers his origin in adulthood. Classic recognition, classic denouement. The baby left at Victoria Station, now grown to manhood and on the verge of plot closure, in dire straits concerning both class status and money, is rescued by an entry in the book of genealogical tables which confirms the fact on which his marital fate hangs – his name is, as the young lady's whimsical necessity demanded, Earnest. The pleasure of the closure is in the shameless parody with which it satisfies the last demand of classic structure: recognition-reversal-denouement.   Wilde's mock is about plotting altogether, in which its pieties are sabotaged at every moment, in every scene, the insidiously meaningless substituting for the acceptably meaningful. Insidious and meaningless though they are, they propel forward the mechanics of the plot, the downright silly doing as well in living up to the weighty responsibility of proper plotting. Perfect plotting, perfect linkage, perfect sabotage.

But how grave, how serious the question of causal structure becomes is realized a few years later, in – one example – Wedekind's *Lulu* plays.[14] Lulu is the *femme fatale* of turn-of-the-century male paranoia. Wedekind exaggerates almost to the point of caricature his time's conventional portrait of female threat. Men in quantity are in thrall. They beggar themselves, they commit mad acts, suicide, anything. Lulu's entourage includes the most faithful of all, the lesbian Countess Geschwitz. In all this, there's an incipient lesson to be learned, clearly; but as clearly, Wedekind skirts it. What is the dramatic career of Lulu? What details accrue in her portrait and gather significance? None. The play is a series of discontinuous episodes – Lulu leaving one lover, suddenly returning, suddenly under patronage of another. The strength of her character-drawing is in its uniform changelessness, which levels the purposiveness of her career and of the play's events. To the extent that Lulu's action bears on their continuity or they on hers, they could be in random sequence. And so Wedekind ends the play with an equally random consequence to Lulu's life. In her career in London as a street prostitute, one of her clients, the last as it turns out, is Jack the Ripper, who after having intercourse with her, cuts her throat. 'My God, Jack,' he comments afterward, 'you're a lucky fellow.' The ultimate cynicism of the narrative underscores the unrelieved inconsequence of its causal pattern, a carefully sustained sneer at the notion of bringing gems of moral judgment to bear on the "meaning" of Lulu's destiny.

But if the sabotage of causal structure was making headway in the late Nineteenth Century, so was the continuous, stubborn and powerful allegiance to that structure. It was the most stubborn of the century's moral idealists, the playwrights who prided themselves most on their courage and forthrightness in attacking "outdated beliefs," who also clung most to its far deeper assumptions. Their pride – the pride of Shaw, Ibsen, Zola, Brieux, Hauptmann – who nicked at the moral and social desperation of their century – lay certainly in their own moral zeal in exposing bourgeois ambivalence toward its own pieties, toward the widening cracks in its beliefs. But if it is true that the characteristic emotional life of Nineteenth Century citizens carried with it inward palpitation and repressed yearning, it was also true that – as the novel's then immense popularity signified – there was an overwhelming feeling of life's stability; to be sure, life's tolerance and absorption of incremental changes – Progress – and also, fundamentally, its reliable rhythms of sameness.   And so underlying the sometimes violent urgings toward reform, change, escape, and so on, was the inherent certitude of logical, foreseeable, governable additions to life's good. And in whom was this double and contradictory sensibility operating?   In the intellectual elite, the Nineteenth Century's great social and aesthetic reforming zealots, the Ruskins, the William Morrises, the Wildes, the George Eliots, the Bernard Shaws. They raged, or soberly chastised, or laughed to scorn the very props that supported the solid ground beneath their feet. And the comfort of that security carried over into the "reforming" drama of the latter part of the century. Our playwriting manuals are still entirely beholden to that enthusiastically virtuous time, when drama was to share or possibly lead in the revolt against the sins and stupidities of social, economic and political – in a word, bourgeois – life. But it did so with its contradictory allegiance to the ground beneath its feet – the assumptions of regularity, coherence, and incremental "progress." The consequence of this deeply-held assurance was our late Nineteenth Century and turn-of-the-century "serious" drama: in substance, unremitting attack against middle class values and hypocrisies, but in its dramatic forms, logical, incremental change, the underlying assurances of continuity.

Now – once more – an apparent contradiction. If it is true that in our time welcome torpor and stable apathy have become distinguishing characteristics of the most private private self, so also has dread. The familiar and felt-to-be-guaranteed conditions of life can vanish, as we've had reason to notice for the past some decades, in an instant. The invasion of that feeling, the feeling of the possibly next-instant-removal of the ground under our feet, provides, like its alternate and contradictory certainty, another basis for believable dramatic "progressions." We may laugh at the murder, mayhem, explosion, car wreck, and disorienting pounce from out of the blue of new threat exploited in films, novels and plays that share a kind of cartoonish grasp of reality, but the norms of popular fiction and movies alike answer accurately to our bottom assumption of reality's instability. And so. Side by side, two opposite assumptions, opposite internalizations of belief, are at work in the idea of 'action' in the drama of the late Nineteenth Century and in the regular drama of the Twentieth – in their melodrama's startling thrusts and parries on the one hand, and in their more elevated 'reform' drama with its incremental progressions – and then in the later Twentieth Century drama (now mostly visible in film) with its outdoing of melodrama's allegiance to outlandish catastrophe on the one hand, and its obsessive, finicky mirroring of the *look* of the real.

And so, there is a deep consonance between the blow-em-up, shoot-em-ups of contemporary melodrama and what we must imagine as the more literate examples of contemporary sensibility. They share precisely the same anxieties, and dramatize the same ones. The nightmares of sudden loss of all moorings, the ground going from beneath our feet. And so, external change – explosion, earthquake, car wreck, bombing – any sudden, massive disasters are regarded as credible enough, likely enough, and pass muster as realistically verifiable. But note: what used to be taken for granted in human motivation *internally* – sudden seizures of love, of patriotism, of civic virtue, of religious awakenings, of murderous frenzy, of moral uplift – these changes must now be nurtured slowly, incrementally, to reach any degree of verifiability. The reason is clear: assumptions about the relation between ego mobility and environmental stability are now reversed. Earlier, in the last century, a respectable manual of playwriting reflected with horror on the notion of sudden external intrusions determining action. It was false, it was too easy, it was a violation of story logic. Ideally, the internal logic of the story conformed to the internal logic of the characters. That is still touted as a pious principle of playwriting, but secretly, nobody writing or viewing takes it seriously. For us, the ultimate dramatic moment is one like the chilling reversal in Arabal's *Picnic on the Battlefield*, in which the innocuous chatter and friendly/familiar pleasures of family picnicking occupy almost the whole of the play until the moment when a spray of bullets from invisible planes above wipes out the entire cast and ends the play. This is the way in which contemporary sensibility will accept most completely the reality of action – total reversal of external situation with no preparation and with absolute consequence.   It is closer to the truth of contemporary belief than in the psychology of the criminal, for example, who has a sudden change of heart and embraces religion or virtue or good manners.   Dramatic likelihood is now more than ever based on an inherent and growing fear that the terms of existence are neither stable nor secure, that they are as likely not to hold as to hold.

***

CHAPTER 3
RETROGRESSIVE ACTION

The essential strategy of "retrogressive" action: tracking events in reverse. By degrees, it recovers truths about the past. Characteristically, it begins with a very late point of attack – a few days, a single day, or even hours before story's end – and single-mindedly spirals down to the story's origins – an originating core of guilt, or the dark beginnings and ultimate explanation of the event's subsequent career. Ideally, and in its most profoundly gripping examples, retrogressive action generates, at each of its sequential revelations, a corresponding *progressive* action. Since the revelations are themselves the significant events, each one becomes the impelling incident that generates the next decision, the next plan, for achieving closure. . Anxious curiosity ends when all lingering uncertainties are laid to rest. Let's look at each of the examples below, and note the enormous range in their formal structures – from classic models to structures that undercut all assumptions concerning the certainties of fact, of sequence, even of coherence.

VARIATIONS

Oedipus Rex

The example of *Oedipus* is prescriptive. The play is structured as a search by the protagonist for the culprit responsible for the underlying crime which has caused the city of Thebes to suffer its current plague. But far from being – as traditional analysis has it – the tragic hero of overweening intellectual pride determined to ferret out objective truth and so suffering retribution for that human "transgression," Oedipus is instead a hunted man desperate to fly out of the reach of an encroaching enemy: a fact. Once he is confronted (by the prophet Tiresias) with the possibility that he himself is the criminal he's seeking, rather than bravely, with pride of intellect, inviting a continuing search, he's terrified of it. It's his terror that provokes, then demands, that he be rescued from doubt. But each succeeding revelation, each one ostensibly intended to reassure him, bears with it the further-encroaching certainty of his inadvertent but dooming culpability. Five moments of revelations of the past, five major reversals, as follows:

1) Having sent Creon to the Delphic Oracle to learn the cause of the city's plague, on his return, Oedipus receives the oracle's answer, at first judiciously – yes, we will hunt out the culprit and banish him from the city. He begins his investigation by summoning the blind prophet Tiresias, and – first revelation – Tiresias, enraged by Oedipus's refusal to allow him to remain silent, blurts out the accusation that Oedipus himself is the culprit he's seeking, the man who murdered his father Laius and wed with his mother Jocasta. Oedipus, recoiling from the enormity and apparent absurdity of the charge, concludes that Creon and Tiresias together must be plotting his political destruction.

2) Creon, angered by the charge, confronts Oedipus. Their quarrel causes Jocasta to intervene, and to quiet Oedipus's anger reassures him – second revelation (to be proved misleading) – that her husband Laius was murdered not by one man but by a band of robbers, and that she and Laius had exposed their three-day-old son on a mountain many years before, and that babe, in all likelihood, is long since dead. Oedipus, not reassured but increasingly troubled, confesses – third revelation – that he left his ostensible parents, the King of Corinth and his Queen, after learning of a similar prophecy: that he would one day commit this double crime of which Tiresias has accused him. In horror of that possibility, he left Corinth, but on his way, did indeed kill a traveler before his solving the riddle of the murdering Sphinx, and so arriving in Thebes as saviour of the city from the Sphinx's ravages, for reward was wedded to Jocasta, its queen. Oedipus determines to confront Laius's servant who exposed that newborn infant, and

so lay to rest the lingering suspicion that he was that infant who fulfilled the horrifying prophecy.

3) For a moment, he's relieved from doubt. A Messenger from Corinth brings news that the King of Corinth died of old age, and that Oedipus, his heir, inherits his throne. And to overcome Oedipus's fear of the rest of the prophecy – that he will wed with his mother – he is reassured by the Messenger,

4) – fourth revelation – that the monarchs of Corinth were not his real parents, that the Messenger himself took him from the hands of one of Laius's shepherds, and brought him for rescue to Corinth.

5) Jocasta pleads with Oedipus not to inquire further, but Oedipus, supposing Jocasta is ashamed of having married a man of low descent, insists on confronting the Shepherd, who confirms – final revelation – that it was indeed Oedipus who was the babe of Laius and Jocasta whom he handed over to the Corinthian herdsman.

It's Aristotle, not Sophocles, who broached the question of Oedipus' "tragic flaw,"[1] and since few critics have had the temerity to say that that isn't the germane question, or is in fact a later Aristotelian question, the play has inevitably served as a capacious dumping ground for debates over human will vs. a controlling providential will, which conundrum is perpetually resolved according to the philosophico-religious persuasion of the arguer. And the conclusions concerning the "serenity" of Sophocles as opposed to his, according to other commentators, "black pessimism," are weighed heavily in the balance of Oedipus and the "meaning" of his "fate." The question can be argued with equal assurance either way, and should therefore be regarded as moot, simplistic and irrelevant. More germane is the frightening drama of Oedipus's gingerly stepping through the maze of his doubts and fears, concluding with the overwhelming moment of his devastating entrapment in certainty. For what gnaws at Oedipus is precisely doubt, and it's the pain of that uncertainty that must, at any cost, be allayed by him. Part of the tragedy's irony lies in the fact that the total success of his discovery is the total accomplishment of his catastrophe.

Citizen Kane[2]

It makes, therefore, an enormous difference that the inquiring agent engaged in the pursuit of those story facts in reverse is pursuing his *own* story, and that each stage of his discoveries has overwhelming impact on *him*. Compare the more usual and far less impactful detective-story pattern, or similarly, the *Citizen Kane* pattern, in which the Inquiring Mind is aloof from the facts, and is moved to pursue them by no more than professional zeal or awakened curiosity.   As a consequence, he's left either merely contented or mildly frustrated over his success or failure in ferreting out that final, most critical of all, fact. In the fleshed out detective story, the culprit, his motive and his means are an open book at story's end, and the professional sleuth has the satisfaction of having figured them all out. In *Citizen Kane*, on the other hand, the final fact remains a riddle – not the objective fact, (the word "Rosebud" on the face of the sleigh going into the fire) but its ambiguous meaning. And so the unsatisfying consequence for the journalist pursuing that final meaning is hardly devastating – more like *shucks*.

But if the detective in the story, or the journalist-sleuth in the film, doesn't experience the level of doubt and torment which his counterpart in *Oedipus* undergoes, the characters in the tale he's uncovering, to some extent, do. The agent's action, then, serves only as the organizing, structural frame for the telling of the real tale, the one that presumably carries the essential impact of the play or film. Note, though, that the retrogressive organization of *the agent's* story of discovering the facts – and the spectator's or reader's hand-in-hand journey with him – may be intellectually compelling, it's hardly integral. It has the tantalizing virtue of telling its tale in discontinuous peeks, but this, at the cost of losing the impact of the frightening emotional investment of Oedipus' journey of discovery. The gamesmanship of the spectator's or reader's interest is a less compelling and certainly a less invested journey of discovery.

Ghosts

In Ibsen's *Ghosts,* there is a third variation of retrogressive action, a uniquely powerful one. It is woven intimately – and classically –

into a tense progressive action generated by the series of revelations of the past. As in *Oedipus*, revelation provoking further revelation becomes in effect the entire present-tense action. But unlike Oedipus, whose burden of guilt and whose confrontation with it are arrived at through his career of apparently random or diversionary acts, *Ghosts* is a study of guilt achieved through intentional acts. The difference is fundamental, and is in fact the difference between a Greek sense of cosmic tragic irony and a "modern," that is, an Ibsenian one. It is his – not Sophocles' – that becomes the model for examinations of buried guilt in modern drama. Oedipus's fate, in retrospect, is read as having been in the cards from his birth – Aristotle's "air of design" [3] – , and whether he temporarily skirts it or unknowingly rushes toward it, whether he hurries or forestalls its discovery, whatever he does, whatever he has done, his retribution waits. Mrs. Alving's in *Ghosts*, whose tragedy is centered in a miasma of cultural and social moralistic beliefs, is a gradually self-accumulated, self-inflicted tragedy, although like Oedipus, each act she performed in her past, each decision she made, was, unknown to her, reaping ultimate retribution.

And so it is not a secret fact or immutable circumstance, as in *Oedipus*, that is discovered, but – a sort of special subset of the pattern of retrogressive action – the story of how a person, being *that* person, accomplishes her ruin. Spiraling down to the core of her being to discover an unknown opposite "self" becomes the most compelling narrative in late Nineteenth Century fiction. It was more compelling and more frightening than the attacks of external dangers, because it was the empathetic sense of the spectator or reader that much the same character was, unbeknownst to oneself, embedded in oneself.

It is this pattern of self-inflicted guilt in the past and the subsequent self-discovery of it – a moral guilt which might have been corrected in the doing but for ongoing self-deception – which is peculiarly a "modern," that is to say, late Nineteenth Century, model for tragedy. But it persisted throughout the Twentieth Century in the structures of the essentially moralising, punishing sermons of "serious" drama. It tends to be a personal, self-enwrapped, self-involved journey of discovery of the shame the self has accumulated in the past. Private guilt. So private that, in Ibsen, for example, characteristically no one else is party to it even at its ultimate revelation – only the self, or the selves who mutually accomplished it. Nor, characteristically, has anyone else had an inkling of its accumulation during the past. The privacy of these journeys may be so perfectly self-enwrapped that characters in the same play remain immune to one another's perception or understanding.

The most profound of these mournful journeys backwards to the core of one's own guilt proceed from one layer of self-recognition to another – a gradual self-uncovering of the iniquity or the hypocrisy or the delusion in which the self has unknowingly lived. Finally bowed down by full knowledge, the self stares at the sum of its discoveries, and in that sum, knows punishing retribution. Those terrible concluding images of pain – Mrs. Alving wrestling with both the desire and the terror of feeding lethal pills to her son, the men in O'Neill's *Long Day's Journey into Night* resignedly, helplessly, watching their mother and wife reliving in drugged fantasy the first day of her married life – overwhelmingly encapsulate the impact of the entire play.

Let's outline the stages of that retrogressive-progressive pattern in *Ghosts*, and follow in detail the Ibsenian technique of "layering" the journey of Mrs. Alving from self-ignorance to self-knowledge. So remorselessly, so precisely, does Ibsen accomplish, step by step, the revelation of Mrs. Alving's fixed imprisonment to her mind-set and its inevitable retribution, that, as an exercise in learning playwriting sagacity, it's worth recapitulating in detail the action's sequence of revelations.

Unlike Oedipus, Mrs. Alving at the beginning of the play is by no means embarking on a mission of discovery; she is, if anything, absolutely certain that she's done with painful discoveries, that she's won her hard battle against the constraints, the moral/cultural "ghosts," under which she's lived her secretly embittered life, and now, thoroughly enlightened, has only one more gesture – a largely symbolic one – to make before a new life begins – benign, untormented, cloudless. Mrs. Alving appears to be the model Nora at the end of Ibsen's *Doll House* so fervently longed to emulate: a determined soul who's battled her way, through introspection and self-education, to genuine moral enlightenment. Again unlike Oedipus, she has no reason to be haunted by doubt; having read all the enlightened authors – Voltaire and Nietzsche and Shaw and Ibsen – she's secure in her hard-won intellectual and moral liberation.

And so, as an entirely passive, uncomprehending agent, Mrs. Alving, far from recognizing or initiating these discoveries, at first quickly retreats from their implications when, for a moment, they surface. The very first phase of the action hints at the strategy of self-delusion of Mrs. Alving's moral life. The small hints – first revelations – that she carefully overlooks in Act One: her son Oswald's physical resemblance to his father; his holding his father's pipe in his mouth precisely as his father had done; his indolence, his air of indifference, his active repugnance toward the grey dullness of the landscape to which he's recently returned, so reminiscent of his father's feelings toward that same landscape.

But a radiant Mrs. Alving is overlooking intimations. She has brought her son back home after ten-years' absence, and on the same day invited Pastor Manders to officiate at the dedication of an orphanage she has charitably built. She takes the occasion of Pastor Manders' visit after almost as many years to disabuse him of his notions of what her life has been since last they spoke, at his parsonage, where he persuaded her to return to her home and her husband, and give up all thought of abandoning Captain Alving to live with the Pastor, whom she loved and whose love he returned. When he congratulates her on the virtue of her decision and her sacrifice, she lets fly.

The catalogue of her sufferings – second revelation – is long. Captain Alving, her husband, to whom she was married unwillingly at the behest of the women who raised her and who looked forward to getting rid of her, was – Pastor Manders learns for the first time – a monster. At first an embarrassment for his drinking and lusting for "the joy of life," Mrs. Alving had no choice in their staid community but to rein him in, and as his behavior became more and more outrageous, she was forced to confine him to their house, and to entertain his drunken lapses while enduring them with disgust. To save her son from the memory of such a father, – third revelation – she sent him away to live in Paris, and – fourth revelation – to save the child Regina whom Captain Alving fathered with their servant – "Let me go, Captain Alving," she heard her servant whisper one day, "Let me go!" – Mrs. Alving secretly paid a tavern-keeper to accept the maid as his wife, and to pretend the daughter was his own, and then eventually brought the child back to her home as her servant. Blessed at last with the death of her husband, she vowed to put aside the precise amount of the fortune her husband had brought to their marriage and to finish all symbolic connection with him, to invest it in this orphanage. And, most important, at last to bring home the son whom she had taught by letter to revere a mythical father.

Every fact in Mrs. Alving's heart-felt confessional is of course significant in this, the play's earliest "revelations," but none of the woeful tale she recites is in fact the truth of those revelations, but their opposite. What neither Mrs. Alving nor Pastor Manders hear in her wrenching recitation is what we, the audience – who unlike those two are alert to clues of self-deception – are expected to hear: that Mrs. Alving is a study in self-deception so profound that it sounds – just as her language and tale convincingly sound – like self-evident truth.

"*Audience alert to clues.*" Here we take note of the other "forward action" in retrogressive-progressive structures, the *audience's* "journey of discovery." Just as with progressive action, there is throughout *Ghosts* the parallel action of the audience's developing perception, and as with progressive action, that development is calculated to follow closely (in Ibsen, rigidly) the "sine waves" of tension-and-release (the technique carried over directly from earlier Nineteenth Century's well-made play practice.) It's a path of discovery at one with, but just as often at odds with, the protagonist's: while Mrs. Alving is avoiding the truth, the audience is sometimes intimating it, and on the other hand, what Mrs. Alving sometimes realizes, she keeps to herself, while the audience remains for a time in the dark. In the instance of these first revelations, the audience's "alertness" can function best if it is already attuned to the moral assumptions Ibsen is, step by step, formulating, in which case Mrs. Alving's self-delusions are an open book. At the time of its production, though, the play's assumption is that the audience is as much in the dark as Mrs. Alving is, and the shock of discovery will strike both at much the same time, the broad hints dotting the action notwithstanding.

What an extraordinarily alert audience would have understood from Mrs. Alving's confession of her married life of torment is that it was inflicted not by her husband, but by her. Just as, in the first episode of *Oedipus*, the factual truth to be ultimately realized is spoken aloud by Tiresias but not believed by the protagonist, so in *Ghosts*, the moral truth to be ultimately understood is borne witness to by the protagonist herself, but not comprehended by her. The story she had inadvertently told is that wed to a man who felt "the joy of life," that is, untrammeled, lusty desire, out of a rigid puritanism – the moral norm of her world – she responded not at all to his cravings, and suppressed and eventually imprisoned him in his own home, and acting companion-jailer to him, kept him so isolated from their community that it was possible for her to sustain the lie of his respectability, though he was wallowing at home in drunkenness and obscenity. Within that home, his options were few, but one – an affair with the maid – was viable; the maid's offspring was packed off to a willing surrogate father and paid by Mrs. Alving for his silence, and the child of the affair was raised to believe the surrogate was her father, and when sufficiently grown, was taken into Mrs. Alving's then widowed home to serve as her maid. If this catalogue of sanctioned iniquities were not enough, Mrs. Alving was guilty of two more. First, her allowing her true love, Pastor Manders, when she sought his protection and made open admission of her love, to persuade her to return to the propriety of home and husband, and then to her sending her young son from home to know nothing of his father but the myth of her invention.

To compare again: In the case of Oedipus, it is his conscious acts that only inadvertently reveal his guilt. What guilt? The very terms of his existence, set in stone from the beginning, make each decision of his life contribute to an accumulation of iniquities. It's the human condition *as such* that alone can bring about so devastating a tragedy as his: willful acts done in total ignorance of their character, a character determined .by the first fact, the controlling fact, of the conditions of his being alive – the determining fact which is shut out from his calculations because of his total ignorance of it.

Here is the sliver of difference between Mrs. Alving's guilt and Oedipus'. In consequence, though, the difference is enormous. *By her own values*, or by values that might conceivably have been operative, Mrs. Alving in her succession of decisions and acts might conceivably have recognized the difference between her labor to remain this side of respectability, and in doing so, the crimes she was perpetrating against life itself. Each of her acts, therefore, like Oedipus', was made in good conscience, accumulating a lifetime of acts and decisions with little consciousness of their ultimate criminality. The slight but enormously consequential difference between the two, however, is that there was no conceivable measure of moral propriety Oedipus could have consulted, given his ignorance of the controlling fact: the circumstance of his birth and abandonment. Not knowing that, all his acts, in relation to credible moral principle, were, in effect, blind guess. The enormous difference, then: hers, controlled moral choice; his, helpless inadvertence.

*

Leaving past icons, let's look at movies of the past century. In using retrogressive patterns of storytelling, how did some of them fare – with how much sagacity, how much effect? And – most remarkably – how far have the most adventurous of them traveled from simply retreading the conventional pattern to destroying its conventions altogether. Let's start with hardcore convention:

Chinatown[4]

The movie, *Chinatown*, Roman Polanski's whodunit which features Gittes (Jack Nicholson), a protagonist in the classic Raymond Chandler-Dashiell Hammett mold of the tough guy investigator shouldering his way through forests of obstacles to his sleuthing, and periodically suffering bruising punishment for his nerve. But like Sherlock Holmes,[5] the characterization of this protagonist is ultimately irrelevant to the progress of his diggings into the secrets of the past or the hidden secrets of the present: their logic, whether it's recovered by Sherlock or Philip Marlow[6] or the newspaper man in *Citizen Kane*, is independent of the sleuth, belonging as it does to the completion of the puzzle itself, not to the completion of either his or our understanding of himself. The puzzle is self-contained; it needs only a guide to take us through it.

And so the sleuth's real function is to play a game with us: he briskly ties together the revelations, some hard-won, some easily or accidentally dropped in his lap, but only rarely shares them, concurrently, with us. When he knows, we don't; we catch up later. As with Sherlock, his smarts leave us feeling stupid, and puzzling to catch up. But whether we're kept abreast or locked out, the new facts visible to us or out of sight, the revelations ride their concealed but logical way to their thoroughly logical conclusion – waiting, undisturbed and unaltered, so that without the bother of the plot-organized quest, we could as easily have been told at the start, in one breath, the final fixed facts. The pleasure for us is in the game of the tease; and when we finally know it all – relief?

Not entirely. Encroaching on the ostensible story of *Chinatown* is another one, and the discoveries of the one become an open door to the other – one that makes the difference between the mild pleasure of grasping the first story's finished design, and the shock and thrill of digesting a story of – possibly even now – disquieting substance. Its progression: tension is built slowly, leisurely, at the beginning depending largely on merely intriguing our curiosity, with Gittes, our sleuth, driving to one unlikely location, then another, then another, gathering information, storing up suspicions, reaching, silently, tentative conclusions. He lets us in on very few of them, but he grows increasingly generous as he gets closer to the lurid nugget waiting at the end of the plot's quest.

Step One: An investigative case of a husband's adultery is offered to him by a woman, one with "money no object." He suspects – though we have no reason to share his suspicion, nor does he give us a clue – that it's a setup. (And the woman, as it turns out, is, as the wife, a fake.)

Step Two: The real wife – Faye Dunaway – stops the investigation, but arouses other suspicions in Gittes – none of which we have reason to share, but follow along, mildly wondering.

Step Three: Gittes, our Virgil, is looking into L.A. water levels, the current drought, the corporate interests that are causing it, and the two top men – partners, evidently, who "own" the waters of L.A. as well as L.A. itself – when – gravest suspicion – one of them is suddenly murdered.

Step Four: Menace. The more information Gittes gathers – still shared only fitfully with us – the more he's met with polite stonewalling, then menace, then strong-arm beatings, until the iniquities of the L.A. water scandal open up: a consortium of two, then one (after the murder of one partner,) is squeezing the economic life out of L.A. by diverting the water supply.

Step Five: Except for the excessively civic-minded, this scandal as a final revelation would be no thrill. But the evil mastermind who is sucking the life out of the city for his personal gain (John Huston) is also the incestuous tyrant holding in lifetime hostage his daughter (Faye Dunaway) and their mutual daughter. Noticeably, the shock and horror of this revelation is at a disconnect from the water-supply scandal, but in the economy of suspense thrillers, it makes little difference – a momentous revelation has to finish the sleuthing plot before it morphs into:

Step Six: Terminal action: in which the sleuth plays rescuer for daughter-wife and her daughter-sister, climaxing in a shootout in which – reversing the happy-end formula – escaping Faye Dunaway is shot dead by the police and evil daddy grabs his screaming daughter-granddaughter for his own, and gets away with it. And so in this instance, the traditional strategy of retrogressive action is diverted from its usual ending – which would be merely the horror of the revelation itself (as in *Ghosts*, or *Long Day's Journey*) and extended instead by the stereotypical "action-movie" ending – the chase, the nick-of-time rescue, the shootout, the resolution, the fade.

SUBVERSIONS

Memento[7]

Probably no play or film but his own (subsequent) *Inception* worked so complex a weave of strategies into the structure of a retrogressive tale as Christopher Nolan's film, *Memento*. An involuted puzzle, it runs three discernible continuities through its action, and as though that confusion were transparency itself, it tells its entire story not merely retrogressively, but in *exactly* reverse chronological order, the last scene first, the first last. But so carefully are its scenes-in-reverse linked, and so clearly is the essential exposition accomplished in the very first moments of the film, that its impact is not so much bewildering as intriguing. To pull it apart is to do a disservice to so carefully interlocked a structure, but for purposes of description, we'll scalpel.

There are three continuities.

First continuity

Leonard, an insurance investigator, after the trauma of his wife's rape and murder, has lost his short-term memory. From that moment on, he's learned to rely on Polaroid snaps, written notes, and his own body's tattoos to keep him attuned to the hard facts of the recent and immediate past, so that he can function as his wife's avenger, and know that he's dealing with real facts, not illusions. It's a strategy of which he's proud. He compares himself to Sammy, a man who, after a car accident, has also lost his short term memory. But Sammy never developed a system for recording what happens as it happens, a routine by which he could reassure himself, as Leonard does, that the world has not gone away, that he exists within it, and that he can function as a purposeful agent.

At the beginning of the story (the film's actual end) we see Leonard murder a man – one whom he's been fooled into supposing is his wife's murderer. The lying cop who fooled him, and whom he then suspects and attempts to kill as the real murderer, in a panic tells him – possibly lying, possibly revealing the truth – that Leonard himself was his wife's killer, that he's induced his own short-term memory as protection against the truth, and that he's invented the story of Sammy and his diabetic wife as a further self-deception. In the next step of the story (the film's preceding scene) Leonard quickly (and carefully?) forgets both the murder and the lying cop's explanation, and congratulates himself on his strategies for controlling his connection to reality, and for staying on course for his revenge.

Second continuity

Leonard in his hotel room is on the phone talking to (he and we presume) a cop. He's narrating the entire story of his investigation of Sammy's and Sammy's wife's insurance claim. He suspects Sammy is faking, and as a conscientious insurance investigator, he has subjected Sammy to a series of tests to catch him out. The upshot of his investigation is his own confession (to the cop on the phone) that he was wrong about Sammy or his wife faking, and that she, unable to bear the pain of living with a mentally absent husband, allowed him to inject multiple doses of insulin into her for her diabetes, counting on his not remembering he had done so a moment before – and so wins her sought-for death.

Is this long phone report one conversation, or many? It's fragmented, in a series of scenes, filmed, unlike the rest of the film, in black-and-white, and told, also unlike the rest of the film, chronologically. Is it Leonard in the present, still working at his job as investigator, reporting his findings (but to the police?) Or Leonard (as the crooked cop suggested to him) fantasizing? The cop at the other end of the phone call interrupts once, to which Leonard, bewildered, responds: "What drugs?"

Third continuity

The story told backwards is the one of Leonard's involvement with "drugs." Unscrambled and told right side up, it's the story of his being drawn into a drug dealer's world, and being duped into carrying out two murders under the impression in each instance that his victim was his wife's murderer. Manipulated first by the lying undercover cop to murder the dealer who's come to pay him off, Leonard is then manipulated by the dead man's lover to kill the crooked cop.

Or is he? No matter how these separate continuities are reimagined and reassembled, none whether the explanations or the "reality" of the events is certain. The narrative is decorated with slight clues negating this reading, just as every other possible reading is hobbled by similar bits of unassimilated "facts." The most glib, brushing aside all objections of fact, is that the whole tale is wrapped entirely in Leonard's subjectivity – all a dream ! – erasing at a disappointing stroke all the script's complexities. But is even that simplistic explanation possible? Just as others are, this one is too.

As retrogressive narrative, *Memento* is close to the ultimate game that can be played with dramatic structure. Its "statement" or "meaning" is entirely latent in the structure itself, a structure whose grounding is finally unreliable and unfathomable. Leonard's mental plight, his wife's death, his being used by a drug ring, hardly register as much more than the given elements of a puzzle. Noted earlier: that "curiosity, puzzlement" is a "less compelling" seduction of spectator's response. But the impelling interest of *Memento's* puzzlements demonstrates sufficiently that, even absent "anxiety" for the protagonist, and absent any particularly exercising moral outrage, a deeply seducing intellectual puzzle can ultimately trap us in the vexations of indeterminacy. Reason's stabilities pushed aside, the effort to recover them can be as compelling or even more compelling than any number of anxieties, or any number of moral outrages for the way things are.

La Moustache[8]

But there's a pattern of indeterminacy more frightening than intriguing in *La Moustache*, the French film of Emmanuel Carrere, which builds its web of indeterminacy by eliminating altogether any reliability in burrowing into the past for answers in the present. In the film, "retrogression" and "progression" go hand in hand, but only to defeat one another as strategies for discovering "facts." What appear to be the givens of the story quickly undermine their own apparent certainty, and leave no reliable residue of certainties at all. Astonishingly, though, this has already become a possible premise for story-telling – a substantial, tolerable-in-fiction nightmare of shrinking absolutes that dissolves the reality of its objects and the certainty of its events, and even the certainties of already-observed transformations. These are real in fiction, of course, only by agreement between author and reader or spectator. But with that agreement frustrated, more than "objective reality" is lost. So is the possibility of "internalizing" the reality of the entire story within a single subjectivity (the story's protagonist, for example, or its narrator) since even fictional subjectivities need at least a minimum of substantial assurance to guarantee what even Dostoevsky or Kafka or Beckett guaranteed – a residue of memory's certainties sufficient to believe them, greatly disoriented though they may be, within the narrative.

In *La Moustache*, a trivial event triggers the eventual nightmare of "losing fact." Shaving off the mustache that his wife had professed to like, Marc is baffled that neither his wife nor their dinner hosts notice the change; but when his wife is put to the question of how she likes the change, she insists that he never had a mustache. To prove the fact that he did, he unearths the record of a phone call with his father in which the mustache was mentioned, only to be reminded that his father at that date was dead. Eventually, the radical divorce of the memories and perceptions they had both presumably shared, succumbs to the fact that their realities are entirely private, permanently uncorroborated, unavailable to the other, and so, suspect. (The story is a precise reversal of the classic opening conversation in Ionesco's "absurdist" play, *The Bald Soprano*,[9] in which Mr. and Mrs. Smith begin their dialogue as utter strangers, then ferret out facts about one another that lead to the eventual happy discovery that they're really intimate, in fact they're husband and wife.)

Strindberg's *The Road to Damascus*[10]

In traditional drama, so radical a loss of stability could be viewed, and was, as a strictly *personal* lunatic aberration, brought on by explainable causes. In Strindberg's *The Father*,[11] for example, the protagonist is reduced to insanity by the devilish ministrations of his wife. But the uncertainties which are the substance of his insanity (concerning his paternity, his manhood, etc.) belong to him alone, not to us, observing. But it is Strindberg too, as early as the Eighteen Nineties, who in another drama dallied with precisely this structure – or non-structure – of radical uncertainty in which the premises of the tale itself, or an episode in it, are built on sand. In a remarkable sequence in the Second Part of his trilogy, *The Road to Damascus*, its protagonist, the Stranger, is in conversation with his mother-in-law which he must break off to attend a banquet in which he is to be honored for his extraordinary achievements in science. During his acceptance speech at the banquet, the dignitaries at his table are one by one replaced by beggars, and the Stranger is confronted at the end of this baffling banquet with the bill, which he cannot pay. After a night in jail, he returns to his mother-in-law's, only to recognize the possibility that since the break in their conversation, only a few moments may have elapsed. As in Strindberg's *The Dream Play*,[12] nightmarish episodes of this kind can be seen as belonging wholly to the Dreamer, the play's maker; but Strindberg's mesmerizing invitation for us to share entirely in his nightmare is – without overstepping the bounds of an over-all rational structure – at the verge of unmooring altogether the assumptions of cause-and-effect, of stable oases of reality, of cores of certainties. In traditional patterns of "retrogressive action," causative sequence, metaphysical stabilities and even moral certainties can be more or less taken for granted. Now drama and film have come to tolerate patterns that are thoroughly unsustainable in "sense." Their increasing upsurge in both popular and art film versions mirror incipient suspicions about the reliability of just such intellectual certainties. Unstable structure is no longer an intolerable supposition.

***

CHAPTER 4
DOUBLE PROTAGONISTS AND "CONFLICT"

IS CONFLICT EVERYTHING?

Conflict, like the Immaculate Conception, came late to the list of eternal verities. It occurred to no one until the very early Nineteenth Century that conflict was the essence of drama, that in fact defined its substance. Here is a sample tribute to its exigency:

> A play is essentially the history of a particular conflict. The story begins with the first inkling of conflict and traces it through a series of peaks as the conflict grows to climax. Conflict (explicit and/or implicit) is at the core of every scene, every character and almost every moment of a play.[1]

There's another and more studied elaboration of "the Law of Conflict," which regards it as a metaphysical principle, beyond story. It is the condition of life itself, which is, according to this definition, a struggle of storing up against perpetual scarcity – a sort of *consumer nightmare* theory.

> The Law of Conflict is more than an aesthetic principle; it is the soul of story. Story is a metaphor for life, and to be alive is to be in seemingly perpetual conflict. As Jean-Paul Sartre expressed it, the essence of reality is scarcity, a universal and eternal lacking. There isn't enough of anything in this world to go around. Time, as Heidegger observed, is the basic category of existence. We live in an ever-shrinking shadow, and if we are to achieve anything in our brief being that lets us die without feeling we've

wasted our time, we will have to go into heady conflict with the forces of scarcity that deny our desires.

One might shake one's head in wonder at how it was possible that so fundamental a principle of dramatic structure never entered the head of either Aristotle – who never noticed it in Tragedy as a genre, or in any particular play – or the heads of any of the commentators of the next twenty-two centuries leading up to the early Nineteenth. And why then? There's a notion of cultural "composition," the composition, that is, of particular historical times. That notion suggests that the patterns of thought, of deep-seated (or as we say, unconscious) belief, had continued to shift so significantly over a period of time before the late Eighteenth Century, that, given the extraordinary events in politics, in commerce, in industrial development, in the changes that had come over the commonplaces of life generally, the period was ripe for a major shift in deep-seated feelings concerning the patterns of human existence and the patterns of human expectation. Existence hadn't been thought of as so exclusively a competitive enterprise before then; it was beginning to then. And that image became pervasive – in philosophy, in literature, in politics, in business, in international commerce. And so much was it to be reinforced during the rest of the Nineteenth Century, that thought itself, human expectation itself, were more bound by the assumption of competitive exchange among mortals than by any other. It was the German philosopher Hegel who in his *Phenomenology of Spirit* first detailed the dynamics of conflicting principles governing existence in his study of history, and in his remarks on drama[2] in *The Philosophy of Fine Art*, particularly on tragedy, and particularly on Sophocles' *Antigone*,[3] which became his model for conflicting protagonists each representing a conflicting principle, and that conflict governing the progress of the drama.

Not from Hegel's example alone, but from concurrent sensibility, the feeling for *conflict as construct*, conflict as governing reality, took hold not only of speculation on drama, but of speculation generally. The notion was adopted fairly quickly into dramatic theory, certainly into Nineteenth Century dramatic practice, and inevitably, it was visited retroactively on the dramas of the past. Plays of any vintage, of any period, seen through the lens of this particular time's imagination, no matter how remotely from this notion they were in fact imagined in their own time, were given contemporary credentials: all now sported *conflict*.

Judging from the competitive brutalities of the last two centuries, there seems little reason to believe that the notion of conflict as the governing principle of drama will be let go of soon. It's still the staple, certainly, of mainstream criticism, mainstream teaching, and mainstream drama. What's in question, though, as we'll have reason to consider, is the existence of contrary sensibilities which have been displacing the clichés of theory and practice to which conflict-oriented criticism and practice have remained impounded. And there's a broader question: Is it really true that every moment of every life is lived in the grip of conflict? Or is it more true that once in a while if not oftener, the governing principles of the lived life escape it altogether, and enjoy or suffer radically different states of being, states which, when incorporated into dramas, give subtlety, penetration and the feeling of the truth to dramas that conflict alone can flatten into one naive dimension or violate altogether?

But, before the Nineteenth Century, play structure was never described, as it usually is now, as a series of ongoing conflicts under the umbrella of an overriding conflict. It was conventionally described as a structure of three distinct parts: Preparation, Complication and Resolution.[4] During "Preparation," motives were set on course, obstacles were anticipated, and sometimes a mysterious secret was hinted at or only partially revealed. During "Complication" (also called "the tying of the knot") motives crisscrossed and tangled, obstacles reared up powerfully and seemed immovable, misunderstandings and tricks multiplied, and confusion heaped on confusion. During "Resolution" (also called "the untying of the knot") the secret was revealed clearing up misunderstandings, obstacles gave way, and motives either reached their goal or adjusted.

"GOAL" MODEL

How much did "conflict" have to do with this understanding of plot progression? Considerable, but it was not seen, as it is now, to be controlling. And it operated at different degrees and on different levels of significance. Because the essential activity, the key propulsion, of the plot was seen as *a campaign toward a goal* – to get the master's wife into bed, or to murder the king and sit on his throne, or to win in marriage the daughter of the miser, or to be revenged on the rapist of wife or daughter, or on the murderer of son or father or wife or daughter. Or, most ambitiously, to win great wealth or power, or both together. So that "Preparation" was seen as the spelling out of the obstacles to be faced, and the laying out of the strategies to be used to overcome them. And here is the difference: the obstacles to be faced in this campaign were not merely active, competitive agents, but more often than not obstacles that were inert, fixed and bafflingly unyielding – Gordian knots – that had somehow to be smashed through or circumvented. What this protagonist – and his plot – needed most was single-minded ingenuity and cunning. Since this plot model was perpetrated largely during the Renaissance and lasted through most of the Eighteenth Century, it should be clear how its creators' life-models were being simultaneously imagined: as cutting one's way through obstacles any which way to reach clearly set private goals.

What was the nature of those "obstacles?" It made little difference to the plot's project whether they were active competitors for the same goal, aggressive obstructers against its achievement, or inert, unchangeable circumstances that stood in the way; all needed the same overcoming or bypassing, whether by strength or stealth. And after confusion was heaped on confusion in the "Complication" section of the plot's progression, it made little difference in the "Resolution" whether ingenuity, cunning, accident, miracle or merely cleared-up misunderstanding was responsible for putting all the plot's ducks in a row – any way out was fair play and good enough, so long as the goal was reached. Machiavelli's Sixteenth Century Florentine comedy, *Mandragola*,[5] is a perfect if cynical example of such a protagonist driving toward his fixed goal with amoral cunning and guile.

Mandragola

Preparation: The young student Callimaco, falling in love with the portrait of a Florentine lady married to an old fool of a husband, has flown back from Paris to win her. He begins by reckoning the obstacles toward winning her bed: she is married, she has a stupid but suspicious husband, and greatest obstacle of all, she is virtuous. He sets out to overcome each of the obstacles in turn:

Complication: By direct and blatant appeal to the self-interest of his servant, then of a parasite, then of the husband himself, then of her confessor, and finally of the lady's mother, all contribute handily to his scheme – a pretense that the mandrake root, an aphrodisiac which on its first use kills, but used thereafter would guarantee the husband renewal of his potency and the birth of a son. Against her desire, the lady is persuaded to succumb to the scheme first by her willingly duped husband, then by her confessor, then by her mother. The passing stranger who is kidnapped by husband and henchman, and put into the bed of the lady to suffer, presumably, the fatal pleasure of the first use of the mandrake root, is of course Callimaco in disguise.

Resolution: The lady, after their night of pleasure, acknowledges that after suffering the stupidity of her husband and the cupidity of her confessor and her mother to bring her to adultery, she will happily surrender virtuous principle for what, with Callimaco, should prove eternally rewarding policy.

"CONFLICT" MODEL

Unlike this model, then, in which a protagonist's announced and clearly formulated desire begins the plot, in "direct-conflict" models, the plot does not begin and the protagonist is not awakened to his role until an active counter force – an antagonist, an Iago against Othello, a Stanley against Blanche, a Bolingbroke against Richard, – is perceived to be operating against him or his good. What's the effect of the difference? In a *Mandragola*-like play, the role of the aggressive "antagonist," if there is one, may be one amongst other obstacles, variable in importance, sometimes less than secondary and sometimes even absent. In *Mandragola* itself, he does not even appear – all the oppositions are simply obstacles – inert, simply there – made up of the fixed realities of human nature's greed or morality's virtue. None are actively contending against Callimaco and none are competing with him for his prize. And so in this "protagonist's-goal-with-obstacles" model, there is possibly and possibly not an active antagonist. In the "equal-contenders" model, the perpetual competition is obviously primary, invariable and essential to the plot's beginning at all, as well as to its continuing life. And so, with the unmistakable triumph of "conflict" as drama's prime ingredient, contending characters, when they went at one another, left no doubt that they meant their fight to shape the progress of the plot in which they were embroiled, and said so. Bolingbroke in Scribe's *The Glass of Water*[6] is crystal-clear: "For twenty-four hours, a faithful armistice?" he challenges, throwing the gauntlet down to the Duchess of Marlborough, and she unhesitatingly echoes: "But afterwards, war!" Dumas fils, generally more civilized in his dialogue, is no more civilized in his plot maneuvering: "Then it's – war?" asks Suzanne in *The Demi-Monde*,[7] and Olivier obligingly concurs: "Very well: war!" even though their contention is many notches below a struggle between life and death. And the habit persists: Albee,[8] a reasonably civilized teller, can't let it alone. To George's "Total war?" Martha responds, like her forbears: "Total!"

In the Jungle of Cities[9]

Even when the battle lines are drawn more subtly, the moment of unspoken challenge is generally as clear as when it's spoken. Brecht, as though inventing for the first time the story artifice of a head-on collision of contending parties, makes the point of his play, *In the Jungle of Cities*, precisely this: that his two protagonists with no past antagonism or even knowledge of one another, lock at once, in Scene One, in a deadly contest in which both intend as in a prize-fight to vanquish the other, and have no other reason for being in the same world than for the sake of that plot victory. "You are about to witness," writes Brecht in his Prologue, "an inexplicable wrestling match between two men…. Don't worry your heads about the motives for the fight, concentrate on the stakes. Judge impartially the technique of the contenders, and keep your eyes on the finish." But what Brecht has inadvertently caught is the essential gratuitousness to which "conflict" can descend, the speciousness of the reasons for it happening at all, and yet − its real and only reason for being − its irresistible pleasure. Like gambling, like Russian roulette, apart from invented reasons, there is no particular purpose for the spectator indulging in the pastime of watching other than for its thrill.

Scribe

Scribe's well-made play made no bones about its pointlessness.[10] The presumed motives for his conflicts were lofty, but his use of them − or generally, his neglect of the lofty side of them − in the playing out of his dramas, was determinedly insipid. Determinedly so, since it was clear to him that in his carelessly comfortable bourgeois society, human combat, focused as it was on the pursuit of private goals, at best gave only lip service to loftier goals, and at worst (after mentioning perhaps once that they were battling, really, for Country, for Queen, for Love and so on, rarely mentioned such a thing again) pursuing the game exclusively for its pleasure and/or immediate profit, not its virtue. It is precisely this subversion of ideal purpose that is consistently characteristic of both the essential amorality of the Scribian playwright's game, and the spectator's absorption in the game. As with a chase, a prizefight or a ball game, the spectator picks a side in dramatic conflict, and − whether everything or nothing is at stake makes little difference − he vicariously roots.

What is he rooting for? His surrogate, his other self, who is shooting all the baskets, pirouetting his screeching car through Brooklyn's streets to get away, trading brain-rattling punches with the other bruiser in the ring, creeping through the jungle underbrush after the menace he has to kill first, or possibly away from the menace who is creeping after him. It can be amusing, it can be heart-stopping, but for the spectator so hooked, it might as well be, and − for the brief moments of the show − is for him, as gripping as the matter of life and death. Why? Why is he so gripped? (One explanation, above, is joined by another. here.) Because having chosen his surrogate by instant, intimate recognition, worry for that interim alter ego and for himself begins. The worry can even become terror. There's a vortex inside that surrogate's plight that sucks the spectator in; the plight becomes immediately his own. The vortex has a double appeal: the self enters into and undergoes the familiar terrors of failure, victimization, injustice, monstrosity, inhumanity, obliteration, or possibly only misunderstanding, mild threat, social unease, puzzlement. But at the same time, riding with those same defeating fantasies, there's the counter-fantasy of their conquest, their assuagement. Watching the ball game or watching the movie provokes the same atavism for conquest, for passing over to the role of victimizer one's accumulated burden of victimization. At their most violent and most extreme, whether the game or the movie, in both pastimes the onlooker suffers alike, and yearns alike, for the happy exchange of the nightmare of being murdered for the eventual euphoria of murdering. To arrive at so ecstatic a redemption, it's worth passing through the extremes of anxiety and the most unbearable of sufferings. Because the melodrama of drama, like the melodrama of sports, surfaces these deepest of human atavisms, it's to the most primitive of its appeals to which the most primitive of its formulas is addressed: double-protagonists locked in mortal combat, one of whom is us.

Strangers on a Train[11]

A transparent example of the formula is played out in one of Alfred Hitchcock's most successful thrillers: *Strangers on a Train*. It's a template for double-protagonist plots moved wholly by "conflict."

First Sequence: Dismissible Intimations.

Gus (who will become us) accidentally meets Bruno (his potential antagonist) on a train trip home. The stranger insinuates himself into our (Gus's) attention, suggesting – mockingly? – that he would gladly oblige Gus by murdering his unwanted wife (how does he know?) in exchange for Gus returning the favor by murdering his, Bruno's, father. Before Gus gets off the train, to get rid of this lunatic stranger, he says mockingly, dismissively, Oh, sure.

Second Sequence: Inadvertent Entrapment.

Gus in an angry exchange with his wife is ready to strangle her for refusing to grant him a divorce, and then, on the phone, says as much to Ruth, the woman he yearns to marry: "I could have strangled her!" he confesses.

Gus gets a call from Bruno, saying he's ready to initiate their "pact." (A bit of interim "psychological" exposition – a favorite one in the Fifties – establishing Bruno as psychotic: at home, he demonstrates for us the murderous Oedipal romance he's enjoying, hating his old man and fancying his pampering mama.) Gus, realizing for the first time the seriousness of Bruno's lunatic challenge, hangs up with a bang, but he, and we, are beginning to sweat.

Third Sequence: Conflict Is Suddenly Overt and Joined.

Bruno proceeds to murder Gus's wife, actually does, and comes to tell Gus it's done, and demands equal response.

Gus's *new situation:* He has only negative options. He had motive for the murder of his wife, Bruno reminds him; and Bruno had neither known motive nor known connection to the victim. If Gus tells police the truth, Bruno has material evidence to condemn him (Gus's inscribed cigarette lighter, which Bruno cadged on the train during their first meeting, and could plant near the dead body.)

[*Note that lighter:* a perfect example of Hitchcock's famous "McGuffin," the secret which will solve the mystery of the plot. It was once, in the nineteenth century's well-made play formula, the letter in the locked drawer, the will hidden in the tree, the lost ticket for the murderer's gun which is languishing abandoned in the pawn shop. During the play's or film's last sequence, the entire energy of the plot will be focused on getting possession of it and revealing its secret. This is the tight "narrowing" of the play's focus – when at its finish, the action is wholly devoted to the scramble, preferably one on one, for that single object.] Gus is left with nothing but the option of hope: that he can somehow imagine a way out of this victimization by a madman. How?

Fourth Sequence: The Main Action: Thrust-and-Parry.

With the conflict between the protagonists now overt and engaged, the "middle" plot action, oddly enough, is not simply a perpetual, open clawing battle between them. It is almost its opposite: a rhythm of deliberate, calculated, unhurried, thrusts-and-parries – exactly resembling, believe it or not, the rhythm of Laurel and Hardy[12] comedy. Recall their comedy's strategy – a strategy of comic genius – and note: first one, motivated by the other's just-perpetrated indignity, considers slowly, then decides inwardly, then nods – and only then proceeds to retaliate: Stan tears, for example, the pocket off Oliver's coat. During this outrageous act, Oliver observes, does nothing while the indignity continues, then when it is over, considers, comes to a silent decision, nods – and then proceeds to retaliate: tears, for example, the whole sleeve off Stan's coat. Stan, following that same calculation, that same procedure, ups the ante – and by the end of their retaliations, they've destroyed step by slowly considered step, their whole house, or their whole car, or their whole neighborhood.

It is precisely this series of considered thrusts and considered parries – each waiting for the other to act, each noting his consequent gain or loss, then considering his options, and finally parrying – that constitutes the "battle-action" between these stereotypically matched protagonists. The pattern is unlike Laurel and Hardy's in only one respect: the rhythm of exchange becomes not only, like theirs, more and more consequential, but incrementally faster; the rush of the action, the truncating of time as the plot moves to its end, is one of the signatures of the well-made play's structure, and of its imitation in film. (But as we'll see in a moment, Hitchcock, by doing the opposite, outdoes the well-made play's impact.)

Thrust: When the police, suspecting with reason a connection between Gus and his wife's murder, call him in for questioning, he has one out: during the time of the murder, he was once again on his commuter train, talking to a man he distinctly remembers. (Establishing this fact, Gus would be entirely relieved of Bruno's hold over him.) They call in the man.

Result: The man was drunk, and on cross-examination, remembers nothing.

Parry: Against Gus's miserably unsuccessful thrust, Bruno parries: phone calls, letters, insisting that Gus, having lost his option (that alibi), now murder Bruno's father.

Thrust: Gus phones Bruno to leave his house, pretending that he will go there to kill his father, and that he's on his way. Approaching the old man apparently asleep in his bed, Gus wakes him, hoping to tell him the truth of his son's plot.

Parry: Bruno, having anticipated Gus's plan, is in bed in his father's stead, frustrating Gus's intention, and

Thrust: Enraged at the "betrayal," he confronts Gus with the evidence – now held in his hand – of the cigarette lighter, which, in revenge, he will plant near the murder scene – in the dark – to establish Gus's guilt.

Parry: Gus – after a set of frustrating delays (the champ tennis match he has to play, the police tailing him to arrest him, their suspect) – has to get to the amusement park – before nightfall – where the murder occurred, before Bruno can plant the lighter at the scene of the crime.

Fifth Sequence: Terminal (Physical) Conflict.

The Terminal One-on-One Confrontation: Both have reached the amusement park, spotted each other at the park's carousel, and both, on the strength of the outcome of their wrestling tussle, will win all or lose all. Carousel breaks down, races, collapses, (what was called in Nineteenth Century melodrama the "Sensation

Scene") while the hand-to-hand fight brings Bruno to accidental death (the cops who are after Gus shoot Bruno instead,) and the cigarette lighter falls out of the hand of the dying Bruno – confirming Gus's story for the cops. (A weakish line had to be added to the script's last moments to absolve the cops of the onus of sloppy shooting. The Chief Cop is heard on soundtrack: "We already knew he was the guilty one.")

So much for the bare bones of the one-on-one "conflict" between two protagonists. But only its bare bones. What is added to that structure, pre-eminently by Hitchcock, is a set of obstacles, irrelevancies, or circumstantial constraints that impede, slow, and divert the intended and expected flow of the action, and paradoxically by so doing, boost enormously its emotional momentum. They are deft, skillfully placed, and perfectly arbitrary, but they make the difference between a merely reasonably logical, reasonably compelling telling of the tale, and a nail-biting one. In *Strangers on a Train*, arbitrary and pasted on though they are, they add to the thrill:

1) Slowing, instead of hurrying the action:

As the plot moves toward final confrontation – this is a Hitchcock signature device – not only is the usual hurtling to the finish slowed, but it's stopped altogether. Gus, a tennis pro, is scheduled for the championship game of his life on this particular afternoon, at the plot's very last hour. The action stops for the match; it's played out in full, all *four* sets, while the plot waits. But if Gus – and we – were in a sweat before this *irrelevantly inserted process* intruded, every moment of its progress adds to his and our desperation to get the damn tennis match out of the way so that he can –

2) The Race of The Tortoise and the Hare:

before the oncoming of night, when Bruno will be able to plant the McGuffin near the scene of the murder – Gus has to get to the amusement park to stop him. The tortoise and the hare nightmare: Bruno is already in the park, waiting impatiently for night to fall, while Gus, try as he might to hurry up, has to crawl slowly through the four sets of his tennis match.

3) A third nightmare: Tightening the Noose:

Once the Gus-Bruno conflict has been joined (in Third Sequence), Gus is progressively squeezed into narrower parameters. In addition to the insistent pressure of Bruno's demand, there's the growing menace of the police who, more and more sure of Gus's guilt, first keep one cop on his trail, then a number of them, and by the last sequence a small army of cops is tracking him to the amusement park. The "thrusts" of his plot-actions, the freedom to implement them, become so tightly constrained that by the last sequence, he has almost no parameters left – only the one that –

4) Nick of Time:

luckily – lets him get to the carousel on time for the finish.

So: (1) an excruciating slowing of the action at the threshold of an anticipated climax; (2) an increasingly encroaching contraction of the protagonist's parameters of action; (3) a race between the protagonist's tortoise and his antagonist's hare; (4) the protagonist's final panicked effort to arrive, finish and win in the nick of time. Overall, the trajectory of a loser's nightmare stretched almost to the limit of paralyzed helplessness, then reversed in one miraculous instant. The control, the perfect manipulation of this emotional trajectory's smoothness, is possible because no matters other than its own maneuverings divert or burden its progress. In its incremental hurry to get to its end, it narrows its focus when it's approaching its oncoming, final collision, divesting meaning's and value's irrelevant freight. Approaching that end, the spectator, abstracting himself entirely from the world of pressing reality, banishes from the mind everything extraneous to the game's or the story's outcome, wraps himself in the deepest pleasures of terror and suffering, and then in the even greater ecstasy of victory over terror and suffering.

He, grateful and thrilled, touches more thoroughly, more profoundly, ecstasies of emotional release than he is likely ever to know in the real world, and, gratifyingly, without practical resonance, without guilt, and without (unless he bets) consequence.

In summary: the conventional structure of a double-protagonist conflict, less used on stage now but alive and well in film, still following Hitchcock's model – which he in turn inherited and expanded from early silent film: (1) There's the awakening, usually a gradual, slow realization of the "me," the protagonist, to the existence of the danger and hostility of the "other," the antagonist; (2) there's the first joining of the issue between them, which remains tentative and unresolved; (3) there's the long sequence of thrust-and-parry in the "Laurel and Hardy" mode of carefully considered tit-for-tat; (4) there's finally the open joining of battle, involving either naked warfare with metaphorical or actual armies, or a classic horse or plane or car or foot chase, energy at maximal pitch, except for (5) the terminal contest of the two protagonists in a one-on-one fight, hand to hand or sword to sword or gun to gun, in which the "me" – protagonist, after near-death or other kind of termination, wins by a hair.

Recognizably, the model is so exhausted that to survive, it's needed massive technological infusion, but for all its mechanical torpor, it remains the most astronomically successful model for entertainment in human history, and so has no pressing urge to change.

MELODRAMA IN EARNEST

But unlike Scribe's and modern mainstream audiences' careless moral indifferentism, early melodrama's audiences did have a stake, and a considerable one, in their choice of sides. Critically savaged, melodrama's lowly audiences had one advantage over their overclass: to them it mattered. The assaults on virtue, the kidnappings, the violations of the helpless, the victimizations of the poor, the exploitations of the unprotected, the starvations and deaths of the abandoned, suffered in group memory and elevated into group nightmare, provoked passion, not amused indifference, when their staged reflection stared them in the face. And so provoked, the spectator-victim's heart raged for justice, sharing the unequal battle, the "conflict," in total emotional rapport with his stage surrogates, and won with them their concluding, equalizing, mutual dream of overcoming life's massively unjust immovables. It was precisely this investment of their emotional activism that rendered *aesthetically* ridiculous both them and the spectacles they wept over and applauded. Aesthetically indeed, since as we've noticed, it's the unspoken but common feature of raw dramatic "conflict" that it must eventually matter as little as possible in the ordinary pass-through of dramatic action in which the game gradually pursues only its own game's end, ridding itself along the way of its originally provoked, originally meaningful baggage. Conflict raw has the fundamental purity of that abstraction, and like all abstraction, studiously avoids the irrelevance of the particular and the real. And when the disturbances of reality do continue to cling, the thoroughly unengaged are bothered by what they regard as aesthetic lapse. Scribe preached that preaching had no place in dramatic entertainment, and the queasy feeling of its encroachment, when it does encroach, moves the unengaged to take umbrage in whatever accommodation they can find in critical jargon.

CLASSIC CONFRONTATIONS

Tragedy, of course, exhibits more terrible engagements, but even then not always with the starkness of head-on conflict. Again, there are subtle variations, some so elusive as hardly to merit the name of "conflict." But we find in some of the greatest tragedies in Western drama, conflict's absolute, fully earned.

Schiller's *Mary Stuart*[13]

Queen Mary/Queen Elizabeth: In one of the greatest confrontation scenes in Western drama, the meeting of the two English queens in Schiller's tragedy, *Mary Stuart*, poses stature against stature – the political power of Elizabeth against the political helplessness of her captive, Mary. But the confrontation ends with the leveling of their inherent psychological prowess as each woman enlarges through argument the greatness of her pride.

Whatever the overt victory of the one or overt failure of the other, at the end of the scene they are matched in their dignity, their will, their unbridled power in opposition. The two queens in this climactic scene represent the ultimate in direct battle, the ultimate in naked confrontation.

The Father[14]

In Strindberg's tragedy, two contenders of equal savagery battle openly not merely in the climactic *scene a faire*, but in every moment of their drama. The male, the Captain, and his wife Laura contend for absolute psychic-sexual domination, two antagonists who, once roused to sexual battle, cannot be diverted until one of them is destroyed. In their contention, though, the wife has lying in wait from the beginning the ultimate weapon against which the father must prove helpless: the sure knowledge which only the woman can have of the paternity of their child.

In the first act, the contention between them begins sanely enough with the sort of question which for rational people seems amenable to resolution: the question of the proper education, the proper schooling for their daughter. What lies behind their discussion, from their first exchange triggered to explode, is the buried, too easily evoked, atavistic competitiveness between male and female. At the critical moment in their contest – implicitly, their silent but perpetual war – Laura brings into play the weapon against which the prowess of the male has no counter. The cunning of Laura's campaign is in her never granting the Captain certainty; his fatherhood is neither confirmed nor denied but only held in question. The uncertainty leads finally to the Captain's "madness," his psychic castration, and at play's end, he is lying helplessly straitjacketed, submissive and defeated.

Strindberg's pattern is closely echoed in Albee's *Who's Afraid of Virginia Woolf?* in which the struggle, once engaged, is also unrelenting and incremental, and leads to the total defeat – not, as in *The Father*, to the male's castration, but – to the mutual destruction of the illusion on which the marriage's fragile bond of male-female love-hate depended for survival. In both plays, the primary and unrelenting place of direct "conflict" is almost ritualistic in its step-by-step inevitability – Albee's play is in fact programmed as a "ritual," a sort of Witch's Sabbath – to the exclusion of all other structural devices, and both serve as models, almost perfect ones, for drama's appeal as the mythopoetic ground for naked, unalloyed, uninterrupted battle, whether with psychic or real weapons of war.

Equally matched contenders produce, of course, head-on collisions. But rarely do other contending protagonists slug it out without intermission throughout an entire play; characteristically, their struggle gathers force incrementally, reaches climactic confrontation in a major scene, and is resolved in the victory of one, or the defeat of both, or the victory of both. But this is too easily said, since permutations in the progressions of conflict range from comic-book directness to subtleties that almost conceal the evidence of its going on. Let's look briefly at some examples of the mightily driven, and the subtly tempered battlers in action.

Antigone

Head to head, then, the progress of two protagonists bent on destroying one another can be seen and applauded, as in Scribe, more for their skills and cunning and weapons and maneuverings than for their moral intent. But what about plays in which their moral intent is never lost sight of, in which their battle is fought with an eye forever on their moral purpose, and in which allegiance to that purpose wholly defines the parameters within which they fight? This, in Hegel's view, is the case in Greek tragedy, and the example of *Antigone* serves as his defining instance of tragic conflict in Western drama.[15] Let's look closely at his example of *Antigone* as dramatic "conflict" charged with overwhelming moral import.

Creon forbid the burial of Polyneices who, in warring against Thebes, was condemned as a traitor to the state. His sister Antigone, out of religious obligation to the tie of blood, violated Creon's injunction and performed the burial ceremony anyhow. Two principles in conflict: on the one hand, Creon's allegiance to the state, on the other, Antigone's allegiance to family blood-ties; both presumably absolute, both unswerving, leaving principles and characters irreconcilable.

But there's a fixed difficulty for principles doing battle in drama: they cannot. For two reasons. First, since principles are not persons, they have themselves no voice and no volition – they need embodiment. But the moment they have it, either the dynamic of the drama or the dynamic of intellectual controversy is imperiled. If the characters are not to be walking precepts, there must be an animus alive in them – motive, disposition – that is automatically heeded by playwright as well as spectator, and the instant it is, argument becomes only a function of motive, an expression or extension of motive. But once argument becomes peripheral to, a mere instance of the playing out of, motive, it has little efficacy of its own. Its logic at once becomes psychologic, and its truth is only relative to the truth of the character's conviction and motive, and not as truth seen justified in itself.

On the other hand, impersonal argument, that is to say, argument coming out of a human mouth that is understood to be true in itself and has no self-referential inflection, lies outside the discourse of drama and tends not to be heard – sometimes not even to be tolerated. In the case of Hegel's model, *Antigone*, the battle of principle between the two protagonists is fought, or rather voiced, only once – in their first confrontation – and subsequently, as in the drama of Scribe, practical maneuverings to overcome the enemy's resistance are substituted for the battle of convictions. It is the failure of *those* maneuvers and their strategies that defeats them. *They,* the characters, are defeated, but both their principles remain as they were, neither won, lost, nor tested.

What we are left with, then, in the head-to-head battles of two equally-weighted protagonists, is their power of wit or their power of will to overcome the other, and whoever wins, it is not within the straitjacketed province of traditional dramatic convention to signify by that victory or that defeat any more or any less meaning or value to the moral banner under which either contestant has fought. Except in intellectual fantasy. And it is precisely in our fantasy of plot construction as inherently providential that winning or losing at the story's end tells us who owns the moral victory. Clearly, a specious judgment, and a specious "ending."

HEGEL AND THE IDEA OF CONFLICT

But that is not exactly the feeling of "end" we experience in plays like *Antigone* in which the thematic resolution is not specious, but profound. And though the double demise of Antigone and Creon is brought about not by the contest of their values, but as in Scribe by the contest of their wills and strategies, it is still the case that the end in terms of significant meaning signifies a great deal more than the same strategies at the end of Scribe's plays manage to signify. The practical rules of battle are the same. Then what's the difference?

Here Hegel has a precisely studied and precisely reasoned answer. It's in the baggage the protagonists carry, the inherent value that *is* or *becomes* character itself in the course of their struggle. Hegel puts it in language of studied obscurity, but it can be parsed: he calls the motives of his ethical hero "the practical content of [his] volitional self-identity." That "practical content" does not define his "soul-life" – that is, his inherent ethical being – until it *engages*, until, that is, it realizes itself "by means of active volition," and so making itself into "an object of the outer world," the world of human affairs and human engagement. Translated, it seems obvious enough: the self becomes a genuinely active agent when it enters into, and engages in, the real world. Not news. But what *is* news is Hegel's concept of that moral agent, that heroic protagonist. His ethical posture is so embedded in his "soul-life" that when it does manifest itself in the real world, it becomes demonstrably the whole of the self, without distinction between the practical "conflict" in which he is engaged, and the moral posture with which he of necessity imbues it. Inseparable from his own being, he bears within him the code of values by which he automatically acts, and by which, winning or losing the prize in his worldly (plot) struggle, his *transcending* the practical defeat or compromise of those values – which are, in Hegel's terms, his very self – *is* his victory, a victory established, therefore, for those very values which define the whole of him.

The final revelation, at the conclusion of this protagonist's journey, is a moment of the purest manifestation of the unity of self and meaning-value. And the splendor of that revelation –

whether in a moment of worldly triumph or in a moment of heroic (or even ignominious) death – transcends worldliness altogether. He *is* the heroic, the icon of ethical heroism, and his values – within him and through him – win that triumph.

How many heroic icons in the Nineteenth Century grew to this stature in the final moments of the fifth act! How many lived through four acts teetering this way and that on the brink of self-revelation, only to reveal their worth in full and dazzling ethical splendor in the fifth! There were such heroes in abundance in the past, to be sure, but the Nineteenth Century, following the gush of Romantic sensibility in its early decades, wallowed in this vision of heroic moral closure in its poetic drama, its closet drama, its bourgeois melodrama (and therefore in its opera), and late in the century in its revival of Romantic moral heroism in the social/political and reform drama which imagined it had turned its back on these Hegelian idealist excesses. And they were, for very good reason, the heroes still most reverenced in Twentieth Century mainstream drama. Why cannot Proctor, in Arthur Miller's *The Crucible*,[16] manage to speak the scurrilous lies to his Seventeenth Century McCarthy Committee to save himself? "Because it is my name!" he cries, dying, but for us, absolved.

THE SPECIAL CASE: "SEPARATED" HEROES

And here we have the secret of that double-protagonist conflict that is *like* conflict, but not quite. Consider the Doctor Stockmanns,[17] as in Ibsen's *Enemy of the People*, who are left with the shattered remnants of their lives, but who nevertheless are seen as the moral victors, holding the unspoiled banners of their ethical devotion higher than ever at play's end. What could be more obvious than that they, as well as their moral devotion, own, unambiguously, the victory – the very victory that is signaled in their defeat? The special glory of these latter-day Hegelian saints[18] is that they are *in no sense* in the same arena as their contenders; they are, in spirit, *somewhere else*. The goals for which they are fighting are not only different, but of almost comic, or almost tragic, irrelevance to their apparent plot goals. And the ironies that attend their victorious demise, not only for Ibsen's Stockmann but

Rostand's Cyrano and Buchner's Danton and Musset's Lorenzacchio and Byron's Manfred and Ibsen's Brand and Shaw's Marchbanks and Caesar and St. Joan and Arthur Miller's Proctor, in no case win plot victories over the "other," but in every case victory, so to speak, "in-itself." And it is very much the case that since the Nineteenth Century, all these heroic failures and their kind are ruefully lauded by their playwrights for their *separation* from their flock, from their time, from their world, and signify by their very being a sometimes moderate and sometimes entire contempt for the world as it is. They are, in their virtue, uniformly, somewhere else.

That note of lonely ethical separation echoes in few historical periods of Western drama more compassionately for us than in Elizabethan tragic drama. There too the fundamentally tormenting sense of a hostile or shredded ethical landscape, one that must be rejected and at the same time accommodated, moves its tragic heroes sometimes to frenzy, sometimes to raging irony. But who, dramatically, personifies their opposite, their "antagonist?" Not always a single character or even – as Stockmann faces – a whole town, but instead, one writ large, in the mass, in "the world." Let's distinguish in tragic oppositions between active agents and this passive, inert, greatest of all, obstacles: "things as they are," or more particularly, structures of morality, structures of belief, which are sometimes hardly nameable, and sometimes overwhelming and altogether imprisoning.

ACTIVE AGENT, INERT OBSTACLE

An active agent standing against "the world's" opposition is familiar enough: Hamlet faces "the world," the times that are out of joint, as they enter the lists against him in the guise of Claudius, of Polonius, of Rosencranz and Guildenstern, and for a moment even of Ophelia. A hydra-headed opposing agent, to be sure, but dramatically active – challenging, mocking, scheming, threatening. These he in turn challenges, mocks, schemes against, even threatens. But the "conflict" between him and these representative agents hardly encompasses the whole of his intangible opposition, which is the world as such, the times out of joint, which are the manifestations – as in the case of Stockmann – of the forest of beliefs and commitments from which he so passionately disengages. We have seen how this fixed, inert enemy functions in the lighter fare of classical comedy, but in tragedy and in the serious drama of the past two centuries, that obstacle, dramatically inert, simply there, is – in tragedy – unconquerable. It's the wall against which all these alienated agents hurl themselves in their own time, and which functions as the absolute limit at which the protagonist's battle, no matter how heroic, falters. It's the inert but adamant obstacle to which the Elizabethan heroes succumbed, as we've said, sometimes with rage and sometimes with sneering resignation, and about which modern heroes, given our faltering religion of ongoing Progress, wisely project their hope of victory into far, far distant futures.

"Obstacle", then, contends by doing nothing, by being there. But though it is the truest, the ultimate, the terminal, opposition to the protagonist, battling only by its inertness, in tragedy it can utterly confound the simple pattern of two active contenders, and leave only one of them – the "protagonist" – in active contention, while the other – the "obstacle" – is the victor before the game has even begun.

***

CHAPTER 5
MULTIPLE PLOTS

Plot, says Aristotle, is the soul of Tragedy, and a single action is the unifying principle of the plot. But the long history of drama in the West didn't bear out his stricture. The contest between single action and multiple action as the structural core of plays, one arguing the authority of Aristotle and the other the authority of popular practice, is in fact a draw: In Italy in the Renaissance, Commedia dell'arte reveled in multiple progressions, Shakespeare and the Elizabethans opted generally for two concurrent plots, but sometimes reveled even more in as many as five concurrent progressions – not all full plots, to be sure, but not all easily accommodated under the umbrella of a single unifying action.

Which is best? Neither. The French neoclassical plays of the Seventeenth Century produced what are arguably some of the greatest plays in Western tradition, and were rigidly devoted to the single action formula; but the neoclassicists in England of Shakespeare's time – the Countess of Pembroke's and Sir Philip Sidney's circle[1] – just as piously devoted to the single-action formula, produced some of the most thoroughly forgotten plays of any time. Both the most outrageous violations of tight-action construction, and the most analy-constricted single-action structures, have each in their way produced masterpieces – and so, no contest.

DOUBLE PLOTS

Heywood's *A Woman Killed with Kindness*[2]

In most Elizabethan dramas, a subplot alternates with a main plot, and frequently – in fact, most often – the one has little to do with

77

the other.   In one remarkable instance, *A Woman Killed with Kindness,* the subplot has so little to do with the main plot that the very basic assumptions of the one confute the assumptions of the other; the two stories remain in entirely different fictional worlds. In the main plot, a deeply Puritan psychology and morality demonstrate the doom of predestined characters to commit sin with no possibility of avoiding it.   The seducer is so thoroughly "unelected" for salvation that try as he might, there's no conceivable way for him to avoid the devil's blandishments; his victim, the virtuous wife of an upright husband, is seduced by her very compassion for her seducer's suffering, thereby exemplifying the dour lesson that   giving the devil the slightest toehold – showing compassion, for example, for a sinner – invites the fiend to drag so misguided a soul to damnation.   The fate of Wendoll the seducer is fixed by his inability to repent, and so determines his inevitable damnation.   The fate of Mistress Frankfort is mitigated by her Christian husband – instead of slaughtering her outright, he allows her the privilege of living in an imprisoning exile and studying penitence while starving herself to death, thereby winning his forgiveness, and engendering the dim hope that his forgiveness will register in her favor in Heaven (although in the Puritan code, there are no guarantees.)

The subplot lives in an entirely different, infinitely more forgiving world.   Its moral and psychological premises are compassionate, and view sin not as doom but as blessing in disguise.   The cruel Sir Francis Acton is blackmailing Mountford into bartering his sister's virtue in payment for is debts, but when the black-hearted Lord is confronted by a brother and sister both ready to sacrifice the girl's life the moment her virginity is despoiled, the example of their lofty Roman virtue makes Acton's hard heart melt, and his cruel demand of seduction is converted at once into a more pleasing offer of marriage.   The two tales are told in alternating scenes, but they're connected by only the slenderest of threads, hardly at all: Acton, we're told, is the brother of Mistress Frankford.   Massive disconnect, and yet traditionally it is more than tolerated, even favored.   Why?

The disconnect in Elizabethan double-plots   stems ultimately from the classical tradition of the Roman comedies of Plautus and

Terence.[3] *Contaminatio,* their practice, was to borrow the plots of two, sometimes more, unrelated Greek New Comedies and bind them into a single action, or at least lead the borrowed plots to a shared resolution. In Terence's *The Brothers,*[4] for example, two brothers, one adopted by a gentle old uncle, the other raised by his own irascible father, play out in their actions the consequences of their opposite upbringings. The parallel tales are intertwined so that they lead to a single thematic resolution: the lesson of "the mean" in the raising of offspring. But the use of separate borrowings in Roman comedy range from the two plots tightly harnessed in *The Brothers* to the far more loosely allied in some of the comedies of Plautus. Both ways have served Western drama well. Neoclassical tradition in both comedy and tragedy demands a unifying logic binding together all story elements into a single plot; popular tradition demands the opposite: not only double plots in violent contrast with one another, but multiple plots that barely hold together their disparate elements. In comedy, that tradition still holds: comedy in film, comedy on TV, double their continuities religiously.

M.A.S.H., Rosanne, Cheers, Golden Girls[5]

No single episode in any of these TV sitcoms features only one story or one mood: there are two. Both may be funny, but if one is gravely so, the other is a laugh and only a laugh. If in one story, Sam Malone is tormented and bewildered by Diane's haughty mockery, then the story tailing it shows, for example, glued-to-the-bar Norm making believe, during an interview for a job in the pub, that he can take the brew or leave it, his withdrawal bends becoming the running gag of the episode. Or in the later sentimental episodes of *M.A.S.H.,* if Pierce is emotionally wrecked by the loss of a GI patient in the unit's operating room, there's on the other hand that determined Lebanese cross-dresser working hopeless strategies on never-to-be-fooled Colonel Potter to get him the hell out of the army and out of Korea. So familiar a strategy need hardly be highlighted; but why – in sitcoms, in Nineteenth Century melodrama, in Elizabethan drama, in popular comedy and drama generally – is it the norm?

Along with its other pleasures, a good deal of social laughter is based on the pleasures of emotional betrayal. Funerals are marred by mourners succumbing to laughter's temptations; so are sermons, so are chastisements. Each instance of it in drama is a reversal – not, as described above, plot reversal, but emotional reversal, which has the same effect and offers the same delight. In the two-part plot, its use is clear. But there are degrees of connection sometimes established between two plots that have little to do with the relief of laughter, and everything to do with their thematic underscoring.

The Changeling

Middleton and Rowley's *The Changeling*[6] is a good example of Elizabethan double plotting. The two plots, as stories, are still entirely disconnected from one another, but they have an inkling of thematic connection: one plot as an ironic, or possibly parodic, comment on the other. The grave tragedy of the main plot – a story of sexual duplicity, self-abasement and eventual murder – alternates with a subplot of farcical or even mad humor, involving sexual jealousy, games of pretended madness, and finally, not murder but merely failed lovers' chagrin. But it's possible to catch a thematic echo of the one plot in the other, so that "changeling" may refer as fittingly to the characters in one plot as to those in the other. It's possible also to note the profound psychological interplay between the characters in the main plot echoed and parodied in the farcical, merely whimsical, role-disguises in the other. So understood, the practice becomes careful strategy, and adds some dimension to a play's tale.

Doll House[7]

But more than added dimension, more than guessed-at interconnections, and more than alternate moments of relief can be double-plotting's genuine function. As in Terence's *The Brothers*, it can be the key to a drama's essential statement, the technique which not blatantly but fairly subtly, structures its complex meanings in a way that would be impossible for single-action plotting to emulate. The master who elevated what was essentially Terentian strategy to a level of intellectual sagacity that few in drama have rivaled is Ibsen. In some of his greatest plays, there is an integrated, almost hidden, enmeshing of two actions that supports and adds extraordinary resonance to his drama's ultimate implications. Take the example of his most famous though far from most complex play, *A Doll House*. On the face of it, the plot seems entirely unified, wholly one; but in fact, it harbors a separate continuity of action that undercuts – almost as thoroughly as in *A Woman Killed with Kindness* – the apparent premise of the play's main action. A group of characters – the three secondary characters – who are thoroughly involved in the action of the main plot, constitute also, among themselves, a distinct and separate counter-action. Let's trace both:

Both plots, apart from their well-made-play underpinnings, are essentially and overtly thematically structured. The story of Nora and her husband Torvald is – as the world has come to know like the back of its hand – the story of the discovery and reification of a value-system that neither were aware of during their marriage, but through the plot crisis they undergo (the forged papers, the letter in the mailbox, its discovery, their rescue from its terrors in the nick of time), suffer the bitter discovery of the fictions on which their marriage was based. Nora sees clearly its anomalies and moves, famously, to find a life free of them, and leaves. Torvald doesn't yet, but in a dim way, is left to hope.

But Ibsen, a committed Hegelian, sees the antithesis of Nora's journey toward truth and freedom. From an alternate perspective, the progress of Nora and her husband might as well be a road to ruin, since the values of Nora's newly-won discovery are at odds with the unshakable realities of human existence (just as, by the way, do the values of those other transcending heroes of Ibsen's *Love's Comedy*[8] and *The Wild Duck* and *Brand* and *The Master Builder* and *Hedda Gabler* and *John Gabriel Borkman* and more.) The play's alternate action, involving its three minor characters, develops a solid case on the other side of moral absolutes, and quietly subverts them; step by step, the life-entanglements of the three characters is made clear – Nora's friend Christine in the hopeless position of a woman who has bravely broken from her moorings and needs a job and a lover; Krogstad who has defied conventional morality to save – a higher morality – his sons from starvation, for which he was jailed and is now ostracized; Doctor

Rank whose love of life and of love itself has left him confronting their price – terminal illness and now imminent death. There's a moment in the play when two of them take counsel among themselves, and wonder if they should risk edifying Nora about her fantasies – and decide no, there's no way out but self-discovery. From the plight of Christine which is introduced early, to the hopeless plight of Dr. Rank suggested last, an arc of thematic progression is accomplished that makes a mockery of the postures of moral idealism.

Does this signify that Ibsen played devil's advocate against the very values for which his plays, particularly *A Doll House*, are still celebrated? Far from it: the positing of moral absolutes against existential absolutes is the very essence of his plays' structures, and the intellectual impasse that such confrontation poses is the very essence of his thinking and his art. Beyond the moralisms with which the reputation of his plays is shackled, the very structuring of them, like the structuring of his thought, defines what is in his dramas the tragedy of existence: a permanent, and infuriating, irreconcilability of ideal value and world-ridden, value-eroding fact. In *A Doll House*, the double structure of the play carefully builds that statement.

MULTIPLE PLOTS

The unity of multiple plots, in their greatest and most original examples, tend to lie outside the domain of plots altogether. Running through as many as three, four or five plot lines concurrently, they have, on the face of it, no unity. But if we study the greatest of these disparate and multi-faceted behemoths, we tend to discover that even those with no discernible plot coherence, have something other than story lines that make them one thing, although in a different sense, and that they satisfy a longing for a considerable breadth of fictional universes, the wider the better, that is the very opposite of the longing for the plot that is visibly and graspably one.

Commedia dell'arte[9]

For the most part, *commedia dell'arte scenarii* in the sixteenth and seventeenth centuries stuck to double plots; they copied them directly from the Ancients (Plautus and Terence) inheriting them from the learned Italian Academies which put on classic or imitations of classic comedies, sometimes with the professional assistance of the companies of *commedia* players. Independent of those sources, there were medieval farces, pastoral poems, and such matter to draw from, and so from these, or from either direct or indirect classical sources, they used texts as templates, and stretched and hacked those sources to accommodate the needs of the actors of the company for one, and the needs of popular audiences to be kept awake for another.

From these practices, they developed an art of structuring their plays that mightily influenced the comic art of the seventeenth and eighteenth centuries. They did so in two ways, both ways opposite to one another. One, the French, or Molière, tradition, that for all its borrowings of *commedia* material, stayed close to the pattern of one or at most two plot lines, and no more, for a single play. The other was an immensely freer form, most clearly exhibited in comedies of Shakespeare's like *A Midsummer Night's Dream* or *The Merchant of Venice* or *Much Ado About Nothing*. What are the elements of this extraordinarily free and extraordinarily engaging form?

Let's begin with two pairs of lovers, either entangled in one another's affairs, or more or less independent of them. Let's add obstacles to their peace: there are only four kinds – serious misunderstandings, hidden secrets, necessary disguises, enemies. Let's add, too, confederates who rescue the lovers from their entanglements. Clearly, the four lovers and their obstacles (fathers, rival lovers, slave-masters, money-lenders, princes, magicians, spirits, etc.) figure prominently in the main plots. But the rescuers and confederates of the lovers (mainly servants, rustics, parasites, fools) over and above their function in the main plot, have an independent life and independent bits of plots (called *burla*) that thread through the play's action as counters or as relief from the main actions. And as further relief, the signature element in *commedia*, its most identifiable ingredient, its *lazzi*, is added, the short comic bits which interrupt the action and exploit the sheer comic skill of the actors, whether physical or verbal or both together. Sometimes added to all this, particularly in *scenarii* involving tyrants or benign magicians, there's a frame action, the play's bookends, the magical ones who stir the pot of the play's entanglements, and unscramble them at the end.

But *commedia* at its freest ran not one or two but as many as four or five concurrent progressions through a single play. Nor were all the progressions in the same comic mode or genre. A *scenario* at its wildest, its form at its most incoherent, could embrace an intrigue plot, a romantic plot, a pastoral plot, a "royal" plot and low farce. Its ideal was to gather into a single entertainment a variety, of comic, serio-comic and serious progressions that invited continual shifts and readjustments in spectator response. If the story of the lovers' entanglements was either serious or tragic-comic, the other progressions added easy humor, embattled wit, vulgar farce, delicate fantasy, romantic ardor, dramatic urgency, the whole finding its unity not in plot but in an indefinable harmony of tone synthesized out of its variety of tones – the "feel," we might call it, the accumulated "aura," of *A Midsummer Night's Dream,* for example, or *The Winter's Tale,* as opposed to *Much Ado About Nothing.*

It was a rare and outlandish structure that flew in the face of neoclassic regularities with their insistence on a single dominant emotional tone for an entire piece. Not all Elizabethan comic playwrights adopted it – there were two schools, Ben Jonson's for regularity, Shakespeare's for this variety. Allardyce Nicoll in *The World of Harlequin*[10] pointed out that if you were to shrivel one of Shakespeare's comedies into a *scenario* nutshell, it would be indistinguishable from a *commedia scenario,* and for some of the comedies, identical. In one of the Italian *commedias,* the Prospero story of *The Tempest* "frames" the crossed lovers' story of *A Midsummer Night's Dream.* In *Much Ado About Nothing,* there's the tragic-comic plot of the two young lovers, the humorous and witty plot of its principal lovers, and the *burla* of the constable-*zanni,* or clowns. And in *The Merchant of Venice,* the commandingly serious plot of Shylock-Portia- Bassanio, the lovers' gamesmanship of the Portia-Bassanio plot, the dramatic and lyrical romanticism of the Jessica-Lorenzo plot, and the *burla* of Old Gobbo and Launcelot Gobbo. *A Midsummer Night's Dream* is the most abandoned of all: it has the four-lovers' comic-romantic plot, the "royal" plot of

Thescus and Hippolyta, the "mythological" plot of Oberon, Puck and Titania, and the *burla* of the rustics preparing the performance of their play.

Chekhov

At its most theatrically and poetically compelling, Shakespearean and *commedia* multiple structures demand a willingness to tolerate not only multiple tales, but multiple realities in one. Modern realism tolerates only one reality, but jostles multiple narratives within a social frame – a family, a club, a bus, a house, a suburban enclave – all contributing to a composition, an *uber*narrative, of psychological and emotional density. The master of this structure is of course Chekhov, in whose plays that density is buried within multiple story progressions, some of which are shared among the drama's inhabitants, some of which remain invisible to others. *The Three Sisters* is probably his most masterful example of a densely textured assemblage of many tales coming together with overwhelming impact, achieved in part because they skillfully avoid, yet finally cohere, as one.

Six stories are told in *The Three Sisters*,[11] roughly adding up to one: the story of Masha's affair with Vershinin; of Andrey's marriage to Natasha; of Irina's loss of Tuzenbach because of the jealousy of Solyony; of Olga's protection of old Anfisa and of herself from Natasha;, and of Natasha's affair with Protopopov. In their intertwining, some are told prominently but with large gaps, and one (the last) hardly at all. Over and above these, there is one story that gives the play its primary momentum, and that subsumes all the others: Natasha's displacing the family of brother and three sisters. Similar to the *burlas* of *commedia* are the minor, but in the emotional and intellectual texture of the drama, significant continuities: Chebutikin's lapse into mental immobility, Kulygin's reports of his satisfactions with his life, Ferrapont's hearing nothing even when he hears. Studied closely, it's remarkable how some of these stories have little impact on the others; seeming to be part of the texture of the whole, they're still of little consequence to other characters in the other tales who neither notice nor care. Some of the characters flaunt their compassion, others do indeed really possess it. Among the several subtle games played among the play's actions, there is sometimes a generous flow of understanding between them, from others a refusal to understand, as well as studied indifference. The use, in other words, to which these parallel tales is put in Chekhov, over and above the strategies of multiple-action storytelling, is the story that cannot be diagrammatically charted but only inferred – the most subtle and in a way the most deadly story told in Chekhov – the story of the flux of human emotional bonding, and its numerous lapses, and its numerous betrayals.

Bartholomew Fair[12]

But there's a different strategy, and a different set of interests altogether, in another kind of multiple progression. As in medieval literature's "field full of folk,"[13] it envisions a great panorama within a single locus. For all its distinctively characterized population, the "field" has an odor and flavor of its own, and is in fact the principle feature of the entertainment – the "field" itself, the landscape not as background but as chief character. Perhaps the greatest celebration of so motley a panorama in Western drama is Ben Jonson's *Bartholomew Fair*. Thirty-four characters, a parcel of puppets, and any number of anonymous passersby wander through the fair set up in squalid Smithfield in Seventeenth Century London on St. Bartholomew's Day. The characters who come: Jonson's characterization of them is done strictly in the traditional mode of comic types – they wear, and we know them entirely by, their external signposts: age, sex, occupation, and as for their moral bent, it's wholly governed by class, religion, money, and appetite. In reality, only the latter two cases govern. In the course of the day at the fair, Jonson strips off class and religion from the most pretentious, so that little is left of their moral "bent," as proper Puritan is reduced by the temptations of the fair to a creature-state of greed and appetite.

But this divestment of humanity's clothing is hardly accomplished in Jonson's normal way with didactic comedy – as in *The Alchemist* or *Volpone*[14] – where in the comedy's first half, there's an accumulation of crimes and misdemeanors, and in the second, a parceling out of fitting punishment. No such arrow flies to its mark; instead, the telling has an indifferently wandering center, a shift of focus from one crowd to another, in what appears to be – but isn't – randomly focused scrutiny on this field of folk, gradually divesting them of the idea of themselves as a result of the fair's temptations. Who are the tempted, who are the tempters?

The field is cluttered with both. At the beginning, condescending to visit the lewd fair is a group of bourgeois Puritans who come variously to spy, to condemn, and to savor. Journeying with them are a pair of young men who need desperately to marry for money, and a young lady, virtuous but sensible, who needs marriage to hold on to her money. With them is a Puritan Divine sniffing out the fair's "enormities," but justifying by the Book his coming to the fair and partaking. He is contending for the hand of the widow who spouts Gospel as well as he does. The names of all of these tell all: The Puritan Divine is Zeal-of-the-Land Busy; the Widow is Dame Purecraft; her daughter is Win-the-Fight who is married, not ideally, to Littlewit. The young woman with the fortune is Grace Wellborn; the two courting young men, Winwife and Quarlous. These are the tempted. What are their temptations?

They're symbolized by its putative empress, Ursula the Pig Woman, a divinity of flesh, gross, gluttonous and pungent, all body, basking in sweat and stink, fire and fat, who cooks and sells roast pig and taps ale. Swarming around her stall is the riffraff of the fair – its pickpockets, its whores, its pimps, its gamblers, its brawlers, its shills, who mix with the respectable and their holiday desires, bringing them all to shameful crises and to their own degraded level. Ursula, reigning spirit, defines the lower limit of human nature in Jonson's field of folk.

A simple dichotomy? It's confused by another set of the fair's inhabitants: Leatherhead's puppets, who at the end of the day perform Littlewit's play, in which Hero and Leander's tragedy is "Anglicized," contemporized and debased to the level of appetite, violence and vulgarity to which the fair's folk have gradually succumbed. But in the climactic debate between wooden puppets and outraged Puritan (Zeal-of-the-Land Busy), the puppets prove that the Puritan is as idolatrous as the mob, all of whom, the amused as well as the outraged, by giving credence to the theatre of the performing puppets, are uniformly idolators, all sharing in the same illusory/immoral worship.

The implications, therefore, of this mix of the world's folk, with their plays of appetite and folly and postures of virtue and censure, so scrambles moral judgment as to leave the world where it found it, none more divine than bestial, none more bestial than divine. The swirl of the fair itself, and the enmeshing of anecdotes of its characters' multiple adventures, say the same thing in image as the debate of puppet and puritan says in argument. The very enormity of Jonson's canvas and its structural elaboration produces a large and tolerant image of the world in moral equilibrium.

Image, then, does the work that plots, no matter how many, can at best merely subserve. The "unity" of Jonson's play, the unity of its "statement," like the subtle unity of tones that make up the "unity" of *A Midsummer Night's Dream*, really lies outside of statement, more felt than known. Plots, when so multiplied, can diminish rather than enlarge their own function, and become on these occasions more like adornments than structural supports.

Nashville[15]

Like the wandering focus of Jonson's play, the twenty-four characters in Robert Altman's *Nashville* are scrambled in a tangle of continuities more or less sewn together in the final sequence – Jonson's last-sequence puppet show matched by Altman's final day of the country-and-western folk's political rally for the "Replacement Party's" presidential candidate Hal Philip Walker. All the stars and near-stars are rallying politically, sure, but also groping at getting into or holding onto celebrity in mass-media culture. Like *Bartholomew Fair*, separate bits of story of each of the participants are tracked until the last day's rally, when an assassin attempts the life of the candidate but kills one of the celebrities instead. The implications of this are as obvious and as muffled as in Jonson's play: the mix of a nation's entertainment and a nation's politics in one pot, displacing the grim and violent realities of national life by festive competitions for success and mass recognition. No more is this underscored than the anti-Puritanism of *Bartholomew Fair*. In both, whatever statement lurks is made without utterance. But most significantly, in both cases, technically, the story progressions used wander so far from regular plot dogmatics that they're on the verge of being abandoned altogether.

SUBVERTED PLOTTING

Prison Is Where I Learned To Fly

They are, in fact, altogether abandoned in a play that gains its conviction and impact from the very absence of any plot dogmatics. To its advantage, there are none. A stage-full of siblings – seventeen – have written letters to their elder sister over the years, letters which sometimes circle, sometimes face squarely, sometimes complain bitterly, and sometimes simply recall with neither bias nor compassion but with pleasure, what they remember and what secrets they know but have always kept to themselves (Catholic upbringing) about the family, about their father and about their oldest brother now in prison. He writes too, exchanges letters with the sister who talks to us, but neither he, she, nor any of the siblings imagine that their interchange of family recollections has any more than momentary, anecdotal interest. The spectator, not being led to any judgment whatever, is bombarded with the shards of literal recall of years of family life, and forms, inevitably, private images of the years of that family's stay. They're persuasive, somberly and happily so, and getting so close to a family's long existence becomes the spectator's way to a deeply private experience, moved that it's wholly recognizable, wholly true, entirely so. The absence of the screen of the drama's mechanics becomes its art's huge gain.

***

CHAPTER 6
ACTION'S FOUR ALTERNATIVES

There are alternate strategies in Western drama, each of which can be counter to the Plot- Action format, which they've qualified and subverted many times over, but are frequently, if not usually, joined with it. Each expands drama's story-telling options. Except for ritual, rarely do any of them function alone, but for purposes of description and example, we'll isolate them as: (1) Process, (2) Ceremony, (3) Ritual, (4) Thematic Progression.

PROCESS

Traditional action moves on the wheels of its reversals, and as we've seen, the most dramatic changes flip through one hundred eighty degree turns, and do so instantaneously. The power and effectiveness of the change is in its total shift of direction and speed. *Process* too is made up of a series of changes, but they're slow, incremental, and without reversal, You may have seen old footage of a milk conveyer belt – one exists – in which a quart of milk is squirted into an empty carton which then moves along, replaced by another carton, and each, in a line, glides into a box, joining a dozen similarly loaded cartons. No cataclysmic changes, but a gradual procedure in which empty cartons become cartons of milk. If you were to watch that process from beginning to end, it would hardly strike you as dramatic, but it is, or can be, riveting, even hypnotic. My own recollection is of a group of strollers on a New York sidewalk watching (I with them) a building construction, one brick laid on top of another, a steel beam sliding into place, etc. The expectation of sudden change – a man falling off the scaffolding, a man shot below the wall – is minimal, and yet the very monotony of the process, its tiny, uniform increments of forward motion is, peculiarly, the essence of what is intriguing about the event. *Process* is what we depend on unconsciously for the guarantees of continuity and certainty: sun rising and setting, things growing, flourishing and dying – things cycling and completing themselves familiarly and reassuringly.

The Long Christmas Dinner[1]

In a major innovation in American playwriting in the Nineteen Twenties, Thornton Wilder's *A Long Christmas Dinner,* a family sits at table for their first course, rises after the last. Every few moments, a character rises and leaves another enters and sits, signifying birth and death – generations being born, dying, succeeding one another, the process synopsizing a saga of decades. The event of the dinner dramatizes time-flow itself, process as such.

The Changing Room

Wilder's is a one-act play. The British playwright David Storey[2] wrote several full length plays devoid of conventional action, entirely in terms of one ongoing process. In *The Changing Room*, a working class Northern England soccer team straggles into the team's dressing, or changing, room, greets, chats, gets into uniform, and leaves for the field to play the game. End of Act One. In the second act, one of the men comes off the field injured, is tended to; the team having lost comes off the field, showers, horses around a bit, gets dressed, goes home. Clinging to and filling out this progression is the chatter of the players, their workaday world and their values, their ways of living in their corner of Yorkshire. The interest of the play, extraordinarily strong, lies largely in our filling in the backgrounds of the men who share in the simple, predictable process of their preparations and farewells to their Saturday afternoon game. *The Contractor*,[3] another of Storey's process plays, centers on the event of a wedding. In the first act, the tent for the lawn ceremony is set up, and in the second it's taken down. Along the way, labor relations, family relations, loom and are delineated against the foregrounded process alone.

But process is more usually combined with action, and, as in Chekhov, the relation between the two can be both subtle and beautiful. It is pre-eminently so in Chekhov, A process is used as the structural frame for each act, and adds – what is especially mysterious in his art – that overriding feeling of the play's musicality, as though his plays are four-movement symphonic as much as four-act dramatic compositions. So much is the process foregrounded that it – rather than the action – governs each act's forward momentum. A multiplicity of actions surface briefly, sometimes passing almost unnoticed, through the act, as though providing notes for the composition of the overarching process. In *The Three Sisters*, for example, a birthday, or rather name-day party, is gathering in Act One as guests gradually arrive, until the end of the act when all the guests are at table, celebrating. In Act Two another party is underway, happily gathering momentum until the moment when it is suddenly brought to a halt by Natasha pleading her sleeping baby's need for quiet – the process snapping suddenly into an "action" – and the rest of the act, the opposite process – the falling-away of the potential party, the company leaving, some fleeing, the now dull and unfriendly house, ending in a mournful grace-note of the youngest sister, Irina, remaining alone in solitary misery. The process governing Act Three is a fire down the street from the three sisters' house, with the comings and goings of the act's participants – some helping, some indifferent, some altogether ignoring, some exhausted by their labors *vis-a-vis* the catastrophe – process governed wholly by an offstage fire down the street. Act Four, like the final acts of *The Cherry Orchard* and *Uncle Vanya*, orchestrates farewells, the process of leave-taking framing multiple actions and their suppressed or quickly flaring attendant emotion, each fourth act closing with musically calculated codas.

Possibly instructive: comparing Chekhov's near-lyrical processes with Ibsen's drumbeat action-reversals. For us skeptics of strongly manipulated action, the gentle controls of an underlying musicality contributes strongly to what might have emerged as conventional sentimentally-saturated tales. But unlike Chekhov's, Ibsen's slight foregrounding of process, and his persistent foregrounding of strong reversals, have given critics occasion to snarl at the creakiness of Papa Ibsen's technique. Chekhov, one of those made uncomfortable by that technique, paid Ibsen polite homage, but could not bear to sit through performances of his plays. Wise directors of Ibsen resort to a dodge – possibly unblessed but sometimes useful – of inserting invented processes that merge with and somehow compensate for the artificiality of his dialogue with its perpetual tension-release patterns and its moment-to-moment reversals. (But in a British production of Ibsen's *Enemy of the People*, heavy overlays of household chores and familial clutchings in the midst of jackhammer action sadly didn't help.)

O'Neill

A single process frames the action, as the title plainly tells us, of O'Neill's *Long Day's Journey Into Night*, where it is used with both symbolic and intensely mordant effect. The play begins after breakfast and ends at 3 a.m. the following morning, the downward spiral of the family's self discoveries mirrored in the gradual disappearance of light and the encroachment of enveloping fog. In O'Neill's *Strange Interlude*,[4] a play better planned than executed, the life of one woman, Nina Leeds, is traced in nine acts from her loss of sexual and psychic harmony, through the stages of her quietly ruthless battle to recover it. At the beginning of her journey, she's lost a fulfilling lover, a kind of God in memory, and her subsequent life is spent in pursuit of the components which would bring her once again to fulfillment – a husband, a lover, a child, a father-friend. Her journey is predatory and amoral. She attains her fulfillment, *belle dame sans merci*, by keeping four men in thrall, drained of their own hopes of a full life. In the play's sixth act – the high point of Nina's successful journey – she is surrounded by the men she so-to-speak keeps captive – 'my husband, my lover, my child, my friend' – and from that climactic moment of fulfillment, her life descends into its late afternoon, when she is left with only her friend, "good old Charlie." The play's profoundly ambitious design, still overwhelming despite some terrible writing, lies in its representing Nina's struggle as the equivalent of a complete life journey ironically analogous to the Nietzschean journey of the tragic hero, who wills his rising like the sun at dawn, reaches his high noon, and then if in his demise, rather than fighting necessity, voluntarily assents to bend his will to the Eternal Will, and so dies the great death. Nina, after a terminal struggle, makes that choice. Paralleling the process of the Nietzschean journey lends a sort of gently tragic context to Nina's life struggle.

King Lear

A single scene, a single moment, can multiply its narrative force many times over by the injection of a process, preferably in counterpoint to the scene's or the moment's action. A powerful moment in *King Lear*[5] juxtaposes a "process" to a moment's 'action.' Poor Tom describes an episode to his blind father Gloucester that is actually not happening, persuading Gloucester of the enormity of the distance he would fall if he attempted his longed-for suicidal plunge. A group of fisherman, he pretends he is seeing, almost dots, so distant are they below, are pulling in their catch, he tells his father. The pretended report of a routine activity altogether irrelevant to the tragic moment of Gloucester's longing for death, so inserted, suddenly throws the normal light of day onto that tense, dark moment. As the tragedy of the play is moving toward its almost unbearable pitch, a window, it seems, is suddenly thrown open for the spectator, who glimpses the ironic contrast between the intensely focused tragic action and the indifferent regularity of the world's routines.

Process vs. Action

Combining process with irrelevant tensions of opposites is now almost standard film practice. It counters the device in Poe or Dickens – Ruskin called it "the pathetic fallacy" – in which sympathetic weather (Poe writes, "On a dull, dark, dreary" etc. "day,") introduces similarly dark events. Characteristic: on the brightest of days amid the pleasures of an amusement park in Hitchcock's *Strangers on a Train*, the murderer stalks. Or in his *The Thirty-Nine Steps*,[6] the hero, in the midst of a tense, nail-biting episode of his being chased to his likely doom, is temporarily trapped in an academic lecture hall during a sleep-inducing lecture on James Joyce, when (British courtesy) working hard not to disturb the lecture, he maneuvers his way out. Camus' novel does it too: In T*he Stranger,*[7] the critical murder occurs on a populated Algerian beach at blazing noon – headlong action played against an indifferent beach crowd worshipping the sun.

CEREMONY

Ceremonies are processes, too, but not ordinary or habitual ones. They may have social, legal, denominational or even no-longer-remembered validation. Their function is not primarily to call to mind ritualized models, although they frequently do, but to channel the customary into more or less formal procedures. Shakespeare as well as all the other Elizabethans leaned heavily on these lurches into high formality while stiffening their verse into rhetorical *gravitas*: trial scenes, funeral scenes, wedding scenes, investiture scenes, royal deposition scenes,[8] even for the opening formalities of battle scenes.

Ceremony provides two excessively familiar and immensely overused dramatic opportunities. It limits, in fact annuls, the idiosyncratic conduct of its participants, at once tuning their language and behavior to the notes of ceremonial functionaries. *Ceremony* also raises the dramatic temperature enormously when it collides with an unanticipated explosion of a reversal in the action. It's a familiar device: the action makes exciting mayhem of the ceremony, and ceremony labors to straitjacket the intrusive action. Film history, for example, has left a long and eventually tired trail of courtroom trial scenes in which the action explodes the propriety of the legal ceremony: it was characteristically sentimental in the Twenties: *Madame X*; gritty in the Thirties: *The Night of January 16*; svelte in the Forties: *The Paradine Case*; manipulative in the Fifties: *Witness for the Prosecution*; powerful in the Sixties: *Inherit the Wind*; tired by the Seventies: *Owen Marshall*.[9] Man or woman on the witness stand holds a secret and a simmering emotion. Cross-examiner grimly follows question-and-answer format. Witness pummeled, tensed, pushed to the limit, explodes. Judge bangs gavel but can't stop the mayhem.

More serious, more ambitious uses of ceremonial are explored in several major full-length plays that are all trials or hearings – the German playwright Kipphardt's *In the Matter of J. Robert*

Oppenheimer,[10] Eric Bentley's *Are You Now or Have You Ever Been*,[11] and possibly most effective of all, Moises Kaufman's *Gross Indecency: The Three Trials of Oscar Wilde*.[12]   In each, rigidity of the trial format is suddenly rent, then recovered, then shredded again, in a regular tension-release pattern.   But in each case, the weight of the play's substance, the sequential (explosive) revelations in the critical steps of its argument, the tense pursuit *battling the obstructions of ceremony* to reveal its own "truth" – genuinely converts argument into drama, and makes clear the value of the ceremonial frame for plays which are in fact essentially not dramas in the conventional sense, but arguments.   This particular structure is truly based on conflict, for beyond the battles of its contending protagonists is the perpetual tension created by the confrontation between two irreconcilable modes of progression, each violating and crippling the procedure of the other, each preventing and then succumbing to the force of the other.

Ceremony used to structure exposition: Coppola's *The Godfather*.[13]   The opening sequence of *Godfather I* does the work of conventional exposition, a complex of many-faceted strands of information: the organization of the Mafia "family", the organization and the relations within the Godfather's biological family, the hates, loves, loyalties, potential disloyalties, and pecking order in each of the two "families."   The frame of all this is a ceremony – a wedding.   The exposition of all the details is smoothly integrated into the sumptuous celebration of the wedding, a carefully delineated, thoroughly staged ceremony which does double duty, itself serving as exposition of the rich upper middle class, socially entrenched, supremely comfortable Mafia style,   and also working its ceremonial frame with unhurried leisure, delineating all the characters and all their incipient stories, the multitudes of information inserted, illustrated, exemplified, the structural control of   *ceremony* enclosing the entire sequence. Equally brilliant, as telling and as richly musical in its structuring is the opening sequence of Michael Cimino's *The Deerhunter*,[14] a wedding celebration also serving as its frame, delineating, with the same lush detail, the same ironic and at the same time celebratory rendering of the values, the loves and hopes, the signs of thorough gratification and creeping desperation, of working class Americans shoring up their self-belief. In both instances, the ceremonial frame is overtly honored, even reverenced – but subtly betrayed, even mocked, yet holds. And in both films, the ceremony is the synoptic image of the value system which becomes, in both, the prize their family of characters struggle violently, even savagely, to hold on to, and eventually, ruefully, they do.

RITUAL

As in the performances of the Mass, *ritual* is a procedure of fixed steps that recapitulates and pays homage to a sacred event or events enshrined in religion or in myth. Through mandatory procedure, it looks to significant validation for its participants. It can underpin the structure – and for centuries has – of dramatic presentation, but with significant variation. It is not merely ceremonial, a usual or familiar or habitual procedure, but first and foremost a predicated event with a formal, controlled, and specially guided structure to appease or emulate a sacred figure, a hero, a god. Its repetition properly done is understood to be efficacious; improperly done, punishable. It has, then, as distinct from ceremony, a different order of sanctity, and invites not just attention, but awe. It doesn't matter whether we submit to it intellectually or spiritually; we automatically accede to its being greatly grave in import. It is not – as in narrative drama – within our authority to judge its efficacy or its protocol. So sanctified is it by tradition, that it at least tempts toward imitative genuflection even from those who have no truck at all with sanctities.

Is Drama Ritual?

For some critic/historians like Gilbert Murray, a common ritual pattern underlies the structure of all Fifth Century Greek tragedies. But how does it bear – or in certain theoretical excursions, seem to bear – on modern drama? Since the Nineteenth Century, there's developed the notion that not only some periods of drama, but all drama, is fundamentally rooted in ritual performance – and when it is not, it should be. Drama, this tradition holds, is only authentic when it functions in two related guises: one, as ritual performance that offers modern audiences the same prospect that ancient drama offered for an entire culture, and for the individual as well:

the prospect of spiritual regeneration or self-transcendence; and two, that dramatic authenticity, like ritual authenticity, demands not merely spectators but *participants* in the communal exercise which is performance.

It's worth examining closely the validity of the notion of drama-as-ritual, since it counters fundamentally conventional notions of drama's cultural function, and therefore its design. Its elaboration in theory outweighs its influence on drama's practice, but its value as a theoretical as well as practical model for playwrights has been considerable during the last century, and it's had impact on film as well.

Nietzsche

The theory begins with Nietzsche's *The Birth of Tragedy*, in which drama is posited as a redemptive therapy that accomplishes aesthetically what neither philosophy nor science nor theology can accomplish alone: a persuasive justification for human suffering. It does so by engaging the spectator in a kind of mesmeric creative act of his own which Nietzsche calls "dreaming." The spectator "dreams" – that is, projects from himself – the creation of the Greek chorus, which in turn "dreams" – that is, projects into existence from *it*self – the tragic protagonists and their actions. What Nietzsche calls "Dionysian chaos," the savagery of earthly existence itself, as well as the untrammeled Dionysian ecstasy of desire is translated in tragic performance into the beauty of the "Apollonian," the measured, structured beauty of the work of art.[15] And so, Apollonian art *redeems* Dionysian chaos. "Only aesthetically," therefore concludes Nietzsche, "can life be eternally justified."[16]

Two elements, then, are central to Nietzsche's metaphor for theatrical redemption: the myth itself, and the spectator's own creation – through a sort of dreaming – of the myth-in-performance. The efficacy lies in the *audience's aesthetic act*, not merely in the drama's recapitulation of the myth. Nietzsche posits a culture with participants capable of such an act through both the depth of its remembered suffering and the poise of its aesthetic imagining. In Nietzsche's sense, merely programming myth/ritual patterns into the plots of plays or films is no guarantee of aesthetic or any other kind of redemption.

Jung-Campbell

An alternate version, one that veers somewhat from Nietzsche's, is the psychoanalyst Jung's. For Jung, all myths, no matter how disparate are fundamentally one, each exhibiting one stage or another of the overarching myth embedded not only in particular cultures, but universally, in the "racial unconscious." Not only myths but all fictions, all dreams, all story-like imaginings are informed by the ur-myth. Both Jung and his disciple, the cultural anthropologist Joseph Campbell, assumed that the ur-myth or their formulaic variations of that myth worked their own efficacy, that their recapitulation in dreams and tales could be harnessed therapeutically to accomplish, for the individual patient, the "integration of the soul." The theory has widespread popularity, but its development has been hobbled by considerable skepticism. In Nietzsche's terms, no matter how many times the story of Dionysus is told, it can be objected that it doesn't have the impact of Euripides' telling unless Euripides or his equal tells it, and the culture listening is capable of the kind of creative, Apollonian "dreaming" that's at one with the telling.[17] Neither Jung's ur-journey nor Campbell's frog-king[18] can, aesthetically, go it alone, since Apollonian poise and measure are not packaged with the myths.

Ancient myth, modern reality

But in modern drama, myth-ritual has for the most part not been used for spiritual redemption, but almost for its opposite: mordant, satiric negations of "modernity." In the wake of the moral disaster of the first World War, what vestige of Nineteenth Century cultural idealism had been left among Western writers and intellectuals generally decayed into moral revulsion. One of the outcomes of that revulsion in the 1920's and 30's was the weighing of modern life and values against nostalgic recollections of the ancient myths and their imagined grounding in belief systems that gave dignity and overall value to life itself. In literature, and in drama particularly, the underpinning of myth/ritual patterns were implicitly bitter, , sometimes   shamefaced, always   ironic, juxtaposing the inherent grandeur of the mythic world with the inherent failure of the modern to emulate it. The most celebrated literary work, the very model for juxtaposing the two, was Joyce's *Ulysses*,[19] the novel in which Leopold Bloom, a reduced Odysseus, aimlessly wandering the streets of Dublin for a day just as the Greek hero purposefully and heroically wandered the seas for ten years searching for home. Among poet playwrights – Auden, Isherwood, Ronald Duncan, T.S. Eliot[20] used particular rituals as the basis for their play structures, a practice that continued for Eliot into the Fifties. In the fashion of the period, the rituals were given heavy Freudian, and in the case of Eliot, theological, overtones which gave their plays their double efficacy as cautionary lessons on the debilitating differences between then and now, and at the same time implementing the psychological/spiritual therapy that was taken to be implicit in evoking cultural myths. A particularly bitter example:

From Morn Till Midnight[21]

In Georg Kaiser's Expressionist play of the Twenties, *From Morn Till Midnight*, its insignificant everyman parodies/emulates Nietzsche's tragic hero in his day's "journey" as well as the sufferings of the Christ. The Cashier (Expressionism's generic naming knows characters only as functions) journeys through seven scenes – the seven stations of the cross. In the first, a woman approaches his teller's cage at the bank to cash a letter of credit. But when her bejewelled hand passes through his window, the shock of its dazzle and the woman's beauty cause him to cry for "Water, water!" and he's "awakened" in that instant – born, so to speak, into "consciousness." And also, ironically, into the negation of the Nietzschean journey. At once, he steals fistfuls of money from the till, and follows the woman to her hotel room. The walls of her room hold an enticing picture of a sensual Adam and Eve, and the Cashier is inflamed to devote his money and his being to his passion for the woman, his Eve. With the Woman's shocked rejection, he suffers the first of his defeats along his *via dolorosa*. At his home – Station Three – he contemplates the proprieties and ceremonies of his lower middle class existence. His daughter at the piano – "Not that!"   His Wife bringing his supper – "Not that!" His Mother bringing his slippers – "Not that!" and with his yearning suffering a second defeat, he rushes on to Station Four – a wide, snow-covered landscape with a single leafless tree, and to the tree, he articulates his plaint, his longing. The answer comes in a thunderclap and a flash of lightning, and the tree, so illuminated, reveals itself as the skeletal form of Death. "Not yet!" cries the Cashier, tips his hat, and runs to Station Five, the Velodrome during a bicycle race, where his yearning is almost fulfilled. "I offer a million marks to the winner!" he cries, and lifts the crowd to an ecstasy of anticipation. And in that untrammeled ecstasy, his own resonates, until the Crown Prince arrives, and the crowd is at once hushed, stands at attention, and sings with fervor the national anthem. Once again his inexpressible longing is defeated, as it is at the Sixth Station, the Cabaret, where death lurks beneath the skirts of one of the cabaret girls who shows him her wooden leg. In the last Station, his new vision of an innocent Eve, a Salvation Army lass, is shattered when she claims the reward for his capture after his public confession of his theft. The play ends with the Cashier impaled against the wall of the hostel, shot by a Policeman, the explosion causing the scramble of electric wires in the ceiling to light up in the shape of Death's skeleton, and the Cashier, arms outstretched in the posture of Christ on the Cross, cries before his death, "Ecce Homo", such is man.

The *via dolorosa* of the Cashier's quest does not bear witness to Christ but to his opposite. "Have you understood me?" writes Nietzsche at the conclusion of *Beyond Good and Evil.* "Christ versus Dionysus." It's the absolute of Nietzsche's Dionysian ecstasy that the Cashier yearns for as salvation, and suffers the tragedy of failing to break the bonds of, in Nietzsche's phrase, Christianity's "slave morality." Under the burden of its universal submissiveness, the hero struggles to emulate the ecstasy of Dionysus and the "great hero's" yea-saying to death, but becomes the failed hero of tragedy's negation. Kaiser mocks the power of modern moral enslavement which cripples the reach of authentic tragic fulfillment, and like most of his fellow-Expressionists, looked grimly toward all the unlikely post-world-war's "spiritual fulfillments."

The Road to Damascus

In striking contrast to the post-war plays, Strindberg's great autobiographical trilogy of 1901, *The Road to Damascus*, dramatizes his failed and subsequently successful journey toward a settled faith.   Its ironies are directed not toward the desperation of emulating the certainties of myth-ritual patterns, but toward achieving them.   The Stranger, the play's protagonist, journeys through the first two plays as the radical skeptic who believes in nothing, but is haunted by the unexplained, by the sense of underlying mysteries, of hidden controlling agents, of crushing acts destined inevitably to be performed.   Irony plays over his certainties of uncertainty, and over the multiple hints of "patterns" controlling his steps toward, then away from, then again toward the goal he's consciously avoiding.   In Part One, he journeys through seventeen scenes. The first is a Public Square, the ninth – the mid-scene – a Monastery, the seventeenth, the Public Square once again.   His steps toward the Monastery are replicated in reverse on his journey back to the Public Square. His journey in Part One accomplishes nothing, but the order of the scenes are built by the Maker behind them – playwright or Divinity -in the form of a Gothic arch. Self-reference is the language of the play as a whole, and the scenes of Part One and Two, and the early scenes of Part Three, are self-punishingly autobiographical.   But in the last play of the trilogy, when Strindberg anticipates a wholly realized destiny, his journey takes him through the seven scenes of his spiritual growth that replicate the seven-story mountain capped by faith. But in the Monastery's gallery at the top of the mountain, his skepticism is itself made to suffer skepticism, and re-baptised, as though a babe once again, he embraces his faith not by quashing argument with the whole rational traditions of Western philosophers – represented in the gallery by rows of their images – but by surrendering to the collisions of all their argument, and so by argument's denuding.

Murder in the Cathedral[22]

Perhaps the most powerful version of ritual drama during the Thirties was T.S. Eliot's *Murder in the Cathedral*, in which Eliot overlays an historical episode with the sanctity of ritual. Thomas a

Beckett returns from France to suffer inevitable retribution for his opposition to the King, Henry II, and at the altar of his church, Canterbury Cathedral, he meets his martyrdom at the hands of four assassins, the King's emissaries. The play was written to be performed on the altar of the Cathedral itself, recapturing the original event, but it had the further ambition of recovering its sanctity by way of the spectator's acceptance of – in effect, succumbing to – belief during the performance itself. It occurs in a moment, one calculated to cause the spectator to recognize that his transformation *had already occurred* moments before his awareness of it. Thomas a Beckett's murder on the Cathedral's altar is followed by a profound cry of pain from the Chorus of Women – "Clear the air! Take stone from stone and wash it, wash it!" – a cry of appalling power over the sacrilege of the deed. But it's immediately followed by the four assassins stepping forward to explain with polite, conversational pleasantry the historical, political and economic necessity for the deed. The shock of difference stuns the spectators into recognizing that *what they had witnessed* had risen to an order of persuasion wholly at odds with the emotionally and morally indifferent rationality of the murderers; they had – they were presumed to discover – shared the event as participating believers, not as objective observers. Eliot's poetic-dramatic miracle was suddenly made known, in effect, in retrospect.

Dionysus in 69[23]

In all these instances, not the "action" but the ritual-pattern is in control of the play's progress, the action necessarily conforming and subordinate to the demands of its ritual design. A much used stratagem in the poetic drama of the Thirties, it was radically revised in the Sixties. Traditional stage action, with ritual restructuring of its referenced story, was entirely eliminated, supplanted by the performance of ritual itself. The Performing Garage's *Dionysus in 69* was prototypical. The story of Euripides' *The Bacchae* was converted into a literal ritual enactment performed with therapeutic intent. But the therapy involved the audience considerably less than it did the chief actor. He, as the Greek tragedy's sorely-tried Pentheus, underwent a "birth ritual" beneath the massed legs of the chorus, followed by his *sparagmos*, his psychological "dismemberment" (satisfying Gilbert Murray's recipe for the hero's ritual passage in Greek tragedy.) The actor, his actor's "mask" torn off and in his own person, is subjected to grueling psychotherapeutic inquisition by the chorus, until, stripped of all his possible mechanisms of defense, psychotically naked, the actor blubbered confessions of his most guarded secrets and self. It was a rite of passage enacted each night, and each night only its consummation could bring the performance to its end. Here, ritual didn't merely control the progress of action; it entirely supplanted it.

Paradise Now

As it did in the Living Theatre's seminal *Paradise Now*, the most influential and the most vilified of Sixties' ritual enactments. Famous, or at least in their first American appearance notorious for its actors being arrested when they walked out of the theatre into Cambridge streets naked at the end of its Harvard performance (they were not, but were so editorially anathematized,) and leered at in journalism for the grungy life-style of the company. The Living Theatre endured a reputation in the US irrelevant to its intensely political/religious orientation. The structure of *Paradise Now* was based on a massing of formal designs extracted from the "ten rungs" – collapsed into eight – of Martin Buber's way to God, as well as the Kabala, Tantric and Hasidic teaching, the I Ching and more. Out of these, a "voyage"[24] was charted for spectators as well as for the actors. Both together underwent a series of ritual acts passing each of the "rungs" on the way to permanent, non-violent, anarchist revolution – in effect, to the freed self. A ritually-structured change through the performance moved both actors and spectators as mutual participants through stages of gradually overcome resistance to their final spiritual accord, their unity in assent. The formal structuring of the piece was rigidity itself, the essence of ritual enactment: in each "rung" actors and participants passed through a "Rite," a "Vision" and an "Action," recharted and respecified at each Rung. In *Paradise Now*, the enactment of ritual entirely supplanted the enactment of a referenced narrative – a radical revisiting, in contemporary terms, of the coalescence of theatre and mass-conversion rite.

But the "rite" went considerably further. It not only tolerated but required improvisation within each "rung." "Audience" at once became hardly distinguishable from the actors, and shared the ritual tasks to be accomplished within each rung before it could be abandoned for the next. In the first, for example, the actors immediately generated open hostility toward the spectators, who were just as immediately swept into verbal battles, physical battles, cued by the offensive slogans whispered, shouted, or confidently announced (offensive in the first rung, shared by the converted in the last). Controlled mayhem – and then, gradually, spectators lost their hostility, joined – inevitably – with the actors in shared fellow-feeling, and when genuine harmony was reached – not before – the rung could be abandoned for the next. As the last step was accomplished, the participants shedding the "need" for theatre, abandoned it, and in their last symbolic gesture, took to the streets.

But along the road of its Buber-esue ritual journey, the Living Theatre was shredding the vocabulary of theatre itself. The moment performance began, spectator and actor lost their separation; active theatre space obliterated distinction between stage space and audience space; acting itself – the mimicry of remembered events – morphed into behavior involved in the moment's event; the goal of the ritual performance itself undid the need for ritual or any other kind of rigidly structured theatre; the life of theatre was to be now outside of theatre, in the street, the metro, the occupied office or bank or factory.

Though it was not the first – there had been a century of *avant garde* theatre in which some of The Living Theatre's practice was anticipated – but in its tour of *Paradise Now* in Europe and America in 1968, it put permanent stamp on the most revolutionary challenges to theatre as an institution of *display and recollection,* pushing it unrelentingly toward the performative-ritual embrace of a paradise *now.*

Star Wars[25]

In a different world, a different mind-set explored ritual-myth, used it with deadly seriousness and no irony, and out of it developed a freshly invented epic-narrative that instructs the story of Lucas's *Star Wars* films. The narrative more or less follows the ur-myth pattern developed in Campbell's *The Hero with the Thousand Faces*. It was a courageous and startling choice – to give spiritual dimension to a mass-market film based on Campbell's "universal" myth. Lucas put it succinctly: to help the young "think about God." The huge success of the films once more brings to the surface Nietzsche's whole question of myth's efficacy in spurring cultural transformation. How much, how little, how – if to any degree – is it self-deluding?

The films – six in the series – create a comprehensive mythology of their own much like Greek or Teutonic or Celtic mythology, inventing a multi-generational saga of wars and dynasty, and focusing essentially, or at least eventually, on one major mythic/heroic figure, Anakin Skywalker. But in the first film created for the series – eventually placed in the saga's continuity as the fourth – that figure is Luke Skywalker, who is the hero – and for which, according to Lucas,[26] Joseph Campbell's pattern was followed consciously and closely. Two major aspects of that pattern are central to its design: the Hero's Journey, and the ultimate religious or quasi-religious factor now universally known as The Force. The Journey's events and creatures, in Campbell's terms, are made up of mythological symbols not so much meaningful in themselves, but which offer a system of correspondences analogous to "the millennial adventure of the soul." Myth-Journey is really, then, the inward journey of the self, which if it succeeds in fulfilling its potential, arrives at personal and communal redemption. As follows:

The Journey Myth

Campbell's ur-myth tells us: The Hero is called to, or voluntarily begins, his adventure; meets with a (supernatural) protective helper; with this guide, arrives at a threshold gate, beyond which is the terrible unknown; fights a battle (dragon-battle, brother-battle, etc.) ; is "swallowed" into the unknown (e.g., belly of the whale, death and dismemberment, etc.); is born again, and, aided by a benign supernatural force, undergoes a succession of trials (overcoming ogres and barriers); gains the reward of the goddess-mother ("mystical marriage"); confronts the ogre-father, but with the help of the female figure (Blessed Mother, Spider Woman) the justice/wrath of the father becomes mercy/grace; wins (or steals) the ultimate boon, the Elixir; escapes by a "magic flight" and, with outside aid, the Hero returns to his community with the restorative Elixir.

The *Star Wars* Journey

With prunings, rearrangements and additions, this pattern is more or less followed – referred to rather than replicated – and revised, understandably, using "war" rather than "journey" as its central metaphor. Luke Skywalker "journeys" from war to war, but broken shards of Campbell's spiritual journey remain.

Luke Skywalker's advance comes about through his joining the rebel movement against the Empire. By chance, he intercepts a message for help to the old Jedi knight, now recluse, Obi-Wan Kenobi (among sources for names is Kurosawa's film, *Hidden Fortress*, much admired by Lucas, and much influencing the look and style of the *Star Wars* films) and after the murder of his aunt and uncle by the Imperial Storm Troopers, Luke and Kenobi join the Rebel Alliance, and travel with its followers (whose names and beloved characters now fill cyberspace and computer games.) Together with Kenobi and Yoda (another recluse, once a Jedi) Luke becomes a Jedi (whose powers of clairvoyance, telepathy, etc. derive from The Force.)

Here, the story draws heavily on Campbell's double-image of the "Father." Having believed that his father was betrayed and murdered by the villainous Darth Vader, Luke discovers that his father *is* Darth Vader, who, together with the evil Emperor, attempts to enlist Luke in the service of "the Dark Side," (it and "the Bright Side," are the two conflicting aspects of The Force – a packaging of God and the Devil in one.) Luke instead turns Darth Vader/Father toward the "Bright Side," and he then, though mortally wounded, kills the evil Emperor; and this is followed by the Rebels' destruction of their final obstacle, the "Death Star," and then victory over the Empire.

The pattern of *Star Wars*, with its overtly "mythic" paraphernalia removed, is recognizably the standard pattern of the conventional action film.   In a sense, this underscores Campbell's point: that story-telling at any level is basically ur-myth, partial, refracted, substituted, fragmented, but essentially there, controlling its "secret" structural cohesion and more importantly, according to Jung-Campbell, the secret of its appeal.

THEMATIC PROGRESSION

For the playwright, the question is not merely, What does a play mean? but How does it get to mean? What are the techniques that structure, gradually, sequentially, the play's statement? How, during the shifts and turns of its action, does it accumulate coherent meaning? The exploration of how "meaning" is read in – or into – completed dramas is reserved for the last chapter, on *"Packaging" Meaning*.   We're concerned here with how the playwright makes the play's "statement," tracks its progression until it arrives at its QED.

Of course, every traditional play automatically carries signposts of gathering meaning along with what is ostensibly its chief business, telling its story. But the particular kind of play we'll be discussing now is one in which the play's "action" is the action of its developing argument. The play as "argument" pursues the resolution of its question, just as more conventional plays pursue the resolution of their plot. But in a play wholly geared to its argument rather than its plot, plot must still seem to be, as Aristotle legislates, the "soul" of the tragedy. So careful is Aristotle to maintain the priority of plot over point that he offers neither discussion nor mention of plays' arguments. Plot, in itself, is the soul of tragedy.

So, in Aristotle's model, it must seem. But many times over in Western theatre, multiple models have been developed that hold plays' statements to be the only authentic reason for drama to exist. And certainly, in some of Western drama's greatest plays, their slow, persuasive, cumulative, and finally overriding argument underpins not only their structure but their calculated intellectual complexity, their power and even their emotional force. The plot as story may be the soul of tragedy, but it desperately needs the intrusion of significant rationale to elevate it to a measure of some value.

Shaw's "discussion" plays[27]

Bernard Shaw, following what he thought of as the example of Ibsen, became the last century's earliest propagandist for thematic structures – what he called "discussion" plays – and although the lessons he thoroughly learned from Moliere's comedy and from Nineteenth Century melodrama never left him, nor his relish for them even to the very last days of his playwriting dotage (see *Boyant Billions*, written in his nineties) he relentlessly championed the "discussion play" as the genre that most fit the new century's intellectual/moral dilemmas.   His combination of traditional playwright's ploys and the strategies of discussion plays produced masterful compromises as well as several of his greatest plays, but he did attempt on occasion to do "discussion" raw – not as Ibsen's *Doll House* did it, as a "discussion" resolving a conventional plot, but in several   instances (*Don Juan in Hell, The Doctor's Dilemma*, and *Getting Married*) and in the structure of particular key acts in other plays (*Caesar and Cleopatra*, Act IV; *Saint Joan*, Sc. 6; *The Apple Cart*, Act I; *On the Rocks*, Act II) "discussion" became the drama, the plot itself, the play's or the scene's "action." He was abetted impressively by a fellow-playwright, Granville Barker,[27] who wrote thematically structured plays – *Waste, The Madras House* – without the comic genius of Shaw, but with uncompromising authenticity.

Man and Superman, Act One[28]

Thematic statement in Shaw is structured as a series of reversals – precisely mirroring, in fact becoming, the action line of the narrative.   The first scene of Shaw's *Man and Superman* is a relatively simple example.   A traditional farce format – characteristic of Shaw – carries the burden of his thematic progression: his characters piling error on error, until a climactic revelation collapses the heap of their follies. But these – again characteristic of Shaw – are not farcical follies of behavior, but farcical follies of belief.

Viola, the sister of the play's anti-heroine Ann Whitfield, is discovered to be pregnant. The discoverers are Shaw's assemblage of leisure-class Londoners – one, an elderly lady who is an authentic Puritan, another a very conventional peer of the realm, and several others variously shocked by Viola's revelation. First: To the Puritan lady's outright condemnation, Viola expresses only her regret that she should think of her as she does, but understands, thoroughly approves, and forgives her. To the others, as one after the other voices opinion by either criticising or being sympathetic to her plight, she makes little or no protest, keeping her counsel, until John Tanner, the play's unabashed ambassador of Shaw's own radical opinions on moral issues, elects to champion – first reversal – Viola's expression of freedom from the constraints of prejudice, and applauds her courageous gesture of conceiving out of wedlock. To this Viola responds with spirit: how dare Tanner make such an assumption; how dare he suppose she is so abandoned a creature as to share his disgusting views! She is – second and climactic reversal – for particular private reasons secretly married, and nothing would have dragged the truth from her but Tanner's revolting supposition of her immorality.

Double reversal – Shaw's favorite device – twice over subverting the audience's suppositions about his scene's assumptions. But the result of the double twist of suppositions is not its whole point. This episode, Shaw's "paradigm scene," anticipates John Tanner's place in the play's full thematic statement. Tanner holds agreeably virtuous revolutionary opinions, and judged from this scene, and from Tanner's *Revolutionist's Handbook* (appended to the text of the play) his views are as properly "revolutionary" as Shaw's own. But in the world as it is, as the thematic statement of the play demonstrates, they are not only genuine folly, but crippling to the world's real work for the future. They're supplanted, by play's end, by greater Shavian wisdom than Shaw's polemic posture tolerates: worldly common sense.   Characteristically, the real Shaw rounds on the apparent one.

Major Barbara

Probably the neatest, most symmetrical example in Shaw of a "discussion play" is *Major Barbara*,[29] a three-way "case to be argued" among the munitions-maker Undershaft (attending to the needs of the body – jobs, profits – but reprehensibly,) his daughter, the Salvation Army officer, Barbara (attending to the needs of the soul at the Army's impoverished working –class hostel, but under delusion) and her Gilbert Murray-like intellectual suitor, haranguing from a soapbox his lessons on Euripides in Trafalgar Square (attending to the needs of the mind, but absurdly.) All three in the end, through Shaw's plot-argument, find conciliation among themselves: the recipe for society's salvation of *mind, body and soul* – all three in one.

Act One: Barbara, despising her father's contribution to social murder and his beer-making partner's to drunkenness, challenges her father to observe her pious labors at the Army's hostel. He takes her bet,   and invites her to visit his munitions factory afterwards. Act Two: At the hostel, Undershaft, sabotaging Barbara's good-Samaritan notions of the Army's labors, offers the Army's General, and she gleefully accepts. the bounty of an enormous cheque, and Barbara suffers the disenchantment of recognizing how money, drunkenness and murder support and betray salvation's labors in her working-class arena. She resigns her office. Last Act: At the munitions factory, Barbara, overwhelmed by the plant's efficiency and tidiness, and overcome by her father's admonition to those like her to use his lethal bounty for peaceful purposes, to "Dare to make war on war," together with the intellect-mongerer Cusins, joins her father's enterprise to ground the business of salvation and education of the benighted poor on a solid financial footing. Characteristically, Shaw, his plot and his rhetoric arguing equally for his fundamental faith,   adjusts the perspective of his humanitarian Socialism to the play of whimsical common sense.

Two further examples of narrative and thematic structure wedded: Pirandello's *Right You Are If You Think You Are*, and Kurosawa's film, *Rashomon*.

Right You Are if You Think You Are[30]

Pirandello's play is structured as a plot in pursuit of the answer to a very large question, but at its beginning is posed as a very small question. The question, more and more baffling, comes to rest at last in its ironic conclusion. A group of townspeople are curious about a family recently settled in its neighborhood, and made up of a man, his wife and the wife's mother. Suspicions about them lead the townspeople to insist on knowing their secret. Ludovic, the *raisonneur* of the play, warns them that they will never find the truth because the truth, in their sense, is not likely to exist: the sum of the facts will not add up to a single truth. By the end of the first act, the husband has persuaded the eager gossips that his wife is mad, but that her thinking she is his wife is necessary to support her illusion, without which she could not live. Ludovic, laughing, affirms that that is the truth. But in the second act, the Mother explains that it is the man who is laboring under an illusion, an illusion she charitably finds it necessary to support for his sake. When the Wife, veiled, appears in the third act, to the anxious questions of the townspeople, she responds that both are right. Each lives with his own truth, and she, subscribing to both, lives with both their certainties. Ludovic, laughing his heartiest laugh, congratulates the inquisitors on having discovered the truth. Like Shaw's play, the play's "argument" is its drama, its logical steps suffering reversals, and logic itself playing dramatic protagonist.

Rashomon[31]

Kurosawa's film *Rashomon* shares Pirandello's three-reversal logico-dramatic action, and like Pirandello's, its hunt for the plain truth remains ironic and unresolved. An elegant bride and her new husband are waylaid by a bandit; the husband, after bravely battling the bandit, is killed, and the bride is forcefully abused. Or are they? In the three separate tellings of the incident to a magistrate eager to know the truth, three versions of the event are told, each with equal credibility. And each version depicts the moral or physical prowess with which each faced their opposition, and most particularly the cowardly or immoral lapses of the other two. But unlike Pirandello's hearty laugh at the end of *Right You Are*, there's no pleasure in the event's failed resolution; it occasions the desperation of the peasant who was witness to the event and had no voice in the telling. His despair is relieved (for sentimental closure) by the discovery of an abandoned baby which he and his fellows will nurture. But for the question of truth, the sentimental ending is no solace. The implications of Pirandello's "truth" are reversed: they are not all "right." Unlike Pirandello's leaving relative truths alone, *Rashomon* leaves moral resolution permanently baffled.

Brecht

Brecht's early *lehrstucke*[32] ("learning pieces"), as well as most of his later plays, are thematic-action structures by another name. Their resolution is characteristically arrived at through a dialectic which shapes the play itself, and steers head-on for that resolution's logical cap. His lessons are set up clearly in his plays' first sequences, tested several times over through episodic trials – each trial more consequential than the one before – and resolved with clear and thoroughly demonstrated ethical conclusions.

In a sense, then, Brecht and Shaw pursued a common aim: didactic drama devoted to explicating fundamental social and political moral questions, structured primarily as argument under the guise of dramatic narrative. But in address and in aesthetic commitment, they could hardly be more antithetical. Shaw remained solidly within the confines of what Brecht was to call "culinary" theatre – the theatre that spoke essentially to bourgeois audiences of considerable sophistication, warped only by the dead hand of their anachronistic repertory of beliefs. For Shaw, the attack against those beliefs was done through the mouths, as he put it, of "recognizable human beings" within the confines of conventional dramatic action structured as argument. Brecht's was a different case.

The aesthetic dilemma Brecht dealt with in the Berlin of the Twenties was shaped by the political and social crisis in Germany that was close to catastrophe. *Lehrstucke* were born out of the intense desire to address the workers' organizations, the political parties, the university students caught up in the battle of ideologies, and, for Brecht, to set its course on the Marxist ideology which he had very recently learned. In the Twenties, both as Marxism and as drama, it was recognizably young, but Brecht's maturity in both political and dramatic thinking led in his later career to being recognized as the century's prime exemplar of drama as ideological statement.

The strategies of his attack were embodied in the now- familiar notion of *alienation*, borrowed from the Russian critic Shklovsky's "defamiliarization,"[33] and the presentational theatrical techniques from the German director Piscator.[34] "The stage began to instruct," he wrote. The intent of alienation was to cause the audience to resist the temptation to project itself *into* the stage event, to indulge in emotional empathy with characters, to the detriment of its ability to "observe" objectively, and so compelled to make decisions, to be impelled to "make changes." In presentation, the stage itself began to "narrate," that is, to do counter-narration, "making its own comment on stage happenings through large screens... documenting or contradicting statements by characters through quotations projected onto a screen, lending... statistics to abstract discussion," etc. Whereas Shaw's "making a case" reveled in complexity, Brecht's making his case reduced complexities to transparent clarity. In its initial intent, at least, Brecht's "theatre for learning" turned its back violently on the conventions of dramatic action and narrative, and signified meaning in plays structured as "lessons" with greatly extended "illustrative" theatrical vocabulary.

The Measures Taken[35]

The last of the "abstract," or wholly didactic *lehrstucke*, and the most violently controversial, was *The Measures Taken*, which poses personal morality against the "community" morality of Party discipline. A chorus of Communist judges hears the testimony of Four Agitators back from a Party mission in China, who confess they were forced to execute one of their comrades, a young novice. After reenacting the mission's adventure, the Four ask the Chorus for its verdict. Their reenactment:

Before setting out, they obliterated their personal identities by donning masks, and required the young man to do the same. But in the course of their mission, this passionate youngster exhibited serious defects: heartfelt sympathy for the impoverished peasants; lack of discipline when attacked by the police for distributing leaflets, and so jeopardizing the mission's secrecy; violent hostility toward a capitalist for wanting to arm the peasants, and so ruining the mission's chance for temporary and useful collaboration with the capitalist; prematurely encouraging a peasant uprising; and in a fit of moral outrage, ripping off his mask and revealing himself to the enemy. In each gesture, the young man acted out of private virtue, and jeopardized the mission of the collective. "I give up," he had announced, "all agreement with the others. I will do alone what is human." The Agitators then made their painful choice – the measure that had to be taken – to execute him. Understanding his errors, he voluntarily offered his assent, and was shot and buried.

Using brutality to counter brutality, or, more pointedly, evil to counter evil, is generally justified by all morally directed causes; Brecht's discovery of it for the Communist cause in Berlin put the case so baldly that it was applauded by few, rejected by most, even in part by the Party itself. Nevertheless, the impact of the "learning-piece" technique in countering a society's ethical clichés was its central animus, and modified and more subtly rendered, remained the Brechtian model for the wide movement in Twentieth Century theatre that addressed, directly and with confrontational impact, social and political questions of conscience. In his own plays, increasingly, the QED became not so much a simple statement of moral choice, but the revelation of ambiguity inherent in moral thinking, and its implicit hypocrisies. And the weave of issues involved in ambiguous outcomes caused his later plays to move closer to his once-muted conventions of dramatic story-telling.

Mother Courage

Precisely in this mould is *Mother Courage*.[36] The titular heroine of the play – or anti-heroine – plies her canteen business on the battlefields of the Thirty Years' War, foraging for her livelihood and at the same time traveling with and protecting her three children. One by one, in episode after episode, she experiences the same unlooked-for and terrifying predicament, each one grimmer than the one before: suffering the loss of her business or of one of her children. At the critical moment in each instance, she finds herself, either inadvertently or by decision, foregoing the child. The image of Mother Courage at the end of the play, now alone, pulling her wagon and crying after a band of soldiers, "Hey! Wait for me!" is an overpowering one, and invites unambiguous emotional response, but the moral conclusion *is* ambiguous. The values she fundamentally lives by – what Brecht designates as bourgeois capitalist values in little – are criminal, but then, inadvertently and equally demonstrated – so is judged her yearning to stay alive.

The Round Heads and the Peaked Heads

One of Brecht's less well-known plays, *The Round Heads and the Peaked Heads*,[37] exhibits an original use of thematic structure. Its full statement depends less on finger-pointing lessons than on paralleling and distancing itself from another "lesson" play – one that profoundly reflects the values Brecht's "lesson" is intent on dispelling: Shakespeare's *Measure for Measure*. The lesson? That traditional 'universal' values in Shakespeare's play tested against reality's likelihoods have the weight of fantasy. The Brechtian sneer, even in the face of Shakespeare, confidently mocks.

The mockery – and the play's statement – lies in the retelling of Shakespeare's story, substituting ordinary likelihood for the Bard's moral afflatus. One after the other, the original play's values slip and slide; love, justice, virtue, honor itself – all of which hold up nobly, consistently, in Shakespeare's narrative, when put to the Brechtian test, shred; their familiar illusion doesn't hold. Largely, the effectiveness of the parody depends on one's recalling almost moment by moment the tale told in *Measure for Measure,* noting Brecht's point by point undercutting of what seemed – before Brecht – Shakespeare's already cynical moral environment. The difference: to the corrupt world of Shakespeare's Venice, Brecht adds controlling class allegiances and motives which consistently corrode the moral frame of reference to which Shakespeare's play and his characters make their appeals, and from which they seek their justification. That frame removed, and its fantasy "universal" values with it, then class power, class consciousness, class struggle shape the values, decisions and beliefs that govern Shakespeare's renovated narrative's action. As in *The Three-Penny Opera*, the thematic statement suffuses the entire play, its statement made far more by its pervasive posture of mockery and bitterness than by an overtly delineated thesis: what Brecht later called "vaudeville," and, mocking his own critical vocabulary, "entertainment," meaning only deft rather than overt ideological inference.

The Good Person of Setzuan

One of the later plays that frames perfectly Brecht's ironic ambiguities in its resolutions is *The Good Person of Setzuan*.[38] At its end, the Three Gods who have monitored Shen Te's progress through the torment of her being "good" and her suffering its consequences, and alternatively, in her guise as her own alter-ego Shui Ta, winning out by being "evil" but suffering remorse for the evil done – as had a consequence – she puts it to the Gods in a prayer: "When I lay prostrate beneath the weight of good intentions, ruin stared me in the face. It was when I was unjust that I ate good meat and hobnobbed with the mighty. Why? Why are bad deeds rewarded? Good ones punished?" The Gods manage by the assiduous use of clichés to answer by not answering, and instead, putting out of mind the evil alter-ego Shui Ta, they sing at the play's conclusion: "Through all the length of days/ her goodness faileth never/ Sing Hallelujah! Make Shen Te's/ Good name live on forever!" to which she cries as they disappear into the clouds: "Help!" The ambiguity implicit in *Mother Courage* becomes explicit in *The Good Person of Setzuan*, and Shen Te's cry for help shares the ultimate bewilderment of Pirandello's raucous laugh and *Rashomon's* peasant's desperation.

Polemic: *Waiting for Lefty*[39]

In the Thirties during the Depression, several playwrights anxious to make their message count, and impatient with diluting or half-burying it in conventional story-telling, left plot format altogether and structured their plays as what they in fact were: editorials urging action. The plays were structured as emotionally-charged arguments aiming for their impact not merely at spectators' nods of agreement but at public action. Addressing the frustration and anger of its moment, in the course of its career, it created a model for activist theatre that grew in persuasiveness and sophistication until it's become an accepted theatrical genre taking on issues in their whole import rather than story illustrations hinting at their larger significance.

Theatrically it drew on German and Soviet presentational techniques – Meyerhold, Piscator, Brecht – but its writing tended to emulate the formats of contemporary journalism in the U.S – *Life, Newsweek, Time* – whose strategies were later, during World War II, reduced to a simple formula for the instruction of officers in the US Army to inspire their troops. Forestalling possible passivity, each step in their outline was geared to overcoming the resistance of the inert. The four-step model outline is, more than likely, altogether unknown to its current theatrical practitioners, but they still, if inadvertently, follow the same steeps: "Story" elements are anecdotal at best, the overall structure is committed polemical persuasion, demonstrating its proof by dramatically and emotionally-supported, and incrementally reinforced, examples, as follows:

(1) "Ho-hum:" An arresting opening; a striking incident; a shocking revelation;

(2) "So what?" The critical message of the polemic;

(3) "For example:" A sequence of dramatic episodes arranged with increasing emotional strength compelling enough to bring spectators to share the argument's closure:

(4) "What will you do about it?"

The outline is simplistic, but one of the first major attempts to stage wholly polemical theatre in the U.S. was powerful enough in the Thirties to make theatre history: Clifford Odets' *Waiting for Lefty*. Hardly written with this formula in mind, it nevertheless developed its argument – as later examples have done – duplicating its progression.

(1)   The theatre becomes a Union hall.   The audience becomes the union's taxi drivers waiting for their newly elected chairman, Lefty, who's negotiating elsewhere with management for an employee's, not a company union such as they now have.

(2)   In the union hall, the company has its own men in charge, outlawing as "reds" any members proposing to start their own union, or proposing a strike to get it.   Members, frustrated, are emotionally charged, but too intimidated to act.

(3)   While waiting, a sequence of flashback scenes demonstrates the economic, political, emotional bind of the workers' plight over the past months, which more and more infuriated but immobilized them,   until the news comes that Lefty's dead – he's been murdered.

(4)   Cast, with audience spontaneously joining in, shout: "Strike!"

Crude, oh, yes, but what accomplished that bonding of cast and audience was the build of the audience's compassion not merely for the suffering of individuals in the flashback scenes – a way-station in its progress through the argument – but for the emotional increment attached to its learning of the painful core at the heart of the taxi-drivers' common plight.   Brecht's "alienation," in principle abhors such "culinary" emotional delights.   But studied closely, the conclusions of his Mother Courage's "Hey! Wait for me!" and Shen Te's cry for "Help!" come about by the same "culinary" path, not by "distancing."   The moral ambiguity uncovered in both of Brecht's endings unquestionably wins our nod of assent, but what wins a much larger share is our "culinary delight" in the individual plights of his two suffering heroines.   The emotional thrust of *anxiety, outrage and frustration* in the development of Odets' polemic wins overwhelming embrace for the thesis itself.   The Federal theatre's *Living Newspaper* productions were produced concurrently, about Depression issues like slum housing (*One Third of a Nation,*) agricultural subsidies (*Triple-A Plowed Under,*), and other "editorials," which had the same thrust as *Waiting for Lefty* and won the same embrace.

Allegory

Everyman[40]

On the face of it, the simplest thematic structure is dramatic allegory. It is not. The late Fifteenth Century morality play, *Everyman*, is the most powerful example that's come down to us of dramatic allegory dramatizing a single action, yet bearing a multitude of levels of meaning. Morality plays' didacticism is still a most effective way of structuring thematic action; through it, complicated concepts are accessible to audiences of any degree of understanding.

But it's a sore temptation, as morality plays past or present did and do, to dismember a concept – political, philosophical, mystical, moral – into separate and equal parts, stretching them over a play's length, and producing not so much dramatic scenes as illustrative segments of an ultimately meaningful idea. Discouraging on the face of it, the practice brings to mind the listic 'firstlys, secondlys, thirdlys' of deeply sleep-inducing sermons, and almost justifies Shaw's warning that allegory consistently applied is plainly unbearable. "The very word," Henry VIII, one of its most tried spectators, famously admitted, "is like a yawn." Not with baited breath but with desperation, we suffer the intervals before "tenthly." And yet the progression can be, and has been, viable, and in the case of *Everyman*, powerful. Why? Because the matter of *Everyman* takes for its subject the paradigmatic course and the ultimate meaning of human life itself, and it does so by going to the heart of the matter at once: "Everyman," says Death at the beginning of the play, "Stand still." In fulfilling Death's injunction to bring, by day's end, his reckoning before God, "meaning," "parable," and "lesson" are compacted into an allegorical journey from Man's "awakening" into life to his judgment after death. The lesson is explicit, reiterated, elementary. But what gave it significance was not its parable alone, but its expansion into its several contexts.

"Meanings" in medieval exegesis of the Bible carried four distinct levels of reference: the literal, the tropological, the allegorical, the anagogical.[41] There is no use supposing that the same distinctions of meaning were visited on secular writing, but *Everyman* seen through the prism characteristic of medieval exegesis, engages meaning on at least three of those "levels." In the literal sense, Everyman's is the journey of one man who is made aware of his imminent death on his last day, desperately closing accounts with the world and readying for his confrontation with God. He discovers that all the worldly things he's accumulated – his Fellowship, his Kindred, his Wealth – avail him nothing, and in his despair (the middle of his journey) he invokes his Knowledge and his lifetime's small measure of Good Deeds for help. His Knowledge moves him to turn to the Church for his salvation, and after confession and holy unction, he, now without his physical Strength or his Five Wits or Beauty or finally, even Knowledge, confronts the grave with nothing to stand by him before God's judgment but his Good (church sanctioned) Deeds, and it's they alone, we hear from the Angel in the epilogue, which earn him his salvation.

Just as there are three concurrent Everymans being tracked – the living man, the community of living men, and the race of men from Adam on, there are three time frames – the single day in a man's life, his entire lifespan, and synoptically, the span of the life of mankind. And all three are wrapped into four concurrent readings – his literal biography, his moral career and its meaning, his meaning as a metaphor for human existence, and the meaning of the place of humanity in the divine scheme. The tightness of its episodic structure is matched by the tight cohesion of its concurrent levels of meaning. Allegory at its best is the tightest, the most synoptic of thematic structures.

Maeterlinck's *The Blue Bird*[42]

Echoing the Middle Ages in multi-level meaning structure, Maeterlinck, the Symbolist playwright who won a following in the 1890's among the intelligentsia who were given to the occult and the spiritually mysterious, put into theatrical form in his *The Blue Bird* a sampling of the philosopher Swedenborg's[43] mystical doctrine. The play depicts the journey of two children, Tyltyl and Mytyl, ostensibly searching for "the blue bird of happiness." In fact, the journey they are on is – in Swedenborg's sense – a search for the lost knowledge of the soul – the unifying knowledge of matter and spirit which was lost when soul and body were presumably separated after Adam's fall. It was Swedenborg's yearning to find the right passage for the recovery of that lost knowledge, and Maeterlinck's play, in the guise of a children's fairy tale, tracks symbolically the journey attempting to reach that goal.

As with the ritual-journeys we've looked at before, or the morality-play progression of *Everyman*, each scene delineates a single step along the way, and its significance is represented schematically. Using Swedenborg's doctrine of correspondences in his treatise, *An Hieroglyphic Key*, Maeterlinck represents in each scene an aspect of spirit manifesting itself through material equivalents – the colors, objects, figures and events in this world symbolically mirroring the hierarchy of beings and intelligences in the other. As each scene depicts a stage in the children's journey – the House of Memory, the House of Night, etc. – it is overlaid with an elaborate decor signifying its particular esoteric meaning. The play's lesson, like *Everyman's*, has to be read through the conjunction of those "meanings." Put unsparingly, they read as follows:

Tyltyl and Mytyl (human innocence) are moved by the Fairy Bérylune (the Divine Spirit) to journey in search of "the grass that sings" (earthly wisdom) and "the bird that is blue" (spiritual wisdom.) With a retinue of allegorical figures (the needs of the body) – Fire, Water, Milk, Sugar, Bread, together with Dog (instinctive fidelity) and Cat (active evil) – they leave the Fairy Palace and journey through the Land of Memory (where their grandparents live (their living tradition); the Palace of Night (where they experience active and passive evil, but where the stages of Adamic, Mosaic and Christian belief first become manifest); the Forest (where the maze of ecclesiastical systems, loving their entrenched power, battle new understandings); the Graveyard (where the buried past lies, but is not dead and is still functioning in memory among the living); the Kingdom of the Future (where "the children waiting to be born" signify the new wisdoms that are yet to emerge.) On their return home (waking from their dream) they imagine for a moment that they have captured the blue bird, but in an instant it turns pink and flies away (their spiritual truth temporarily grasped, but permanently elusive.)

So self-enclosed a system of parallel meanings-and-referents is clearly not intended for exposition, but finds its "truth" in the perfect symmetry and perfect comprehensiveness of its design alone. Like mystical systems generally, the more cosmic their design and the more apt their "correspondences" between the terrestrial known and the super-terrestrial unknown, the more "truth" is attributable to its claim of revealing a – or the – universal landscape of existence.

Subverting thematic structure: Jarry's *Caesar-Antichrist*[44]

The innocent, wide-eyed pieties of *The Blue Bird,* using the pattern of a journey, sustain a measure of narrative momentum, but the form itself struggles against the static temptations implicit in allegory and in symbolism, with their fixity in scenes made up essentially of conceptually layered diagrams. Wholly giving way to this temptation, and indulging not only in the fixity of sequential diagrams but in the mystery – in fact the studied obfuscation – of meaning, is one of the most complex, esoteric, maddeningly hermetic works in Western literature. Maeterlinck exploits essentially one code, Swedenborg's, but Jarry's *Caesar-Antichrist* wallows in many: symbolic and emblematic languages embracing the picture-cards of the Tarot pack, the escutcheons of medieval heraldry, the agitated symbolism of the Book of Revelation, Cabala, mathematical and occult systems, private sexual and scatological encodings, all serving a supertext depicting the epoch of the Antichrist's reign from the time when it negates the epoch of Christ (at sundown) to the time it is itself supplanted (at sunrise.) Assuming, as in *Everyman,* the universal operation of recurrence, (the overlaying of time-frames – day, epoch, eternity) and as in *The Bluebird,* the structured hierarchies of correspondence, each act, and each scene of each act, is a multilayered, more or less static portrait of a time-space-event. One example: In the structuring of each act (this, taken from the symbolism of the Cabala:)

> "Each of the four acts corresponds to one of the symbolic letters that make up the sacred word *Yahweh*;

the unpronounced Hebrew name of God – *yud, he, vov, he.* They share in the cabalistic symbolism of each letter with respect to their mathematical sexual significances and their corresponding meanings in the cabalistic *Book of Creation.*"

Overlaying this structural pattern, or corresponding to it, are the four suits of the tarot cards, which themselves are sometimes represented by objects from a different frame of reference. The controlling patterns of the four letters of the name of Yahweh, and of the tarot's four suits, are multiplied – there are many that, at different levels of control and subordination, schematize every element of the work's structure.

The fixing of its sequences' symbolically-layered scenes is its essential preoccupation rather than dramatic momentum. Instead of using a strategy of gradually revealing "meaning," it assumes a concept of overwhelming scale and near-universal inclusiveness that makes no attempt at gradual self-revelation, but serves only as the implicit control for the schematic construct of the entire work. It abandons altogether emulating the flow of narrative movement, and emulates instead the stolidity of photographs.

Further: Jarry mocks not only the givens of dramatic composition, but the givens of composition itself. Overwhelming these complex but apparently fixed and stable meanings is his fundamental operative term: *instability.*[45] In Jarry's *"'pataphysical"* system (his definition: an "imaginary system of imaginary solutions") all elements are in flux, meanings can autonomously invert or self-negate, and opposites can function as equivalents. In *Caesar-Antichrist,* they do, and all the stable symbolism that resembles the orthodox practice of the Eighteen Nineties' Symbolists is blown to the moon by a private delirium that mocks its own laboriously simulated gravity.

What, then, is Jarry doing among examples of dramatic structures dedicated to sequential thematic enlightenment? He's pivotal. It was from the Eighteen Nineties to the early decades of the Twentieth Century when the fictional and dramatic constructs of reality – evidenced in plots, in dialogue, in character constructs and in "meaning" constructs – reached a level of complexity that capped Western fictional tradition on the one hand, and on the other was the instrument of its collapse. Jarry in every particular anticipated Joyce's novel *Finnegans Wake*,[46] which signified, like Jarry's play, the climax and the suicide, in one, of creative writing's intellectual monumentalism. The two "artificers" – Joyce's word – most adept at their erection were the very ones who sabotaged their enterprise. Along with several other early "artificers" of Modernism, two of the avenues of the Modernist enterprise were opened. The first was *zero constructs*: the emptying of all constructs, beginning with no inhering suppositions whatever. The other was self-enclosure: fictions and dramas that went a step beyond the Nineteenth Century's Art for Art's sake to the hermetically sealed, no part of whose function was its own revelation or explanation. Not the use of the thing, or the display of the thing, but as Joyce put it, "The ding hvat in itself id est," (or *"what the thing is in itself."*) One of the earmarks of early Modernism: the pride of suicidal integrity. Jarry, although nobody noticed, created a far greater, far more far-reaching revolution in *Caesar-Antichrist* than in his more familiar *Ubu Roi*.

*

So much for the doing and undoing of thematic structures. With them, it's possible to make concepts reverberate dramatically with meaning and feeling; it's also possible to so overlay the very idea of structuring and conveying meaning as to demonstrate by their mockery the inanity of their existence.

***

CHAPTER 7

CHARACTER

DEFINING DRAMATIC CHARACTER

"Character" is a construct. The construct of a dramatic character is a *reference* to "person," but it is in no sense a reproduction of "person." It is a sort of deliberate distortion of what one sees, hears and experiences of others for the sake of a more important obligation than to literal portraiture. One can replicate in one's head the very tone, the very wrinkles, the very smell of an intimately-known person, and the dramatic portrait that emerges will still be fiction, still elude the literal, accurate representation of person, because, whether one is aware of it or not, the inescapable commitment of the writer is to *concept,* or series of concepts, not to portraiture. Character description is determined not by the fact of "person," but by novel formulations assembled from the happenstance of psychological and moral beliefs of one's own time together with, paradoxically, all the formulations of the past. Not unlike other aspects of drama, vestigially and illogically, the idea of "character" has stayed actively with us in all the mythic, folkloric, philosophic, theologic and "scientific" constructs endemic to Western tradition, and, with respect to "character," none of them have remained wholly accepted nor wholly abandoned nor wholly denied nor wholly forgotten. For the last century or so, the felt "rightness" of character portrayal has leaned heavily toward literal replication of tone, accent, wrinkles and – well, not yet smell – of our pictured characters. But this preference for the particular look or sound of the familiar is a novel cultural earmark of our own time, shared by few other periods, which by far preferred only metaphors for the essential features of the construct. Historically,

126

we're alone in needing accurate closeups in 3-D. Nevertheless, behind our costumes of the "real," there remains the reality of the *construct*, not the photograph.

CHARACTER AS "HISTORICAL ACCUMULATION"

Only historically is it possible to describe – and then only roughly – the shape-changing progress through which the idea of *character-structure* has run, catching out the significant moments of those changes, and so tracking how gradually the idea added up to our normally contradictory, frequently ephemeral, highly theoretical, usually superficial, largely impossible notions of how the psychology of dramatic characters is constituted, and how that psychology should make them behave on stage. We will approach the notion of "character-construct" and what it has gradually added up to in contemporary drama through a quick tour of those *key moments in drama's history* that were most critical to its changing definition and its perpetually-altering understanding. And lightly note as we go the cultural conditioning that evoked the models – the governing "constructs" – by which our patchwork idea of "character" is now known. But first: a few animadversions against Aristotle, the "father," so to speak, of important misapprehensions about "character."

"CHARACTER" IN ARISTOTLE'S *POETICS*

Aristotle's *Poetics* has the longest history and the greatest influence of any document in Western dramatic criticism, and his "principles," as they've been more and more codified during that history, weigh heavily on the teaching and practice of playwriting still. What is probably the most important question of all is the degree to which what has been called the *moral fallacy* in criticism weighs on Aristotelian prescriptions for character. Despite the attempt to distance himself from Plato's condemnation of poetry in general, the prescriptions Aristotle offers in the *Poetics* for appraising human behavior in drama are fundamentally not different from Plato's moral judgmentalism.[1] Plato banishes poets from the ideal Republic on the grounds that (1) poets represented humanity at two removes from the Real, (2) that, impiously, they represented the Gods as causing human misery, and that (3) the very showing of evil men and evil acts leads to their imitation.

Aristotle's suggestions on "character" in the *Poetics* hardly share these opinions, but more subtly, they share the same judgmental perspective. Far more carefully calibrated, "character" is still shown within a quintessential organization of values at one with the middling range of human conduct, as in Aristotle's famous "mean" not too much, not too little, but just right, the system of proper conduct calibrating toward the middle. This particular lens through which Aristotle observes has gone a long way toward establishing cultural norms for judging character, but the greatest of Western drama has as often as not ignored these "norms," and explored characters in frenzies of indifference to such judgment. But criticism more often than not has lagged far behind, indulging in uniform condescension toward, and judicious dismissal of, the excessive, the lunatic, the murderous, the incestuous, the blasphemous, the vengeful – in a word, the actual domains of human experience in tragedy. Aristotle's discussions of tragic characters and tragic destinies successfully skirt engagement with any of these qualities and conditions by treating them only to the formulas of classification supported by his judgmental scheme. And the tradition of classical criticism has learned, from his example that tragic behavior and ineffable emotion in drama are best judged coolly – as excessive, or unjustified, or inappropriate. But in fact, the bones and marrow of tragic experience remain out of the range of the *Poetic;* some of the most profoundly conceived characters in Greek tragedy, within his terms, often become merely condemnable if not dismissible.

"GOOD," "APPROPRIATE," "BELIEVABLE," AND "CONSISTENT"

These are Aristotle's four criteria for characters acceptable to tragedy. But had he been living during the time of the three great tragedians, Aeschylus, Sophocles and Euripides, he would have had a terrible time persuading them to believe him. All of Aristotle's excluded kinds figure prominently and purposefully in their tragedies. "Of character," he says in the *Poetics*, there are four things to be aimed at. First and most important, it must be good. Now any speech or action that manifests moral purpose of any kind will be expressive of character; the character will be good if the purpose is good. This rule is relative to each class. Even a woman may be good, and also a slave; though the woman may be said to be an inferior being, and the slave quite worthless. The second thing to aim at is propriety. There is a type of manly valor; but valor in a woman, or unscrupulous cleverness, is inappropriate. Thirdly, character must be true to life: for this is a distinct thing from goodness and propriety, as here described. The fourth point is consistency, for though the subject of the imitation, who suggested the type, be inconsistent, still he must be consistently inconsistent.

Even if with high-minded charity we pass in silence over Aristotle's views of women and slaves, the remoteness of his criteria from our own is manifest. But they are in fact almost as remote from the idea of characterization in Greek tragedy. There's an argument – which we will make below – for Aristotle's significant distance from Fifth Century tragedy, which he in the Fourth Century was observing from an already altered perspective.

As an example of inconsistency of character, he points to Iphigenia in Euripides' tragedy, *Iphigenia in Aulis*,[2] who at her critical moment, is about to be sacrificed by her father at the behest of the goddess Artemis. Suddenly, out of the blue, it seems, she embraces her assassination as a wished-for martyrdom. But "Iphigenia, the suppliant" in the early scenes of the play, Aristotle complains, "in no way resembles her later self." In Aristotle's view, nowhere in the logic of character "consistency" is there room for internal reversion from a preset motive. Only the incidents of the plot may undergo radical change, and only through such alterations of incident can the characters undergo "recognitions" and in that way reverse their motives (i.e., Creusa, in Euripides' *Ion*,[3] in the nick of time discovers that the victim she's about to kill is her son, and so, sensibly enough, changes her mind.) It makes, therefore, little sense for a character like the passive suppliant Iphigenia (in one of the truly magnificent passages in Greek tragedy) with no change of circumstance from the one that threatens her with death, to manifest an extraordinary conversion that recognizes (whether we think well of her change of heart or not) that the sacrifice of her life at this moment for the Greek cause would give greater meaning to that life than rescue and marriage and long living. The case of Iphigenia altogether eludes Aristotle's notion of "consistency," just as the representation of women and slaves in the tragedies in no way squares with his notion of "propriety."

Aristotle's concept of propriety in conduct is wholly related, as it is in Plato, to the appropriate status and function of the citizen of the City-State, and in both Plato and Aristotle, that status is seen, and consistently described, as fixed. But it is not – certainly not in Fifth Century tragedy. Consider: in the urban life of Fourth Century Athens, a cosmopolitan society developed with a more certain feeling for the stability of the separate classes, and an understandably self-flattering way of characterizing those differences – they're low, we're not – and the gradations in judgment that naturally follow. Along with that feeling of our-class-and-kind certainties, it's reasonable to deal – as Fourth Century drama does – with fixed types, recognizable not so much in their individuality as representations of a class or type in the aggregate. But in the previous century's tragedies, which deal, if anything, with radical not to say harrowing changes of condition and circumstance, and deal endlessly with the very instability of role and class – in other words, in the painful dimensions of tragic life – is there a stable posture of the role, or of the psychological fixity, of women? None. Their representation and place is frequently at the heart of the debate in a tragedy rather than settled, closer to the core of tragedy's questions than to a settled understanding. And "slaves" – who are they, not in tragedy, but in Fourth Century comedy?[4] Lower class labor, somewhere between *lumpen* and full-fledged proletariat. As in every culture except perhaps the sentimental fringes in the Eighteenth and Nineteenth Centuries, they're held in easy, comic contempt as merely powerless, vulgar and poor. But who are they in Greek Tragedy? The Queen Hecuba,[5] the Princess Tecmessa,[6] the royal Cassandras,[7] Andromaches, and their followers, the Trojan Women: all now

captives, and so, slaves. In tragedy, the endless play of irony −
tragic irony − concerning their condition as opposed to their worth
makes it folly to equate condition and state with "character." The
very anomaly between the two is at the heart of the tragic
circumstance endured by Medea,[8] for example, a princess terrified
by her apprehension of the oncoming indignity of abandonment −
a condition which spells helpless suppliant, beggar, fugitive − were
it to occur. Or Electra,[9] princess, cast by her mother and her
mother's lover into the situation of slave, or contrariwise,
Clytemnestra[10] in the role of surrogate king, exhibiting authority,
"manly valor" and intelligence, and in Aristotle's words,
"unscrupulous cleverness" − in his formulation, all prerogatives of
the male. But the very question that hangs like a deadly curse over
the whole of the *Oresteia* is precisely the one of male-female
prerogative, not resolved until the end. The powerful portrait of
Aeschylus's Clytemnestra is the perfect example of what Aristotle
would rule out as "inappropriate," a character not to be represented
in tragedy.

Typology, with its fixed functions, squares only too perfectly not
with Fifth Century tragedy, but with the urban New Comedy
developing in the Fourth Century, which concerns itself exclusively
with casts of characters made up of next-door neighbors meeting
and visiting on city streets, acting, judging, and being judged in their
middling circumstances by their middling morality, wholly
abjuring, if they ever felt the urge, to emulate explorations of
character disjuncture, extremes of suffering and painful choice
endemic to the previous century's tragedy. Those who might be
examples of that suffering − the raped girls and wives whose
reputations, after the recognition of the real facts, are judged
redeemed by the men who raped them − are generally kept offstage,
plot facts rather than characters to be known, and explored.

The lesson? Clearly, the very idea of "character" as understood
in the one period may have only a loose fit if any at all over
another. Aristotle's formulations, fitting for Greek New Comedy,
and even for the long tradition that that Fourth Century genre was
to create, is by no means a universal guide, and certainly not for
drama that reaches beyond the boundaries of what can be
sympathetically comprehended by judgmental typologies.

Pursuing further the idea of "character" and how it functions: There are contexts in which it's been understood to have genuine meaning, in practice and in theory, so that we can arrive, if not at a single definition, at least at a smorgasbord of its theoretical varieties and practical possibilities.   One of those contexts we've already belabored, and so we'll let further discussion of it pass: (1) "Character" as a sum of moral judgments.   Two others must be considered at length: (2) "Character" as an accumulation of historical and traditional understandings; and finally, (3) "Character" – in one of its latest versions – as ungraspable, or as displaced, or as non-existent.   We'll begin, once again, with a view of Greek tragic characters, possibly as controversial as Aristotle's.

"MONOLITHIC" PROTAGONIST

The philosopher Hegel described character in Greek tragedy as 'monolithic.'[11]   What he meant was that a character such as Agamemnon could be described only as "an Agamemnon," not a particular kind of person as opposed to another kind, but simply as himself. Oedipus too is not, according to Hegel, to be defined by his "pride" or his rational nature, but simply, again, as an "Oedipus." To some extent, Hegel is right. In Homer, "hero" is the essential characteristic of the hero, the very essence of the man, known usually by his courage on the battlefield. In other words, there is a primary characteristic that wholly defines the "worth" of the man, and secondary characteristics do not weigh significantly against that worth. It is this sense of the heroic that is still with us, but considerably downgraded – relegated for the most part to the fantasy heroes of action films.

But Hegel meant more: the Greek protagonist was "monolithic," he explained, because each one embodied a single ethical posture and goal: they are "entirely and absolutely that which they will and achieve" and nothing more. They are, therefore, "monolithic" in that "they do not choose" – that is, having no reason to imagine that they are confronted by ethical alternatives, they cannot weigh alternatives, and so they are nothing but a single intention driving toward a single determined resolution.

Is this true? Far from it. So far, in fact, is Agamemnon, for example, from Hegel's portrait as to represent its precise opposite. Twice over in the course of Aeschylus's tragedy, he is caught in a double bind – between two contradictory but absolute injunctions in the face of which either choice leads to inevitable doom. And, just as for a half-dozen or so other tragic protagonists, it's a given that he must make that choice and suffer that doom. But side by side with tragic protagonists so caught are those – like Creon or Antigone – whom Hegel's characterization more accurately fits.

Does Hegel's lapse matter? Not entirely. In either case, the tragic figure is defined essentially by his ethical situation and by nothing else. "Monolithic" we can say in that altered sense: each signifies a single ethical situation – and no more. What matters is that Hegel is defining the protagonists of Greek tragedy as representing ethical positions without multiple, bewildering complexity – a condition he preserves for his description of tragedy in a "romantic" age, in which he includes the Elizabethan, a period in which tragic characters were, presumably, overwhelmed and paralyzed by a plethora of ethical options, and further confused by private emotional torments.

Classic-Romantic: with respect to the idea of "character," Hegel's distinction held for many, and for some, still holds. The classic simplicity of the singly-focused, ethically oriented Greek hero, and the complexity of the emotionally-fraught, ethically disoriented Romantic hero – a description that fits far more accurately Hegel's contemporary, early Nineteenth-Century soured anti-romantic Romantics (Byron, Buchner, Kleist, Musset) than it does the more focused though on occasion ethically tormented Elizabethan tragic protagonists.

PROTAGONISTS IN CONFLICT

But what Hegel attributes to the Elizabethans was in fact already happening in the plays of Sophocles and Euripides: not ethical tensions alone, but emotional tensions, thoroughly analyzed and exploited, colliding with ethical absolutes or colliding among themselves. Sophocles' Deianeira (in *The Women of Trachis*) tormented by her jealousy of Heracles' lovers, debating sending the poisoned garment to him, and at the same time, her violent self-hatred, and then her self-punishment afterward; the tormented Medea[12] making her final decision over her sons, debating moral absolutes against her absolute lust for revenge.   In fact, the multiplicity of motives and emotional urgencies in both women transcend the easy match of motive against motive or ethical demand against demand.   Private, intensely personal motive; separation and confusion of motives; unbidden motive – as though arising out of nowhere (Iphigenia) – savage motive eroding justification (Hecuba in Euripides' *Hecuba*.) overlapping motives of rage at injustice and morose self-pity and proud forbearance and gross greed for mere sustenance (Philoctetes)[13]: the private psychological, even pathological, and the demandingly ethical, are so enmeshed in one another in later fifth century tragedy that Hegelian aesthetic characterizations of that tragedy, fit the reality of Greek tragedy's characters awkwardly at best.

GREEK TRAGEDY CHARACTERIZATION

What was happening to the presentation of "character" in Athenian tragedy throughout the Fifth Century was increasing particularization.[14]   The drama more and more invited articulation of small psychological differences, subtle distinctions in human behavior, a drama moving away from the spectacle of large symbolic public acts to one of actions moved as much by the rationale of intimate, private feeling. The social polity was turning away from knowing itself as the citizenry of Pericles' awesome city-state,[15] and more toward the feeling of a private citizenry suffering increasingly under the privations of an ongoing war, and the state's gradual drift toward powerlessness. And from Aristophanes' satiric comedies and Euripides' bitter tragedies, one gets the sense of a state losing its moral compass.   By the time of Alexander's conquests beginning in 336 B.C., the Empire had shriveled to the status of a client city, and recovering from war's catastrophes, the citizenry busied itself with its private concerns, its rapidly-reviving commerce, its intellectual pursuits, its cosmopolitanism.

FOURTH CENTURY MASKED CHARACTERS

And as the culture became more cosmopolitan, the notion of character became more various, as various as society itself. The 'monolithic' heroes of great ethical intent and great public import are gradually displaced, as the representation of character begins to match the variety of the citizenry's functions. It was in the fourth century B.C. when actors began to wear masks with carefully articulated features, and in the century's introduction of New Comedy – the model we still think of as our generic form of "drama" – the masks were for the first time representative of particular types and kinds of the human species. To extrapolate from Pollux's (Second Century AD) treatise on masks,[16] they were broken down as follows: first by gender – male or female; second, by age – young, mature, old; third, by occupation or function – cook, slave dealer, prostitute, lover, matron, etc. marking the higher and the lower social orders, representing occupations from the menial to the dignified and relatively noble (though the cast of characters was restricted to the lower and middle classes.) There was one further defining characteristic: moral/behavioral bent, the direction toward which the masked character's behavior tended, as: boorish, cunning, temperate, kindly, greedy, etc. And so character now became a sum, and fit into these four descriptive categories: a *man, middle-aged*, who is a *slave-dealer*, and *greedy*, for example. Using these four variables, the number of masks described in Pollux's treatise – more than a hundred – leaves considerable room for significant variation.

THE "FIXITY" OF CHARACTERS: ITS BEGINNINGS

The masks, as the exact and delimiting definitions of the comedy's characters, require that once a character enters into the action of the play, he remains fixed in his characterization. Since he holds to these characteristics until the end of the play, what we currently imagine as a character's 'journey' or change is foreign to this tradition of comedy. Moliere is fully its heir. No characters in his plays undergo any fundamental change whatever, nor are any of his characters delineated beyond the four delimiting terms of New Comedy.

But it is here, in Fourth Century New Comedy, that Aristotle's end-of-play *reversal – recognition* truly comes into its own. The comedy ends with the discovery that converts the assumed facts into the real facts. ("Now, my master, that we learn it was you who raped your masked wife at the *saturnalia,* we know she is not an abandoned whore and the son she now bears is not a bastard, but your own son. So she, fortunate woman, can take her rightful place once more in your home.") But the reversal by no means signals his "change of character;" only his decision. The husband doesn't change his fixed moral bent. The new situation confirms and responds to his "bent" for demanding the strictest moral behavior in his wife, and his decision – now that she, having been raped by him alone, is proved virtuous – to take her back into his home, reinforces his husband-demand for strictest moral behavior in a wife.

This four-item checklist is the strongest and most abiding tradition of characterization in Western drama. It was carried over into Roman comedy intact – the Roman plays being essentially slight variations on their Greek New Comedy sources – and then wholly resuscitated in the Renaissance, whose middle-class urban comedy norms remained the model for urban comedy characterization through the eighteenth, nineteenth and twentieth centuries. And it is still today the basis for characterization in popular comedy, and exists entirely unaltered from the original Fourth Century B.C. model in TV sitcoms: sex, age, social place, and fixed moral bent. There are several interesting – and irritating – reflections to be made on this way of defining character: (1) its attached values, (2) its exclusions.

(1) *Its attached values*: Fixity of characterization is at one with fixity of values. In comedy, there's a moral rule-book for each class and kind. A servant is good or bad, appropriate or inappropriate in a different way from his master. Best servanthood exhibits loyalty, obedience, and – in a word – servility. But a master with the same propensities would hardly be a good master. A servile master? Precisely in this respect does the notion of character in Aristotle's *Poetics* (written c.335-323 B.C. concurrently with Greek New Comedy's advent, after 336 B.C.) reflect more exactly his contemporaries' comedy than it does the tragedy of the century

before.   It's the class divisions of cosmopolitan Athens out of which the fixed divisions of behavioral and moral difference rigidified.   At least, it did so in the moral dreamscape of comedy, whose resilience has lasted for centuries, and lasts still.[17]

This static concept of character was perfectly, sometimes exquisitely, realized in one of neoclassical comedy's great periods: English Restoration comedy.   So completely did the formulas of fixed characterization govern, that before a character entered, he was frequently summed up in a brief portrait which the French called a *caractere*,[18] a speech or so of succinct description of his bent, classified according to the then-current operative categories of formal fool, French fop, decaying beauty, and so on.

Caractere derived originally from Theophrastus, Aristotle's disciple and successor to his direction of his school, the Lyceum. In his treatise on "Characters," he catalogued the fixed habit, speech, and resulting kinds of behavior of each type, and either stated or implied his place on the social scale.   An example:

> *The Boor:* "His genuine grossness. His shamelessness and disgusting jesting... In a theatre he keeps clapping when everyone else is finished, and hisses the performers who have taken the fancy of the rest of the audience.... When the market-place is crowded he goes up to a stall where walnuts or fruits are sold and stands eating away from pure greed, talking all the time to the seller.... He passes the remark as he stands at the barber's or the perfume-seller's that he intends to get drunk.... And when people are at their devotions and pouring libations, he lets fall his cup, and laughs as if he had done something witty.... When he desires to spit, he does it across the table at the cupbearer."

Petulant, in Congreve's *The Way of the World* is a particular kind of fool, a Restoration fool, who pretends to the fashionable, amoral life of a "true" wit, of which he is barely half.[19]   His advance report by his paired friend Witwoud, who makes up the other half, pretends he's trying not to slander his friend:

WITWOUD: Petulant's my friend, and a very honest fellow, and a very pretty fellow, and has a smattering – faith and troth, a pretty deal of an odd sort of a small wit…. And if he had but any judgment in the world, he would be not altogether contemptible…. I can defend most of his faults except one or two….

FAINALL: Too illiterate.

WITWOUD: That! That's his happiness. His want of learning gives him the more opportunities to show his natural parts….

COACHMAN enters: Is Master Petulant here?… Three gentlewomen in the coach would speak with him….

WITWOUD: O brave Petulant, Three!…. To tell you a secret. these are trulls that he allows coach-hire, and something more by the week, to call on him once a day at public places…. You shall see how he won't go to 'em because there's no more company here to take notice of him. Why, this is nothing to what he used to do: before he found out this way, I have known him to call for himself.

FAINALL: Call for himself? What dost thou mean?

WITWOUD: Why, he would slip you out of this chocolate house, just when you had been talking to him. As soon as your back was turned – whip he was gone, then trip to his lodging, clap on a hood and scarf and mask, slap into a hackney coach, and drive hither to the door again in a trice; where he would send in for himself – that I mean – call for himself, wait for himself, nay and what's more, not finding himself, sometimes leave a letter for himself….

MIRABEL: I believe he waits for himself now, he is so long a-coming. Oh, I ask his pardon!

At his entrance, Petulant at once illustrates his *caractere*, filling in with particulars the Theophrastian report which preceded him.

(2) *Its exclusions*: But how much inquiry and exploration, we may ask, is made of his past, or of the dynamic of his behavior? None.

The facts of his past bear only on his immediate plot situation (delayed inheritance, beggared by an unfriendly will, income dependent on an ancient ruin's favor, or chafing under the burden of a cast-off mistress), but never on a deep-lying, invisible, governing motive operating relentlessly from the past. He is seen entirely and understood wholly in his presentness, the sum of his characteristics at once apparent, all perceived at a glance, with no hint of anything lying unexplored "within," or "below." Character, then, not perceived in depth, but all of it equally apparent, equally present. But by the time of Seventeenth Century Restoration comedy, something had been added:

"HORIZONTAL" CHARACTERIZATION

Four-part "listic" characterization widened its list, so that relevant items beyond the four basic determinants became more numerous, more subtly and expertly distinguished from one another, and most particularly, more integrated into the game of character appraisal. The judgmentalism derived from Aristotle added massively to its checklist by joining the intellectual and social preoccupations of two centuries of leisured societies: when a whole class was – and saw itself more and more, as – at perfect liberty to look away entirely from mundane care, and expend its energies (at least as it represented itself in its comedy) on the refinements of manner, of social address, of intellect, of social punctilio. It happened during the gradual transition over two centuries from Baroque to Rococo sensibility,[20] when what had begun a serious inquiry into the understanding of human affairs gradually devolved into a pleasurable but fundamentally enervated game of multiplying and organizing subtleties of observation of human actions together with multiplying and organizing subtleties of social discourse.

Precision, not merely multiplication, was the game. Exact definition became the model for distinguishing this characteristic from that, this mode of address from another, this moral stance from that. The pleasure in weighing these differences lay in separating what was almost identical, seeing them not only as strikingly different from one another in definition, but in value. The expanding checklist became in itself a value; those who could manipulate it with the peculiar sagacity required for its gamesmanship were either its arbiters or its benefactors or both.

The "Jane Austen" paradigm[21]

By the beginning of the nineteenth century, the game had reached its apex – most particularly and brilliantly in the novels of Jane Austen. Her female characters were studies in their fitful education in reading "character" during their apprenticeship – their gradually learning to read accurately their characterological checklists for men. Gone is the crudeness of the readings of one another by the characters in the Greek and Roman comedies – he is impetuous, she is forlorn, the old man is jealous – and instead there is the careful weighing by these young ladies of the imagination, bearing, taste, judgment, forthrightness, conversation, manners, and/or breeding of the young man under scrutiny. After much study, for example, a question might linger concerning his forbearance, or he might be suspected of a touch of obsequiousness, or even more damning, a shade, perhaps an overplus, of insolence. The gentleman might have a certain wit, but his intellect might not entirely govern his wit, and certainly not his dinner-table conversation. Close scrutiny, scrupulous valuation, particular judgments attaching to each of the basic character giveaways observed by possibly charitable, possibly unforgiving eyes. But Jane Austen as author is the ultimate judge of her fictional judges. Her narrative study is the education of her heroines – how they learn to do these calculations just right. At first failing, they gradually gain sagacity, the stumbling heroines bit by bit realizing their judicial shortcomings, ponder corrective evidence, and by novel's end gain both judgmental precision, and the ultimate reward for their sagacity, a husband.

"Vertical" characterization

It takes a certain genius to sustain the sunniness of Austen's outlook on human psychology and to maintain the necessary blindness that accompanies it. The Nineteenth Century drama that followed was rarely blessed with that genius (Oscar Wilde stands almost alone) though some of its greatest novelists were similarly blessed (preeminently, Trollope.) Still, they were flying in the face of – to put it too simply – an opposing sensibility far more dour, far more given to foraging well beyond the psychological-moral middle ground of rococo burrowings. It was a tradition that had more to do with tragedy and serious drama than with comedy, a tradition that begins, way back, with early classical examples – oddly enough, with the most neglected of the great tragic dramatists of Western drama, the Roman tragedian, Seneca.

SENECAN PSYCHOLOGY

Seneca has been blamed for everything that went wrong with Elizabethan tragedy:[22] its boring rhetoric when it was boring; its ghosts; its blood-curdling melodrama when it curdled the blood; its superfluous one-man chorus. It was T.S. Eliot who first credited Seneca's influence with something positive: his poetic/rhetorical model which, Eliot argued, lent dignity, even sublimity, to Elizabethan tragedy's texts. But there was something far more powerful to be gleaned from Seneca than his rhetoric or even his Stoic philosophy: his characters' psychology, which entered into Elizabethan tragedy, whether unspoiled from his example or from more peripheral influences. It is startlingly modern, and therefore when it appears in Elizabethan tragedy, it is recognized by us as at once familiar and believable.

Unlike the powerful emotional life of tragic figures in Sophocles and Euripides, which Seneca in the same tales replicates, the frenzy, or at least the persuasion of emotion in Seneca's tragic figures, seizes them so entirely as to obliterate ethical motives altogether. An unlooked-for psychological factor enters into their actions; one that wells up, unnamable and unbidden, from the depths of their being, and overwhelms all reason and all restraint. Example: Atreus, in Seneca's *Thyestes*, plans revenge against his brother:

> This crime I long to do is worse than hate.
>
> I own it. In my breast a tumult reigns,
>
> It rages deep within, and I am urged,
>
> I know not whither, yet it urges me....

This shall be done, this evil shall be done.

What evil? I know not yet.

There is a passion in my heart,

Wilder than I have ever known, beyond the bounds

Of human nature. It rises, and urges on

My sluggish hands. I know not what it is,

But it is something great. Be it what it will,

Be quick, my soul! This crime must be

Fit for Thyestes' fate, and worthy of me, of Atreus.[23]

At the furthest remove from rational self-control – which was the ideal of the Stoics and of Seneca – is *ira*, wrath. It is ungoverned, boundless, beyond reason. It *is* evil, the thing itself, outside of harmony with God.[24] Atreus's speech is a deliberate structuring of the path of *ira* working independently of human autonomy. A rage, Atreus recognizes, is rising out of the depths within him, "beyond the bounds of human nature," hurrying him "I know not whither."

It is this sense of another power that lies dormant within the self, that emerges and altogether overwhelms the self, that distinguishes not only Seneca's psychology but the psychology of Elizabethan tragic figures when they reach ethical impasse – when nothing serves but frenzy itself as both motive and outcome. Characters run mad, characters murder without restraint, characters yell to bring down the heavens, characters become the opposite of their ethical selves almost in an instant and reach, like Atreus, ecstasies of sadistic ingenuity. They become, like Seneca's, something almost beyond what is recognizably human, but it's precisely in this guise that we recognize them as responding to human urgencies that surpass, that can hardly be encompassed by, ethical or even familiar, human limits.

Beyond the "horizontal" characterological "lists," or rather below them, lies this hidden world of human motive that will be reimagined by Western drama in its many guises until it has become familiar, and more and more in our own time, "scientifically" verified. Let's explore those guises, from its Seventeenth Century tragic manifestations, to the delicacy and sentimentality of its Eighteenth Century redactions, to the tormenting dichotomies of its Romantic versions, to the multi-leveled structuring of its late Nineteenth and Twentieth Century examples, when it reached its para-scientific, or possibly pseudo-scientific, claim to being objectively analyzable. A single drama from each of these critical junctures in the development of this "vertical" construct will serve to illustrate.

RACINE'S *PHEDRE*[25]

"I hate my life, and hold my love in horror," confesses Racine's *Phedre*. Even greater than her illicit passion for her stepson Hippolytus is her revulsion against herself and against that passion, and to blot it out, she longs for only two things, silence and death. Many heroines before Phedre, and heroes as well, having recognized its sinful nature, hated the compulsion to which they were bound. Its enslavement was as inescapable, as unrelenting, as that inflicted by angry, willful or jealous gods in Greek tragedy. But what had been in Aeschylus controlling ethical compulsions (Agamemnon's, Orestes', Prometheus's) had already reverted in Euripides to divinely-inspired compulsion of desire alone, desire in itself (the Goddess of Love Aphrodite's compelling of Euripides' Phaedra.).

Whatever revulsion Euripides' Phaedra feels toward her uncontrollable desire is intensified in Racine's, in whom the powerful constraints of Christian sin have become so entirely internalized as to leave no distance between the restraint of external codes and those same codes deeply imbedded in personal psychology. Internalizations of potential guilt, guilt lying in wait within the self to plague and punish likely, even not yet imagined, or already executed, infractions of desire, becomes the universal, uniformly imbedded characteristic of all figures in Western tragedy, from the Renaissance to the twentieth century, who are considering murder, incest, adultery, theft, betrayal, suicide or sacrilege as a possible next move. Whether before, during or after, in anticipation or following the fateful event, tragic beings characteristically lacerate themselves by imagining, anticipating or executing orgies of self-punishment *over and above* the punishments they anticipate from a social or heavenly source.

This marks the dichotomy of all these characters: the separation between their ostensibly rational selves and the internalized content of their "souls." Should they move in any of these anathematized directions, the burden of sin instantly rises to confront the reason. Whether it is Racine's Phedre or Lillo's Barnwell or Heywood's Mistress Frankford or Shakespeare's Macbeth or Webster's Bosola or Lessing's Sara Sampson or Schiller's Franz Moor or Goethe's Margaret or Dicken's Fagin, all – on the verge of sin or after its transgression – confront the awakened power of their guardian souls.[26]

The dormant Christian soul in dramatic characters was awakened very early – as early as the tenth century in Hroswitha's play of *Paphnutius*.[27] In it, the drama of the soul's critical emergence from within is given powerful, all but literal representation. The monk Paphnutius comes to save the soul of the prostitute Thais. She invites him into her chamber, but he asks, Is there another chamber? Brought into a second one, he still asks, Is there another? Thais, recognizing the chamber he's come to enter, falls to her knees: Lord, I have sinned, she confesses. When the chamber of the soul is brought to light, its power is at once manifest. No matter how hidden or dark it had been, when the light of God finds entrance into it, it is illuminated, becomes primary motive, and fetters the character to its ends.

THE HEART'S CONVERSION

Exceptionally fortunate, though, can be characters in the drama who are so fettered. Two contrary notions of the soul run parallel in Christian tradition.[28] On the one hand, there is the soul conceived as inherently sinful, at every moment in danger of succumbing to devilish temptation and damnation. On the other, there is the soul inherently virtuous, even in its most desperate circumstance, always eligible for the blessings of salvation. When Puritanism in England and Racinian Jansenism in France were effectively subordinated to the sentimentalism of the eighteenth century, the benign soul not only supplanted the sinful one, but changed its name. The "soul", for purposes of sentimental psychologizing, became the "heart," and was newly defined not only in its psychology, but in its physiology as well.[29]

The "heart" had many guises. It could be dark, even black; cold, even frozen; bitter, even desperate; mean, even vicious; careless, even profligate. In all these guises, it was closed to good, either in deed or intent. Like the sinful soul, it could lie hidden forever in its darkness, subject to all seven of the deadly sins. But unlike the sinful soul, the heart's awakening did not lead to self-flagellation and punishment, but to instant blessedness, instant virtue, instant improvement. How did this miracle come about? When the heart was "touched" – either by virtuous example or by apprehending another's undue suffering – in either case, the evidence of its response was immediate and physiognomic: the eyes – long known as the windows of the soul – perceiving these touching examples, signaled the frozen heart, which warmed and thereupon melted. Its liquefaction produced tears which, as they poured through the eyes, demonstrated the ultimate proof of the heart's conversion into the warm heart which had been cold, the open heart which had been closed, the radiant heart which had been black, the generous heart which had been selfish, the pious heart which had been profligate, the kind heart which had been vicious. The moment it was triggered, sleeping virtue upsurged on the instant, and proved to sentimental spectators or readers, if proof for them was needed, that the benign "heart" so functioning was in truth, and universally, at the bottom of human nature.

Several examples

In the midst of Restoration cynicism in England, the novel conversion scene in Colley Cibber's *The Careless Husband* caught its audiences unawares: they wept. They did so after observing long-suffering Lady Easy come upon her libertine husband sleeping in the arms of their maid, and noticing that he was in a draft without his wig, she, overcoming indignation and jealousy, gently placed her neckcloth on his naked head lest he catch his death. Lord Easy wakes to discover his wife's selfless act, and instantly, his heart touched, his formerly cynical prose becomes piously reflective:

> "How low a hypocrite must that sight have proved me!
> The thought has made me despicable ev'n to myself. How
> mean a vice is lying! And how often have these empty
> pleasures lulled my honor and my conscience to a lethargy,
> while I grossly have abused her, poorly skulking behind a
> thousand falsehoods.... How contemptible a figure must I
> have made to her!... and yet with what amazing prudence
> has she borne the secret pangs of injured love, and wore an
> everlasting smile to me!" [30]

And later, when he confesses to Lady Easy, she asks, weeping:

> "Oh, my dear, distract me not with this excess of
> goodness."

To which he appropriately responds:

> "Nay, praise me not, lest I reflect how little I have deserved
> it... Give then to my newborn love what name you please,
> it cannot, shall not, be too kind, – oh! it cannot be too soft
> for what my soul swells up with emulation to deserve.
> Receive me then entire at last, and take what yet no woman
> ever truly had, my conquered love."

Hearts had been touched in Western drama before the eighteenth century, but never so flooded with proof of their benign function. Elizabethan characters like the abandoned Sir Francis Acton, in the sentimental subplot of the otherwise puritanical play, *A Woman Killed with Kindness*, is witness to an extraordinary demonstration of male integrity and female honor, and like Lord Easy in *The Careless Husband*, converts on the spot from villainous cruelty to an overplus of virtue.[31] Sentimental novels and "tearful" stage comedies thrived on these moments of conversion; but for us, their significance and their lasting influence go far beyond these sobbing pleasures.

The gothic dungeon

Once this two-tiered construct was fixed in cultural imagination as a reality, the defining space of the interior self enlarged into a second – other – self (concurrently, Hartmann's "unconscious," decades before Freud's, was born.)[32] And it was that self that became the source and controlling agent not only of the most heartwarming, but also of the most terrifying motivations in dramatic story-telling. Soon enough, in the Nineteenth Century, that buried self became primarily a house of buried secrets, secrets both from the world and from the conscious self as well.

Below the castle in the gothic novel, or in a dark structure beside it, lies the dungeon holding the prisoner who, possibly for years, has never been unchained lest his guardian's secret guilt emerge.[33] The chained victim bears the evidence – is the evidence – of the evil of the castle's master. Not until the novel's end, after the forces of good have penetrated to the castle's deepest recesses, does this villain, frantic to keep invisible the evidence of his guilt, give up his secret at the cost of terrible retribution.

The gothic novel's dark castle is a paradigm of the Nineteenth Century's fictional structure of villainy. Villainy's secret lay in hideous but invisible repose at the bottom of the ego's being, showing over and over again, inadvertently, bits of evidence of its existence. But not until the end of its story is it entirely revealed in its horrible nakedness. In popular melodrama, that secret was merely a plot-secret (the villain's possession of an old letter, a hidden will, a many-years-ago death-bed confession), but in the century's more sophisticated fiction, that assault against the castle's gates, or fiction's gradual penetration of the succession of rooms within it, gives way at last to a terrible psychological secret: the castle proprietor's secret sharer is the ego's deeply buried other self. The mask of Dr. Jekyll gives way to the reality of Mr. Hyde.[34] Story becomes the story of character-uncovering. As Henry James codified it, when character is ultimately fathomed, the story is over.

Full fathoms three

But when is it fathomed? Mr. Hyde, the doppelganger, the secret sharer, the hidden Other – that alternate self is commonly only one level, one layer, below the apparent, and can either be dredged up after lengthy shadowing – Henry James's way – or even kept in fairly full view from early in the telling as the familiar, the emblematically portrayed second self, of the protagonist.

Frightening in ghost stories, awesome in sudden villainous-character revelation, terrifying in Victorian tales intimating lurking sexuality and/or murderous intent in the Suspected One, the melodrama of the moment of discovery had less to do with the subtleties of character portrayal than with the exploitation of spectators' delicious fears. The *unconscious* comes into its own only when "character" posits a level of self below that fearful level, a third level, where the examination of a character is so entirely focused on internal operations as to become a complete and separate drama, deeply within that single self, so deeply as to be secret, unknown, unavailable either to the self or to anyone else, and frequently, at story's end, not even wholly but only darkly revealed to reader or spectator.

Character "development"

What shapes and ultimately defines the unique character of this intensely private self? It was Rousseau in the eighteenth century who most effectively popularized the notions that paralleled and supported this peculiar structuring of character description. For Rousseau, character wasn't a given; it was neither fixed nor permanently describable. It was instead the result of – his word – "development," a gradual accumulation of a lifetime of benign experience or more likely – for him – an accumulation of the ravages of civilization's warping of mankind's native innocence. Major innovation: the very idea of character "development" began as reproof, as evidence of the hard dealings by which the ego was perverted by social belief and social reality. From the beginning, fictional investigation of the equation between the developing self and the civilized world judged the world at fault.[35]

Wherever the fault, the past became the present. The density of experience accumulated within the self harbored the past's culpability – the culprit of its incapacities, its private miseries that verged sometimes on terminal pathology, on the frustrations of men and women of particular and exquisite sensibility which ended in their madness or suicide or brave but futile gestures or dumb resignation: Hebbel's Maria Magdalena, Anna Karenina, Emma Bovary, Hedda Gabler.

Character dynamic

The dynamic operating beneath the surface of this story-telling was powerful in the way that Nineteenth Century progressions of every kind were understood to be powerful: their subterranean burrowings, their forward thrusts, their irresistible force, images that governed the century's notions of machinery, history, causality itself. "Development" was informed by images supplanting the Eighteenth Century's sense of existence. Then, existence – and time – had not been felt as hurtling forward, but as more or less at rest, its progression hardly in a hurry, and history's future rarely imagined as hurtling into a dark unknown which trembled with the possibility of salvation or shipwreck. By the end of the Nineteenth Century, the most ambitious dramatic story-telling had honed the patterns of character dynamic in which the thrust of decision and plan and justification were no longer governed merely by the plot's machinery, but by the long history of the sufferer's interior development. In drama and in the novel, "character" told the story of muted prisoners suffering quietly in their passivity, of aggression biding its time, burdened by the formative, frustrating weights of both the past and the present. Frustration festered, then exploded. *And moral perspective shifted* from the mere judgment of the character to the judgment of the *propulsions* surrounding and making inevitable these acts, these gestures, these ultimate fatalities.

And so the image of history's dynamism was recapitulated in the powerful forces subliminally controlling fictional characters' actions and motivations. The subtext of fiction (in the dramas of the Post-Romantics like Buchner and Hebbel, and – after the wasteland of mid-Nineteenth Century drama – in the Naturalists and Ibsen) shared in the dynamism of those Nineteenth Century philosophies, social sciences, psychologies, which told the story of the muscular thrusts and parries of powerful forces against which the individual will fought to escape and win its own way, and in the novel and in the drama, tended to demonstrate the futility of the ego's struggle. It was a world of tragedy that celebrated the heroism of its yearnings to escape imprisonment and defeat, and ended characteristically in pyrrhic victories.

Three characteristics, then, three ambitions for characterization: there was the layering of character in triple density that clothed its ultimate secret; the accumulations of past history that accounted for its present state; the large and hidden dynamic forces that controlled the progress of this single being's layered saga. Given the ambition and complexity of such an ideal of portraiture, how often could it be fully accomplished? In the drama of the later Nineteenth Century, at a guess: only once or twice. Its greatest playwrights, Strindberg and Ibsen, in two or three of their greatest plays, fully realized characters so densely conceived.

Ibsen's Hedda: Triple density

An example: Ibsen's Hedda Gabler returns from a boring, distasteful, sexually repellent honeymoon with a husband for whom she has all but open contempt. The daughter of General Gabler, she's stooped in her marriage to a narrow academic who has plunged her into his hopelessly bourgeois world – the house he's bought whose blowsy interior for Hedda smells of death, the unspeakably commonplace aunts one of whom is actually dying, and a slim household budget which precludes her expectations of a butler and coach and brilliant salon. In the opening passages of Act One, she speaks little, responds with diffidence, is hardly civil to husband, maid or Aunt Julia. We know her only from hints, slight gestures – a particularly cruel one against Aunt Julia. But through her façade of shrugging indifference and polite incivility, there are two moments when we glimpse a concealed Hedda. Early in the act, when she is alone for a moment, we see her with clenched hands suddenly striking the air above her head, a caged creature in profound pain, and later talking to her visitor Mrs. Elvsted, an old forgotten schoolmate who had been in awe of her glamorous, sophisticated, older schoolmate, when Hedda bursts out, "If you only knew how poor I am!" and quickly diverts attention from her outburst.

This Hedda is a not unusual portrait of the bored, tensed, frustrated married woman who had already become iconic in middle-class "serious" plays by middle-class playwrights like Henry Arthur Jones and Arthur Wing Pinero, who afforded a measure of sympathy together with a measure of disdain for this favorite heroine of late Nineteenth Century domestic tragedies.

But beyond this stereotypical Hedda, there's one who lives a silent but inwardly violent life of perpetual and perfect self-contradiction: one who is poised to wager her life, exploit her sexuality, control other destinies, subvert propriety, obliterate, if it were possible, the limits and the sheer deadliness of her existence; and the other Hedda whose every gesture, every intent, is frozen in timidity, invisibly suppressed. Ibsen contracts into the comparatively tiny space of polite social behavior the enormity of the codes accumulated over decades of Western social conduct, the truly invisible "ghosts" of Hedda's tutoring that calibrate social distinctions with unerring and deadly judgment; and it is Hedda herself who is both their dupe and arbiter.

Inwardly, then, she's achieved stalemate. The violence of each yearning, act or gesture is accompanied at the same time by its studied constraint. Opposites act in tandem: Strong sexual arousal in the past, during private episodes with Lovborg, were hinted at, whispered, denied while being almost exhibited under General Gabler's gaze, and at the point of fulfillment, vehemently prohibited. And now, in maneuvering for Lovborg to act the surrogate for her own lust for heroic abandon (and at the same time lust for its opposite, the destruction of his and Mrs. Elvsted's rehabilitated Lovborg) a whispered lie to Lovborg, a slight pinch and quiet warning to Mrs. Elvsted, a skillfully performed air of disinterestedness, and her project is launched.

The skill in her performance of balancing an invisible exercise of near-criminal viciousness against her visible performance of fidelity to perfect moral and social restraint collapses in the face of Ibsen's ungenerous plot conditions: first, she is pregnant; her revulsion against this ego-oblivion that shares in the uniform commonplace of human existence is matched, in fact exceeded, by her revulsion against the trap of ultimate victimhood: the gross failure of her project for Lovborg's destruction/redemption has put her in the grotesque position of her potential criminality being salvageable by accepting the sexual bargain offered by Judge Brack. "Death rather than that!" she replies to Judge Brack. "Death" rather than what?

The smothering of her freedom – Dionysian freedom arrayed in Apollonian splendor. The vine-leaves she imagined would be in Lovborg's hair when he returned from his evening's test were to be worn by a mere surrogate; the wreath was in fact her own. This is the Hedda who finally emerges, who finally – as the playwright Giraudoux used to put it – "realizes" herself. And so: Pyrrhic victory – her death is a transcendence; she means it to be a Dionysian/Apollonian transcendence over the vulgar constraint of being definable, of being known for whom she was not: mere person, mother, wife, mistress, and worse – a scandal-ridden accomplice, a bound victim. At the last, she pays homage to the nobility of transcending gestures, regards her husband and Mrs. Elvsted from her distance of the already-dead while they, still merely living, toil over Lovborg's scattered papers; leaving them, a maenad now, playing wild notes on the piano, and with exquisite self-portrayal, she brings the silver pistol to her temple. As with Ibsen characteristically, the ambiguous ending: its absurdity, its tragedy.

And as we've already noticed, Ibsen's Rebecca West in *Rosmersholm*,[36] and Mrs. Alving in *Ghosts*,[37] become known, like Hedda, through similar Ibsenian strategies of sequential revelation.

Strindberg's Miss Julie: Multiple causality

But in Miss Julie, Strindberg uses a different strategy for dramatizing his character's complexity. She's made up, like Hedda, of multiple and complex motives – motives at different levels of intensity and significance – but in Strindberg's drama, they operate not sequentially but simultaneously. They're multiple indeed: Miss Julie's actions are governed from moment to moment by a complex of accumulated influences, controls, motives, that reach back not only into her own past but into the history of her family and even her family's forebears. In the mythos of Naturalism, heredity's power governs, and in the orthodoxy of Zola's "scientific" Naturalism,[38] the combination of that heredity and the environment experienced in growing up, determine the action and psychological composition of character. But it's not only the history of private experience that can so govern, but the moment at hand – its accidental immediacy – the accidental intimacy of human relations, the accidental insinuation of a word spoken or a command given, and in Miss Julie, the accident of the sudden intrusion of an irrelevant event – a midsummer night's celebration. Feeding into the accident of the moment are the many long-burrowing causal determinants that, ignited, so to speak, by their relevance to a particular moment, may create tragedy, revelation, even ecstasy.

Miss Julie finds herself in one of the dwellings – her cook's – on her family's estate with the family's valet, Jean. Their presence there is not predicated on any particular motive on the part of either, merely the result of a not unusual outing in which Miss Julie and her attendant end up in the temporary convenience of this dwelling. Since Strindberg's Jean has the richness of background and memory and motive of Miss Julie, the drama traces the meshing of their two so-to-speak multiple "beings," each step of their conversation taking them further into the duel of roles which becomes, by play's end, a suicidal encounter for Miss Julie, and a momentarily triumphant afflatus, but one quickly punctured, for the valet.

It's the conviction of Naturalism that chance – even chance – is inevitable. And if one were capable of tracing that meshing of motives and influences and hidden controls in such a fatal encounter as Miss Julie's and Jean's, the mystery of character inevitability might actually be revealed; but no such consolation is likely to result from any amount of scrutiny and investigation. Why not? Because the psychological, the historical, the environmental factors in the armory of one, and a similar enormity of factors in the other, and the swiftness of their shifts of applicability and irrelevance, are so great that the likelihood of fixing all the sums, all the conclusions, is almost impossible.

What is it, then, that properly "characterizes" Miss Julie? Her every gesture, every act, every word, is significant beyond itself. We attend not so much to the person on stage as to something behind and beyond her literal self and literal behavior. We look *into* Miss Julie, not merely at her. The "character" is interior to her self-presentation. What are we following through her career in the play? Not, certainly, the accumulation of details that register as her external behavior, but the continuity we ferret out that illuminates her sequence of motives. Does each one rise out of the one before in an 'action-chain?' To an extent, yes, but what is far more in control of her moment-to-moment responses is the pattern of motives that have accumulated throughout her life. In Miss Julie, her stage 'character-life' began when she was born, and even a generation or so before. To know her is to know what "caused" her, the sequence of motives that have moved her conduct from the day she was born until the day we observe her suicide. Addressing the valet Jean, she is the cock of the walk, the aristocratic martinet, in charge. One word, one gesture from him, and she is helpless, humbled, servile. Another word, another gesture, and she is once again the Countess Julie. What connects these different people? We understand – what the Restoration had neither resource nor interest in understanding – that there is a complete logic of behavior in these apparently illogical changes, and we scrutinize her behavior to discern that interior logic, and remain, so to speak, tensed until we can make sense of that interior. The discernment of the dynamic operating within is the object of our interest, the dynamic based on the invisible – her past life, her parent's life, her class controls, her sexual controls, as well as her "accidental" immersion in this place, this moment, this creature who accompanies her.

In Western tradition, this turn-of-the-century construct of character is, to date, certainly the most ambitious and the most complex of any that Western drama has so far imagined. It was at one with the building of other constructs in other contemporary fields of speculation which at the end of the Nineteenth Century corroborated a shared feeling of having not only accumulated material but intellectual stores in abundance. But the deluding assurance that civilization's pinnacle was close to being reached was subject to a grim and iron law: at the back of the century's ripened thesis, time's winged antithesis was hurrying near. In the early decades of the Twentieth Century, when character depth and character complexity had become solemn articles of faith, in the unconventional and *avant garde* drama developing throughout its early decades, all the props, bit by bit and step by step, that justified these constructs, suffered gradual collapse.

CHARACTER AS DIMINISHED, DISPERSED, OR NON-EXISTENT

We've already noted how at the very beginning of the Twentieth Century, Wedekind's Lulu was bereft of "development," remained uniformly unchangeable throughout her drama, and although, paradoxically, she exhibited no volition of her own, had powerful and mordant effect on her random circle of votaries.[39] Unlike Hedda, she consciously initiated nothing, yet the action of the play was still, and entirely, generated by her. Interior character structure, so painstakingly built in Hedda and Miss Julie, is altogether absent – a central force in the play's structure with no interior volition, and yet as consequential to the play's action as Hedda herself.

The Gentle Lena

There's a story in Stein's *Three Lives* of "The Gentle Lena," an immigrant German servant girl in Baltimore at the turn of the century, who has the same internal passivity, the same negative volition as does Lulu, but taking negation in character structure one step further, Stein gives Lena no effect on the world at all. Unlike Lulu, though her situation changes radically, and she is employed by a string of employers, she has no impact whatever on any of them. The inconsequence of her existence is underscored at her death – abruptly, as a consequence of nothing told before, she gets ill, and dies; and in its telling, her tale, like Lulu's, registers no authorial "meaning" at all. It commands only the authority of its assertion that the event, and the character of Lena, are so.[40]

The emptying of character's volitional internality, and the study of its existence with no reference to its consequence or meaning, is the abjuration altogether of the very predicates, as we're familiar with them, of late Nineteenth-Century story telling. But as we've also noted, those predicates are as operative now in mainstream story-telling as they were then. What has changed is not, certainly, the allegiance to this nostalgia, but simply the enlarging – enormous enlarging, in fact – of conceivable alternatives, and like action-structures, character-structures (if they can be so designated) moved into new terrain, most particularly toward their own undoing.

The Symbolists

Side by side with the development of the complex Ibsenian character, Eighteen-Nineties Symbolists, severely undercutting the exploration of character "depth," settled for   uni-dimensional characters, dramatic icons, returning deliberately to earlier models – medieval in particular – for characters who were essentially little more than a motive and a voice. Such characters in themselves were not meant to be a visible depiction of their own whole reality – they shadowed that reality, constrained to exhibit little of it since what it was in its entirety lay at a considerable distance, within, beyond, its corporeal show. When the Russian director Meyerhold in his early Symbolist days staged *Hedda Gabler* in St. Petersburg,[41] he deliberately denuded the play of its complex textures, and substituted what amounted to masks for characters, both they and the production's scenic elements given one or two significant colors to suggest – not to reveal – the play's mysterious context which was, in Symbolist belief, beyond the scope of representation. And so what remained to show of "character" was image, gesture and voice, themselves deliberately minimalized, each performed in a single key. This restricted stage language implied immensities of meaning somewhere else. Where? Wherever it was, it was not in the ultimately rational, ultimately comprehensible world of Ibsenian psychological structures. Given its character, then, the world of Symbolist meaning could be pointed *toward*, but never fully revealed, and dramatic representation was invited to constrain its rational yearnings, and instead, accommodate its sensibilities to the haunting mystery of meaning's veiled evocation. It was the new century's first step in shifting theatre language toward signification and away from representation, and its consequences for the portrayal of "character" were enormous.

The Avant-Garde

In the avant garde movements – futurism, dada, expressionism, surrealism – "character" in the round effectively vanished with the collapse of literal representation. In Expressionism, it was reduced to functional abbreviations (The Mother, The Poet, The Cashier,

The Laborer); in Dada and Futurism, when it was not erased altogether from performance texts, it was, at best, the author-performer's own voice (Tzara reciting his own manifestos,[42] or Vladimir Mayakovsky performing his drama called *Vladimir Mayakovsky)*[43] or a mocking pretense of peopling the text with names that were no more than ciphers without connotation, reference, or appreciable function; again, in Dada and Surrealism, substitutions for the entity that had been "character" became inanimate objects, or parts of the human body,[44] or most significantly, cartoon-cutouts of human forms or (in the German Bauhaus theatre) geometrized costumes over humans, representing person as a geometrical function moving in, effecting and being effected by, space. Obliteration and near-obliteration of the human dimension of "character." Why?

Neither whimsical nor meaningless, these movements responded with disgust and rage to what they recognized as the untenable fantasies of conventional intellectual – political and moral – postures at the turn of the century that were leading to cultural catastrophes, and soon led to the devastation of world war, and in response erased, with a peculiar combination of utmost seriousness and zany mockery, the fundamental structures that sustained those postures. They were, primarily, the structures of reason itself – logic, coherence, sequence, the "pyramidal" way of building theory toward summary pinnacles of abstraction – the common, and for the *avant gardists*, the self-deluding – rudiments of rational thought. "Character," as one of those theoretical constructs, went with the rest. In the attempt to build new constructs skirting rationality, the *avant gardists*, with respect to our particular interest here, "character," essentially reduced or removed – in a word, flattened – its traditional features which since the Renaissance and by the end of the Nineteenth Century had left it basking in an accumulation of virtues and grandeurs with which it habitually and extravagantly celebrated itself. It was one among the several altitudes of civilized self-congratulation here crushed.

"I"

One feature remained and strongly asserted itself – the Poet's self, the Poet as the poem. the poem as the all-embracing, all-inclusive, revelation of self.[45]   In   the novel, that ambition produced the greatest and certainly the most comprehensive compositions of the early Twentieth Century, the Poet in effect engrafting his text on his own, and out of his own, body – in a novel, for example, that literally embraced the entirety of the novelist's world and self (Proust's *Remembrance of Things Past,*) or his mind's entire landscape (Stein's *The Making of American*s,) or even himself in the guise of all of human being in all of its existence (Joyce's *Finnegans Wake.*) And in the drama similarly, Strindberg in his expressionist *Dream Play* ("The characters split, double, multiply, dissolve, condense, float apart, coalesce. But one mind," he explains in his Preface, "stands over and above them all, the mind of the dreamer,") in *The Road to Damascus* and in *The Great Highway* – created models for the later expressionists' dramas which, like his, totally encompassed the internal myths of the "Poet's" own being.

Schreidramen, some of them were called, the Expressionist's "screaming dramas" in which not only was the central role coopted by the writer himself, but the play became an untrammeled personal outcry in which the other characters served only as buffers, personal projections, within the landscape of a dream- or nightmarelike reimagining of the writer's torments. Characters as signs, relevant only to the drama's central voice, with no further reality or existence.[46]

Character fragmented

The breakdown of *unified selves* in the presentation of "character" led to multiple and aberrant – some merely whimsical, some profound – representations in drama and fiction. What were probably among the most profound, certainly among the most provocative, were Beckett's fragmentations of the self in his fictions and in his later plays.[47]   When the ego can be felt to be the equivalent of – in fact, to be – the entire fictional landscape, by virtue of that very inclusiveness, it can also be felt, and seen, as fragmented, made up of multiple and separable elements – itself, in fact, constituting an entire cast of characters. In Beckett's *The Unnamable,* his selves become not merely descriptive but volitional entities, each with a voice and a role, in an internal drama. It's as though they are resurrected from the morality plays of the late

Middle Ages, when the separable entities of the single self — Soul vs. Body, or, as in *Everyman, S*trength, Discretion, Beauty, Five Wits, Knowledge, did battle with one another, or journeyed in company with one another, or merely engaged in friendly dialogue with one another.[48] When ideology reaches the stage of entertaining explicit and comprehensive definitions of the elements that make up man, and whether they are theological or philosophical or scientific in their pretension, those elements are inevitably enrolled in dramatic representation of the psychic landscape of the self. The key, in their conversion to dramatic characters, is in their imperceptible transformation: they are no longer merely descriptive but volitional — that is, the magic of the mind lends to what had been only inert elements, the separate forces of lifelike, willful, even disputatious, internal contenders.

CONCLUSION

Beckett's, and others like his, were hardly the most pervasive of the uses or understandings of the nature of "character" since the end of the Nineteenth Century, but of the many adventurous paths along which the concept has traveled since, and of the variety of extraordinary uses to which it has been put, none has been as predominant, as pervasive, as the one which is perhaps the most questionable of all: the agglomeration of all the constructs that have served dramatic representation in the West for the last twenty-five hundred years. None have been abandoned, all live vestigially within carefully unexamined notions of character construct that currently serve under the banner of "realism." But in the long history of dramatic characterization, the terms that have been assembled to enclose the operations of the psyche within systems were essentially framed and guided, and still are, by moral didacticisms more than by anything else. In addition to the historical constructs we've touched on, such as the soul's and the heart's operations for good and evil, there's a plateful of others that have blossomed and never gone away, such as Plato's willful steeds,[49] the French reason-passion-will triads, the English four humours,[50] the id-ego-superego's private infighting,[51] all dealing with the same interior reality of human behavior, all formulated according to myth-designs at a substantial distance from that reality, since no vocabulary can conceal the fact that we have as yet no match in language or fact for that so-far-wholly-elusive reality. As we've pointed out before, psychology as we know it and use it in social discourse and in drama still remains largely morality; and no culture, certainly not ours, certainly not in its fictions, certainly not in its drama, has yet escaped that spurious enmeshing.

***

CHAPTER 8.

THE ACTOR AS PLAYWRIGHT

But you can't fight City Hall. Common usage, common knowledge says we *do* understand what we're talking about when we're palavering about "character," defining it, justifying it, evaluating it, and putting it into plays and films and novels and even into autobiographies. For all the culturally remembered and contradictory fantasies with which current notions of "character" are burdened, for all its long tradition of essentially ideological formulations with which it is cumulatively endowed, there is lurking under all of that, and inadvertently taking it all into account, and at the same time ignoring all of it, what we recognized in the early pages of this study as essentially operative among human beings understanding one another in any culture, what Gertrude Stein recognized when she, after much struggle with just such diagrammatic formulations as we've been cataloguing, concluded – by way of giving up – "Every peasant woman knows all the psychology you need to know to understand Hamlet."

It's that kind of understanding that spares us – as well as actors acting with one another onstage, or audiences during performance silently conversing with those same actors – the grim necessity of analyzing what need not be analyzed, what for all its scrambled formulations is grasped without formal understanding, and in fact bypassed altogether with the confident assumption that what one understands of intercourse the other does in the same non-language, and so one passes from the first questions: What do you mean? and Who are you? to the more pragmatically serviceable question: What is my answer to you? automatically sharing the wisdom of the equally pragmatic nun who once explained:

"Whenever I'm asked to explain the existence of God, I always say, Let's start with the second question." All of which makes possible an actor's getting a script in hand, and imagining it's available to normal human understanding.

THE ACTOR FACES A SCRIPT

Of course, he could be wrong. An actor may get a script, read for his character, study it closely, and no matter how hard he tries, find that there's no there there. A one dimensional character? Not even. There's a name, there are words, but there's no person. It will happen too, and all the time, that he will discover the tantalizing fact that playwrights, even great playwrights, no matter how conscientiously they've conceived and written their plays, set down fewer hints of their character's own moment to moment life than the actor, to make him come alive, plainly needs. And it happens all the time that, no matter how often an actor makes the discovery, he will always blanch and wonder how the black marks on the page will be hint enough of the human being he must of necessity discover encoded in those black marks.

Of course, there are different levels of wonder. Apart from the blank texts out of the mouths of non-persons, there are the texts that omit great swaths of information about the characters who are, in the hints that are otherwise offered, dense with personality, motive and emotional life. And there are, in the very greatest dramatic texts an actor confronts, so many hints, so many layers of person, that the problem is not one of inventing but of separating, articulating and delineating. What to do?

CHARACTERS WHO ARE "NOT THERE"

Let's begin with the first instance: no there there – characters, that is, who are only a slight function, and with little if any independent life of their own. The actor, of necessity, becomes the playwright. But in this instance, it must be with considerable restraint. There is the hard-to-resist danger of over-writing.

A blow to actors, but characters are not, even in plays emulating literal realism, developed for their own sake, but only in so far as they are needed as functions. What is fatal for a major character must be the objective of so minor a one. To serve his function, he needs only the tag of his identity, for which three of the four character attributes inherited from Greek New Comedy tell everything: his sex, his age, his occupation.[1] Moral bent? Only to this extent: his intention on entering, which is to make his announcement – "Madam Wishfort wishes to know, sir, are you at home?" – expeditiously.

Just as the life of incidental and minor characters is not to be found in an imagined catalogue of their current complexities, it is not to be found either in an invented chronology of their many years' journey to this exciting moment. What must be fixed in that moment is two things and two only: his state of being the moment before he enters (calm, upset, angry, out of breath, laughing, drunk, sick to his stomach, or, emotionally, perfectly neutral), and the very good reason he has for interrupting what is going on on stage.

THE ACTOR INVENTS: TENSION OF OPPOSITES

But when an actor is burdened with a considerably larger role, yet still as one dimensional as the footman's making his announcement for Lady Wishfort – to make such a character comes alive, he has work to do. But he has guidance from some of the most enduring characters in literature, all "structured," so to speak, in the same compelling, extraordinarily believable, extraordinarily effective way. Characters, writes Aristotle, must be consistent, and if not, they must be consistently inconsistent.[2] The latter is closer to the truth. Consistently consistent characters tend to have little life. More compelling is the counter-tradition, in which characters are built on a *tension of opposites*, sometimes so extreme as to make it almost impossible to imagine their belonging to a single person.

The value of this device is fairly obvious for the playwright; it is exactly as useful – and available – to the actor. What follows is a set of suggestions from playwrighting practice adaptable by the actor – given the actor's care not to become more of a practicing playwright than common sense need allow.

For that one-note, one-dimensional character – the serial killer in the movie of the week, the ghoul from the world of the dead, the *femme fatale* in soaps, or even the one-note characters in more considerable plays, like Gregers Werle in Ibsen's *The Wild Duck*, or Don John in *Much Ado About Nothing*, or Aaron in *Titus Andronicus* – the actor is ahead if he introduces into his portrayal the exact opposite of the given. The killer's manner in *The Silence of the Lambs* is judicious, reasonable and kindly when he is not going about his serial task; the *femme fatale* is pleasant, affable and open; Boris Karloff's monster and King Kong are loving, friendly and compassionate. Whatever the choice, it is effective to the degree that it is contradictory or irrelevant to the one-dimensional given. Don Quixote, a prime example, is, on the one hand, a chivalric knight of supreme and unadulterated honesty, integrity and courage. On the other, he is a lunatic. At one and the same time, these two opposite characterizations, performing one and the same act, are judged, irreconcilably, as saint and ass in one. It is precisely the permanent irreconcilability of judgment or of definition that sustains the vitality and universality of the role.

Another example, but based not on the tension of irreconcilable judgments but on irreconcilable motives, sustains the same permanent puzzle, the same irreducibility to definition. Hamlet on the face of it is saddled with a single plot motive, the revenge of his father's murder. In this respect he, like the original Hamlet in Saxo-Grammaticus' more primitive tale,[3] or like innumerable other revenge heroes, is single-minded and is so understood. But in addition to his absolute intent on revenging his father's murder, Shakespeare's Hamlet has the additional intent of *not* performing this revenge – it is deeply inopportune, it is "hire and salary," it belongs to a questionable code – it is, in a word, to be avoided. A complete tension of opposite motives in the single character, as though he were two opposed characters clapped into one. A more manageable and more naive arrangement might have been to tell the tale of Hamlet wanting to accomplish the revenge, and a counter character, a Brutus to his Cassius, as determinedly not wanting it, or not wanting it in the same way, or countering his strategy, and the two poised to defend and fight for the rightness of their opposite intents. In the action of the plot, one counters, frustrates, overcomes the actions and justifications of the other. But Hamlet argues and acts these contraries alone, and so he is volatile, alive, afire with clashing contradictions, permanently elusive to summary definition.

Two examples, then: Don Quixote and Hamlet. One an example of opposite judgments on the part of the spectator, the other opposite motives within the character himself. Further examples: Sherlock Holmes. On the one hand, he has the plot function of a purely ratiocinating machine, a mind on one track fixed in its ability to deduce; on the other, he has irrelevant external characteristics: takes opium, plays the violin, both hardly reinforcing or corroborating his essential function. The appeal of the character lies as much in how in one sense we observe him and in another how we understand him. The external and the plot characterizations are at a remove from one another – not opposite, but irrelevant. Nero Wolfe too is a detective and, irrelevantly, a gourmet cook.[4]

In the Forties and Fifties, the device became a staple of popular comedy. *Arsenic and Old Lace* is a farce about two very dear old ladies who are engaged, as a charitable hobby, in feeding elderberry wine laced with arsenic to stray gentlemen who are down and out.[5] This is, to be sure, a ham-handed use of the device, but it became a staple of the period's comedies and even some dramas, and still does service in this crude way on stage, in films and in sit-coms. The Nineteenth Century of course relished the device in its more lurid melodramas: the grotesque or ghostly outside, the human yearning within: *The Phantom of the Opera, The Hunchback of Notre Dame, The Flying Dutchman, The Wandering Jew.*[6]

And so, as a rule, characters who come alive are based on a real or perceived inconsistency, either on two opposite intents, or two contradictory perceptions or judgments of them, or the inconsistency of, or irrelevance between, their plot function and their external characterization. The more extreme the tension between the two, the more effective the characterization. But, a warning: if the tension is at such an extreme that it is intolerable to common sense, then like an overstretched rubber band, the tension snaps, and credibility is gone.

Much of this can be accomplished in a moment as well, if not throughout a performance.   For example, a character of considerable dignity, overcome by grief and being comforted by a well-meaning friend, suddenly turns on his friend and yells his response (written as a grateful "Thank you") with what seems to be venom from the bottom of his soul. "THANK YOU!!" He is at once someone other and more "layered" than the character we had supposed. And so – the worst choice an actor can make is to play consistently into the character's consistency. He registers only as a descriptive adjective, and an overly-familiar one.

A superb instance in Gorki's *The Lower Depths*: The 'Baron,' Nastya's pimp and lover,[7] beats her mercilessly, and in the last act, when she is screaming at him out of her rage and pain, he laughs at her – a totally abandoned, we judge, son of a bitch. Almost at the next moment, he is confessing to Satin, in private wonder and pain, that his whole life adds up to little more than a changing of hats, a changing of roles, none of which have meant anything to him.   At one moment, his sickening brutality; the next, his wondering introspection.   And sentimental Nastya, when the Baron pulls out of her hands the sentimental novel on which she dotes and over which she wipes her tender tears, responds to the Baron's gesture with a screaming obscenity.   A person, not a posture.

EXTERNAL CHARACTERIZATION

When we look at the photograph of Stanislavsky in his makeup for the role of Gaev in *The Cherry Orchard*, or of Henry Irving playing the haunted Matthias in *The Bells*, or of Olivier in his reportedly four-hour makeup for *Richard III*, or of the portrait of Olivier's black man so aggressively delineated on the face of his *Othello*, we worry.[8] If they carried onto the stage so deliberately spelled-out a portrait of their "characters," did they also carry on at their first appearance as much of the baggage of their "character-concept" as they could manage to fit into that first fresh makeup and that first revealing pose? Let's hope they didn't entirely follow the practice of some actors, on silent screen and on stage early in the twentieth century, who arrived displaying their whole story about their roles in that one look.

We may laugh at the silent-film preservations of this miscalculation, but are still regularly underwhelmed by the 'great' actors in the 'great' performances in the 'great' roles in our own moment who succumb to the same strenuosities. It's a fault readily recognizable in some of our 'great' and 'greatest' actors, a fault not of their greatness but of their fundamental yearning to o'erleap.

Suppressing that yearning, it's useful for the actor in his "playwriting" function, to stay closer to its radical antidote: to think of a character's externality as not entirely relevant – his looks, dress, manner – and assume that externals more or less take care of themselves, on the conviction that character does rather than is. However the actor may bother to decorate his role with his choice of externals, all that finally matters for the life of both play and character is the sequence of his actions and decisions. Elementary though this truism may be, it's worth dwelling on it for a moment at least, since roughly three-fourths of bad acting is based on this simple misapprehension – the error of remorselessly playing the quality or style or condition or age or nationality or physical quirk. If it weren't so, most of us would never have suffered the pain of seeing a comedy by Shaw or Shakespeare or Oscar Wilde or a Restoration comedy done in so unrelenting a "style" that, in order to maintain its consistency, overlooked every nuance of action for the sake of facade. One need only watch the opposite kind of performance – in which the actor is less than scrupulous about "style" or period or manner, and though the result might not be altogether efficacious, it would certainly help make – and does make – performances come alive.

RIGHT AND REASONABLE

Let's for a moment commit the cardinal sin against the Brechtian notion of the actor's alienation from the subjectivity of his role by maintaining critical distance from it. Let's pretend instead that an actor has no particular awareness of his character's condition, not entirely aware that he is drunk or despairing or grey with age or poor or British or ideologically misguided – but aware of one thing alone: that he, in the guise of the character he's playing, is perfectly right and perfectly reasonable. Every action, every word, every gesture he makes is with that one certainty in mind , and that everyone else with whom he contends in his scenes and in the entire play is at best only approximately right and reasonable, and more usually, questionably so. Let the actor assume that he is so centered in his own inner certainty and inner necessity, and that from that subjective center, everything he says and does is justified and justifiable – whether he is sneering or raging or explaining or lying or murdering – and he becomes at once persuasively a whole person. He is not defining himself as different from his character's own felt norm. Characters, like people, are buried inside their own subjectivity; they are not performing objective descriptions of themselves. The center, the reality of their being, lies inside that subjectivity, not outside.

So acted, the spectator's articulated judgment would merely be the same as – and little more than – it would be for friends and acquaintances: adjectival reduction – that he's lying, he's bitter, he's self-deluding, etc. But that's far from the end of the spectator's knowledge. In reality he comprehends a great deal more that cannot be verbalized easily. Given the actor's persuading him that everything he says and does in his circumstance is perfectly appropriate, perfectly right, perfectly reasonable, the spectator's trust in his reality is absolute. And it's out of that trust alone that the spectator's more sagacious judgments of a character's belonging to humanity is actually born.

BOUNDARIES

To put to bed the problem of "externals:" all that is necessary for external characterization is that one does not violate the broad range of audience – that is, cultural – images and associations. You cannot portray Hamlet as a salivating lecher, or Ophelia as an old crone, but it's astonishing how close one can get to the boundaries of possibility and yet thrive. The much-debated, much-cogitated question of Hamlet's "character" in this sense, for accurately portraying the "real" Hamlet, is dismissible. Gielgud's romantic hothouse plant back in the Thirties, Olivier's Nordic snob in his Forties film, Smotunovsky's two-fisted, in-the-thick-of-the-tough-world's activist in Kozintsev's Nineteen Sixties film, and Mel Gibson's straight-shooter in his Nineties film: not one or the other style of Hamlet is deeply at issue in the performance of the play. What is at issue is only whether in his behavior he's believably alive or dead – a contingency that is not dismissible, and is satisfied only by the actor's evident coalescence with the internal dynamic of his action.[9]

DIGGING FOR THE PAST

Excavating a character's past: that, for major and actively motivated characters, will tell the actor who his character is, certainly where he comes from, certainly how he's come to his current state of being, his current "motivations," will it not? Well, sometimes. In Chekhov, in Ibsen, decidedly so. In Shakespeare, for the most part, don't bother to look. Let's consider Shakespeare's Cordelia. At the outset, in the very first scene, she has already made a decision, and we actually "know" her "character" from the moral bent of that decision. It is a choice of extraordinary integrity and honesty, but it's also a startlingly inappropriate one, given the circumstance of the moment. From that initial decision, she is doubly characterized for us, and we quickly form our double moral judgment: integrity perfect, common sense dubious. In terms of "character," she is thus far wholly a moral proposition. We may ask, what else is there in Cordelia that is definable? Her past? Her interior motive? We can only guess or invent. But are such things touched on or even suggested, in this scene or anywhere else? Absolutely not. Unlike Strindberg's Miss Julie, for whom the pertinent and suggestive questions go back to her beginnings, for Cordelia, such questions have no relevance at all. In Shakespeare, what is relevant in the lives of almost all his characters begins when the play begins; other than establishing their current plot circumstance and their initial intention, their past has no relevance for discerning who and what they may be. In this sense, his characters possess no meaningful past, and none is needed to contribute to their characterization. "Once upon a time, a King determined to retire, and to divide his kingdom among his daughters." That, and no earlier Lear, is his "beginning." He was born at the age of fourscore and upward.

But within the framework of the play itself, Shakespeare's characters have extraordinary dynamic. Unlike those Restoration characters, or his contemporaries' comic characters such as Ben Jonson's or many in his own comedies who tend to have none, his major tragic figures have psychological substrata almost as rich as Miss Julie's. From the "facts" of his past, we do not learn why Lear responds to his daughters' treatment of him by crying, 'O fool, I shall go mad!'. The shattering enormity of his rage alone tells us the kind, certainly the level, of motive and yearning operating in him. But the past life and preparatory history of motive are not specified. We are not told, for example, that Lear comes from a long line of kings all of whom were so proud that none dared speak to them with any less ceremony than kneeling low, foreheads touching the carpet. We're told nothing of the habit of mind that causes him to respond as he responds. We discover it, or impute it, from the evidence of successive present-tense moments from which we draw two conclusions: the moral component of his behavior, about which we make instant and also instantly renovated judgments, and the hugeness of his emotional resource.

RELEVANT PAST, RELEVANT DEPTH

But unlike Lear or Cordelia, for characters like Hedda Gabler or Miss Julie, understanding them begins with the beginning of their functioning past. Hedda and Miss Julie have pasts that go back even beyond their years, and throughout their plays remain appallingly present. These are characters densely textured, and long-lived in terms of that past: the Noras, Heddas, Mashas, Ranevskayas. And so there's considerable detail that it's possible to explore in understanding such characters, but there's also considerable detail useful for the actor to invent – the labor of the actor adding to the labor of the playwright, in effect collaborating in the writing of the play. To what effect? It's the actor's invention, over and above the playwright's, that gives unique signature to roles of these dimensions. It adds what truly matters

– the moment to moment life, the *present-tense* stage life, in performance, that belongs to this actor alone. He takes in, to be sure, the lessons of the play's "facts," does the hard work of ferreting out the story of the character's complex motives and buried past, but it's his invention alone that gives unique specificity and explicitness to what is implicit in the play's design. Of course, neither close analysis nor unique invention mean anything unless they become manifest in performance, and sometimes the most telling evidence of that uniqueness appears only briefly, only in moments – but they can register as profound revelations. If they are merely "original," they mean little. The new is easy and dismissible; the profoundly accurate is hard, and becomes memorable. Legends have accumulated about great actors of the past putting their signatures on play's moments that had otherwise been always neutral and opaque, and suddenly become illuminated by a single gesture, a subtle distancing from another character or from an object, a sudden tension or outcry or a so-to-speak sudden investment of the self, of the body, of the voice, or a subtle, almost invisible, play with an object – such things suddenly revealing in a flash a depth of insight into the play's action, into the character's invisible, unarticulated reality, into an overwhelming revelation or even a quiet suggestion of deeply embedded counter-meanings. Eleanora Duse's floating a green handkerchief over her face and into the air during Judge Brack's verbal game of seduction and Hedda Gabler's languid avoidance of his overtures; Duse's deep flush – Shaw took admiring note of this – in Sudermann's *Heimat* when she is meeting again the lover who abandoned her; the toe of Nazimova's shoe caught in the light, as she sits at her desk pretending absorption in a photo album with her ex-lover, and suddenly the toe moves upward, the only visible response to Lovborg's whispered 'Hedda Gabler,'[10] the slight movement countering her "Sh, they will hear you!'; Nazimova at her entrance shaking hands with Aunt Julia, but looking slightly up and to the left, Aunt Julia, as a presence, casually eliminated; the shattering animal howl out of Olivier's Oedipus when the herdsman confessed, 'The man accursed, my lord, was you;' and an extraordinary still moment in the last act of *Uncle Vanya* when

Olivier's Astrov, caught in a long moment after farewells with nothing left to do or say but with time still to be filled, fills it slowly and meticulously buttoning one button of his greatcoat after another, working quietly to last out the embarrassment of that empty space of time.[11]   It's a long journey to such insights, following on many questions asked and many decisions made.

QUESTIONS

Let's consider some of these questions – the most usual, the most fundamental, the least novel ones, and note how their scrutiny – turning them this way and that – can make novice playwrights out of studious actors. First, the questions that inform all choices, that are at the heart of a character's action: his desires and beliefs. What is the most believed, the guiding principle beyond all others (God, money, law, love, family, self, reason, justice, none, humanity, and so on)? And the most familiar question of all: what does he want most? But let's add to these (the questions that really make the difference:) what is the intensity of the want and of the belief? What is the degree of scrutiny, of deliberation, over the want? And finally – thinking around the character one is playing – is there a difference between what he wants and what he thinks he wants? What he feels and what he thinks he feels? What he knows and what he thinks he knows? Answering the first question alone – what does he want? – can lead to possibly accurate but possibly only flat-footed actor's playwriting. Particularly for the greatest of the realistic playwrights whose characters are not only fully rounded but also stuffed with ambiguities, long and careful scrutiny followed by private, distinctly personal solutions, can make for actors who as playwrights join in reasonably comfortable fellowship with, let's say, Chekhov.

Two characters from Chekhov, Solyony in *The Three Sisters* and Trophimov in *The Cherry Orchard*, will do as well as almost any others in Chekhov to demonstrate the purchase an actor can get on characters by worrying these questions.

Solyony

For Solyony, the character who kills Tuzenbach, his rival, in a duel, the significance of the answers to those questions can be telling.

Can be, but depending on the dormant playwriting skills and creative imagination of the actor, can also be murderously ungratifying. The actor may conclude, let us say, that Solyony believes in (1) facts, hard facts; (2) in poetry and its spiritual elevation; (3) in his own strength – brute strength – as positive values. These are Solyony's certainties, the actor may decide, and are the character's arsenal of weapons against his supposed enemies – the unenlightened, the lesser, who are, for Solyony, the rest of the world. How does the actor know, or think he knows, these things? From the evidence of the text, to be sure, but also – and this is the ultimate test of the actor's perspicacity as a contributor to what is missing, or at least is unspecified – in the text. The links between the givens, the actor's devisings.

(1) Solyony's belief in *facts*: In the First Act, during the wrangle of Solyony, Tuzenbach and Chebutikin involving weights and measures, Solyony is certain, he remains certain, and is on the verge of violence when the others give up the innocuous factual question with a laugh. What is significant for Solyony that goes beyond decorum, beyond courtesy, is the actual rock-hard fact. Later, he becomes entangled in an altercation with almost everyone present in the house, about the University of Moscow. There are two, he insists, the old one and the new one. The others are comfortable with dismissing the difference and calling it one university, but Solyony, because of the levity with which they dismiss both his claim and the subject itself, puts himself altogether in the social doghouse when he shouts: "And if you don't believe me, I'll leave!," giving him no alternative but to leave amid their laughter. He's made a fool of himself, but why? Because of his devotion, he believes, to an ideal – facts, facts are facts.

(2) His deep belief, his devotion, to the poet's persona, the poet's ambiance. Evidence: he sees himself, he says, as the Romantic poet Lermontov, Russia's Byron. Though Solyony is boorishness itself in his general behavior and style, his inner sense of himself is tinged with romantic sensibility. Why? the actor asks himself. His possible answer: Because poetry redeems what is gross. The actor knows how much Solyony is devoted to that redemption from his last speech in the play, when he is leaving for

his duel with Tuzenbach: He's perfumed his hands, but still, he comments in disgust, "they smell of death." A telling touch – his deploring his own grossness.

(3) At the same time, his other belief: in the value of his sheer, physical, overpowering strength. How would the actor know this? When Solyony returns to the party he left in hopeless dudgeon, trapped by the folly of his insistence, no one is left, they are all gone. All but Irina, whom he proceeds to woo. Then in a very knowing, very Chekhovian scene, the more his approach to Irina revolts her, and the more bluntly she rejects him, the more his insistence grows – stronger, more boorish, more domineering, until he is caught in the same self-entrapment as in the scene of the two universities in Moscow. The unrelenting, overpowering insistence of his demand finally puts him in the absurd position of challenging her with a threat: "If you refuse me, watch out! Watch out!," – insinuating that his rival Tuzenbach will pay with his life – the sorry end of his, the romantic lover's, endeavor to win her.

What further can the actor discern, or invent, for a shrewd, telling portrait of this, on the face of it, ridiculous character? Let him turn to the last question above: What is it that Solyony only thinks he believes as distinct from what he truly believes? How can the actor tell the difference? Well, first, from the consequence to the character, then from the beliefs he pursues most, and finally from the ones he pursues least. His first love is his reverence for poetic sensibility. Is it? No. While he is imagining himself as the poet Lermontov, he is going off to kill his rival who is also his most tolerant friend. The murder of Tuzenbach is not the best route to the love of Irina. Far from poetic sensibility, far even from the urgings of common sense, it is only the lunge of his inherent brutality, his dominating force, that urges him. But the relation of Solyony's illusion of himself to the reality of his dynamic can occasion, if the actor so determines, a subtle play of personality more ironic and tragic than merely absurd. That relation in Chekhov's characters – between what they believe and what they imagine they believe – is one of the most fascinating probes and most pleasurable inventions in which the playwright-actor can profitably indulge.

Trophimov

For Trophimov – the 'eternal student' in *The Cherry Orchard* – as well. He believes (1) that he is in love. That he is totally in love. That he is Romeo. (One must never take for granted in a Chekhov character that when he says he's in love, he is.) And (2) that he is struggling for a better world, for a glorious future so much more beautiful than the nothing in which we live. And (3) that he has great compassion for others, that he *is* compassion, for their problems, their weaknesses.

How do we know that he is in love? He is, certainly, we say, because at the end of Act One, he pours out his love to Anya, a love expressed in terms of their future together and the future of Russia. They are one. Sunset. Mist. The most romantic scene in all of Chekhov. Ideals: Love of Anya, love of the future, love of Russia. In Act Three, we see him with Mme. Ranevskaya during the anxious party when all are waiting for the news about the sale of the cherry orchard. Trophimov is compassion itself toward Madame as she pours out her heart about the horror of her life in Paris, about her lost child, her abusive lover, protesting, 'But I love him, I love him!' But for Trophimov, the moment of sufficiency has arrived for performing compassion. It entirely gives out, and he talks bluntly to her of her folly. Then she turns on him and recites how he is seen by others – the eternal student, self-deluded, accomplishing nothing – and in this onslaught, his self-image is assaulted if not shattered; he storms out of the room, and falls down a flight of stairs. Chekhov undercuts the sorrow and possible tragedy of Trophimov's shattered self-image. He is suddenly, and   completely, an ass.

But is he? At play's end, he does go off with Anya to what may conceivably be their glorious future, departing from the effete Madame Ranevskaya and her retinue. And we may wonder: Are his ostensible beliefs really or only the illusions of belief? Is he really in love with Anya or with only the idea of being in love with her? Will he really be in the vanguard of those who will change the face of Russia? With Trophimov, certainty wavers. He is the eternal student, we may surmise, the eternal wastrel, or possibly the play's one note of enduring hope. The role is played both ways, and since Trophimov is an especially critical character in the design of the play, the way in which he is played bears heavily on the analysis of Chekhov's political orientation – a debate that has its futile, and even conceivably its useful, side.   When Andre Serban directed the play in New York,[12] Trophimov was indeed the hope of the future. At play's end, his and Anya's leaving was almost danced, in almost balletic motion, and was clearly to be taken seriously. The alternative, of course, is to play Trophimov as one of the more rueful aspects of the play's end, his and Anya's departure signalling little more anchor for hope than Mme. Ranevskaya's return to Paris. The actor has, or at least may have, the latitude of deciding, his choices confused by the almost perfectly balanced and almost perfectly bewildering indications for Trophimov's characterization.

Obviously, the range of these questions can be extended considerably, but what matters is this: the more such questions an actor confronts, and the more his answers bear on the present-tense behavior of the character in performance, the more subtlety, precision and reality is likely to find its way into the performance, most particularly if one is playing roles in Chekhov, Ibsen, Strindberg, Gorki, or other playwrights of realistic plays with richly stocked, subtly detailed characters. But – it must be remembered that such advice pertains only to plays in which the characters are presumed to be, and are encouraged to believe that they are, living far more in the real world than on the stage. Under such a set of illusions, the actor then properly joins the playwright, extends his probing beyond the givens, textures the character with decisions and choices of his own, adds invention and nuance to what must, in the nature of writing such dramatic texts, remain only bare indication, bare suggestion. Until characters are fully clothed and fully lived in the continuity and immediacy of the moment to moment of performance, the writing of them is not remotely finished.

PLAYING WITH MOTIVE

We must not for the world contradict Stanislavsky's notion of the "spine" of the action, the contribution of each of the characters' actions to that "spine," and so forth.[13] But there *is* a way in which this understanding of a scene's or a play's action can be used so naively as to work against the believability of character, scene or play. Two problems: (1) Two actors confront one another. If each one begins with a fixed notion of his "I want," his "I'm fixed on achieving this one thing," and each one pursues his contrary intent unaltered from beginning to end, and (2) each one, driven by maximal conviction, conscientiously pursues this "I want" at a gathering level of intensity, then all scenes become the same scene, and all characters quickly become the same character. It is the most likely fault of solemn exercises in improvisation. All the actors begin at high levels of intensity which gain incrementally, and devotion to their fixed motive is set in stone. The consequence? Basic atavisms quickly take over, and if naïve actors are not interrupted in their flight, every improvisation would end in murder or fornication. The questions that yearn to be addressed are (1) the degree to which the intensity of an overriding motive is in fact operating, and (2) the degree to which it is *not* uniform, *not* fixed, but subtly qualified, endlessly redirected, endlessly altered from one moment, from one exchange, from one interim reversal to the next. These alterations of direction and degree are the basic, constituent elements of realistic action, and not only constitute the reality and life of a scene, but are in fact the genuine action of the scene, and also the precise signposts that signal major (not, of course, all) distinctions among characters. To revert to Chekhov, the intensity, for example, with which Masha is attempting not to be part of the spirit of celebration and good cheer early in Act One is extremely low; the intensity with which Irina is enjoying this moment is very high. But if Masha is being utterly, conscientiously, morbid in her intent and Irina is being utterly, conscientiously, euphoric in hers, (as they so often are in bad Chekhov, and decidedly were in Lee Strasberg's Actors Studio production) they move toward coalescing into the same register on the Richter scale of emotion.[14] Consequently: if all characters are operating on that same level of devotion to their primary motive, every scene turns into a melodrama of unearned emotional intensities. The whip applied by directors is often, "more energy, more concentration," though the more such energy and concentration are overtly in the minds of the actors, the less believability there is likely to be in their performance. Variations in this respect are among the most telling in the language of characterization.

PLAYING WITH FOLLOW-THROUGH

The flow of interior response and of shared interchange between characters that is too subtle to put into words: follow-through. Playwrights of reasonably realistic plays tended – and now tend less and less – to dress their dialogue with those helpful signposts that actors have wisely learned to ignore: passionately, sadly, cheerfully, angrily, lyrically, bitterly. O'Neill, over-anxious as he set it down to have his dialogue done exactly as he heard it in his not-always-impeccable ear, went overboard.   His vision of performance, the vision of a non-actor laying down precise paths within which the actor was to tread, went so far in the last act of *Strange Interlude* as to instruct his Nina to say each of her lines – her last thirty-seven – as he put it: "Strangely." Given such piloting, the actor is impelled to invent his own roadmap.

As in – an example: One talks, the other listens. The speaker is making overt but also hidden demands. Not only on the face of it: 'Believe me, I'm only trying to help you,' but also silently: "See what I see exactly as I see it, value my stance." The listener, while listening, is sifting, weighing the implied demand, sometimes focused or partially focused or not at all on the other's urging. At the tail end, and as a consequence, of the ongoing life of this silent chain of responses is the overt reply. Not to the speaker alone, or possibly not to him at all, but to the result as well of that internal journey.   That is the actor's continuity as distinct from the dialogue's – far more detailed, far more subtle, far less in the programmed thrust and parry of the words themselves. Accord and rejection, the play of different shades of attention and inattention – there are some actors who have the extraordinary ability to register just such subtle stories in the interstices of the story, just such sequences of nonverbalized response.   Not surprisingly, the life of such response becomes the life of the scene, and the character becomes one with whom the audience unwittingly engages in as silent, as detailed, a colloquy.

***

CHAPTER 9

DIALOGUE

What we read about dialogue in the *Poetics* is confusing.[1] In so far as it pertains to speaking *logical thought*, it shares that part of Aristotle's *Rhetoric* which deals with debate (proof and refutation); but in so far as it pertains to *emotional persuasion,* the other part of the *Rhetoric*, it has to do with moving listeners to "pity, fear, anger, and the like." Clear enough. But then – a confusing proviso: "when the object is to evoke the sense of pity, fear, importance or probability... *the incidents should speak for themselves without verbal exposition*"- as though Aristotle were whispering over centuries into the ears of film script writers and film directors: favor image and action, cut talk. The rest of his discussion of dialogue hasn't to do with dialogue *per se*, but with the rhetorical categories it shares with all forms of verbal expression. We will not be considering dialogue in those terms, but in terms of the functional support it does and does not mean to provide for the structuring of a drama. Let's begin with the understood distinction between what dialogue is when it *is* strictly functional, and what it is not.

NOT DIALOGUE

Question: Why are the *Dialogues* of Plato not dramatic dialogue and the dialogues of Bernard Shaw are? Or, to put it another way: Why is the dialogue-exchange in one rational argument not dialogue and that of another such exchange is? Here is a characteristic Platonic exchange, between Socrates and Protagoras. Having already debated long on the question, What is virtue? and Socrates having already made foolish – as was his wont – several attempts by Protagoras and the others to define it, they are approaching the close of the argument:

> PROTAGORAS: What the coward aims for is precisely the opposite of what the brave man aims for. For instance, the brave are willing to enter battle, the others are not.
>
> SOCRATES: Is this willingness an honorable thing, or disgraceful?
>
> PROTAGORAS: Honorable.
>
> SOCRATES: Then if honorable, we agreed earlier that it is good, for we agreed that all honorable action is good.
>
> PROTAGORAS: That is true, and I still think so....
>
> SOCRATES: Then do the cowards act with knowledge when they refuse to approach what is the more honorable and better and pleasanter thing?
>
> PROTAGORAS: If we say so, we shall confound our former conclusions.

Socrates' strategy of winning agreement point by point, and then building from each agreement the next accord, leaves Protagoras eventually confessing surrender:

> PROTAGORAS: You seem to be bent on having your own way, Socrates, and getting me to give the answers; so to humor you, I will say that on our agreed assumptions it seems to be impossible [that men can be utterly ignorant and yet very brave.]²

Which was a proposition, of course, that Protagoras had advanced earlier in their exchange. But what is the intention of the dialogue? Socrates, having brought Protagoras to his knees, so to speak, voices it:

> SOCRATES: I assure you that in asking all these questions I have nothing else in view but my desire to learn the truth about virtue and what it is in itself. [Plato, "Protagoras," *Dialogue,*(380BC), tr. Benjamin Jowett]

The dialogue has for its aim the discovery of the truth of a proposition, and like dramatic dialogue, it does so for the eventual bearing it might have on conduct. But the bearing it has on immediate conduct is merely this: Protagoras, congratulating Socrates on his keenness in argument, looks forward to talking further on these matters at some future date, and Socrates, late for an appointment, professes to have stayed only "as a concession to the blandishments of [his friend] Callias." Still, had they reasoned their way to the bitter end of controversy, that end would only have been a logical conclusion, not an act. Reasoning in dramatic discourse aims at a consequence for conduct – a plan; it moves toward an act. And so the course of reasoning is not only the weighing of propositions, but the weighing of intentions, each proposition considered as a probable or conceivable step toward what is to be done next.

Consider Don Juan's dilemma, which occasions the two-hour dialogue in the third act of Shaw's *Man and Superman*, the episode frequently played by itself as "Don Juan in Hell." The dilemma: Should he remain in the bourgeois mediocrity of a Hell administered by a complacent Devil, or voluntarily abandon it for an apparently equally mediocre pious Heaven? The four engaged in the dialogue each talk to the point of Don Juan's perplexity, weighing considerations bearing on his decision. The dialogue as dialogue has been praised endlessly for its verbal music, its intellectual brilliance, but what is most remarkable is that a dialogue that incidentally covers far-ranging questions of civilization's morality holds word by word to the frame of dramatic discourse, and never becomes a feast of speculations for their own sake. The intention of the scene is fixed, its aim is set, and it drives unswervingly toward Don Juan's eventual decision.

A condensed version of the same strategy: Hamlet's "To be or not to be," deliberating on whether to go on "being," and concluding that, in the face of the ultimate mystery of the after-life, our deliberations "lose the name of action." Which action? The one he must or must not undertake in the pressing future. The great monologues of deliberation in French Seventeenth Century drama almost all share this formulation: alternative posed against alternative; decision all but impossible; and yet after argument with oneself, a decision desperately attempted (although sometimes, tragically, future circumstance laughs at these decisions, and produces a quixotic result.)

Lesson: Functional dramatic dialogue moves toward a decision, a plan, an act; non-functional argumentative dialogue moves only toward its logical conclusion. The latter is persuasive and instructive in the context of argument; the former is persuasive and moving in the context of human behavior. Since it is human behavior that we primarily watch and judge and applaud or sorrow over in drama, the persuasions of argument alone have little power in that context to engage our attention or feeling. And so dialogue that is nothing but logical argument merely resembles, but is not, in the strictest sense, the functional language of drama. We'll examine genuine dialogue in its several modes under three headings: (1) its "four faces," and "Realism's" problems with them; (2) its "three levels;" and (3) its traditional "boilerplate."

DIALOGUE'S FOUR FORMAL FUNCTIONS

In the plays of Ibsen or Racine or Shakespeare or Tennessee Williams, in plays as we traditionally know them, dialogue faces in four directions; it serves, in other words, four separate functions. First: Dialogue is talk, emulating or – more responsibly – elevating the norms of conversation. Second: Dialogue funnels facts to us about "back story," about the character of characters, about anticipated events. Third: Dialogue shares plot momentum in moving the action forward toward closure. And fourth: Dialogue participates in gradually structuring thematic meaning.

Even before the play is over, the spectator's restructuring of the chronology of the play's events has begun. Its chronological sequence is reordered into logical sequence, memory discarding what it does not need. In its fourth function, dialogue builds implications, implies play's purpose, crafts hints of the play's "meanings." From just under the surface of the text-as-conversation, are those broad hints at what the burden of the dialogue, irrespective of plot, really bears: the play's point.

DIALOGUE AND REALISM

It was not until the end of the Nineteenth Century that the advent of a novel notion, "realism," determined to put an end to traditional drama's blatant artifice. Among its many attempts at tactical housecleaning, it tried desperately to accomplish all these functions of dialogue at once and unnoticed by pretending that all the dialogue's functions were bubbling up out of the norms of ordinary speech. But in doing so, "realism" blatantly subverted its own ideal, and produced dialogue that in its early days was, and sometimes still is, hopelessly, even comically, artificial. In its need still to emulate the purest of action patterns – Nineteenth Century melodrama's – the new "realism" never trusted itself to wander far from melodrama's ideal of effective drama. Even in the midst of its proud sneers at melodrama's lowness, whether through Zolaesque Naturalism or Ibsen's later prose dramas, the longing to keep the dialogue tight as a drum, the multiple but separate functions of the dialogue contracted into lines simultaneously serving its multiple purposes, made its artifice sadly transparent. The degree to which the pure pattern was pursued in the drama of the late years of the century is most evident in the dialogue of its most enduring playwright, Henrik Ibsen, whose habitual practice of straitjacketing his dialogue within this pattern is not his most endearing trait. The Master labored to make each line of his play face in as many of these four directions as possible: to be believable as conversation, to provide referential points toward meaning and thematic explication, and lead – as do the White Horse in *Rosmersholm* and Nora's macaroons in *A Doll House* – in a direct line to the play's ultimate significance.[3] Example: A characteristic exchange in the opening scene of *Rosmersholm:* Rebekka and the housekeeper Mrs. Helsbeth are watching Rosmers from the drawing room window as he is returning home:

> MRS. HELSETH: You see, Miss? He's beginning to use the path by the mill again.
>
> REBEKKA: He used it the day before yesterday too. – But I wonder whether -

MRS. HELSETH: Will he bring himself to cross the footbridge,

do you think?

REBEKKA: That's just what I want to see. (Pause) No, he's turning back. Today, again! He's going by the upper road. A long way round.

MRS. HELSETH: Well, good lord! you can't blame him for not wanting to cross the bridge, Miss. When you think of what happened there -

REBEKKA: They certainly cling to their dead at Rosmersholm.

MRS. HELSETH: Do you know what I think, miss? I think it's

the dead that cling to Rosmersholm.

REBEKKA(Looking at her): How do you mean – the dead?

MRS. HELSETH: It's as if they kept trying to come back; as if

they couldn't quite free themselves from those

they left behind.

REBEKKA: What an idea! What put that into your head?

MRS. HELSETH: That would account for the White Horse, you

see.

REBEKKA: What is all that about a White Horse, Mrs. Helseth?

MRS. HELSETH: It's no use talking to you about it, Miss; you

don't believe such things.

But she will, and we will too. The heavy hand of foreshadowing has been laid onto the dialogue, and waits its turn at stipulated roadstops to reemerge and note again the bridge, the reluctance of Rosmers to cross it, the dead clinging, and – most mysterious of all – that White Horse. The building blocks for thematic realignment of the action are laid in with a vengeance, and the talk of the characters does not so much come out of their mouths as out of the store of indicative matter needed to set the action's sights firmly toward the plot's and themes' closure. Dialogue so harnessed to an end beyond its current occasion, with "significance" crowbarred into its continuity for the purpose of future revelation, has small claim to the sound and accent of actual talk, though that, sadly, had been implicitly its claim. In its own time and for much of the Twentieth Century, though, Ibsen's craft was enormously admired for its extraordinarily tight structuring, every word squeezed into the pattern of his dialogue's quadruple filters.

DIALOGUE'S STRATEGIES

Dialogue formatted as tension-release

In American playwriting, the model for this model is of course Arthur Miller. A heavy burden is laid on his early plays that derives from Ibsen's example. In *The Crucible*, in *All My Sons*, in *A View from the Bridge*, the talk emulates the tight structuring of the plot, and additionally, exploits the pattern of tension-release with incremental leaps from one level of tension to the next.[4] The dialogue is nudged strongly in the direction of climbing its steps toward climax; the scenes tend to end in explosive reversal-revelations. Every scene, every exchange, labors under the inherent contradiction of attempting to be literal talk, but it is essentially overstructured talk earnestly duplicating the sequential levels of tension demanded by the pattern. And so in plays conscientiously following this model, the unresolvable problem of the dialogue remains the problem of transparent artifice, characters attempting to talk believable talk when in point of fact they, who are in this respect essentially plot-objects, are talking plot-structure alone.

Replicating the emotional pattern of *tension-release* in its smallest exchanges – keeping the emotional momentum of that device alive in every tiny moment, every conversational exchange, is Ibsen's habitual practice. And it's from this practice that many playwrights in the following century, with greater and greater anxious care for their credibility, wisely fled. Here's the model full-blown in this exchange between Mrs. Alving and Pastor Manders in *Ghosts*:

Mrs. Alving, provoked by Pastor Manders' ignorance of the facts and his moral obtuseness in denouncing her past behavior as wife and mother, decides to tell him the brutal truth. But she doesn't simply tell him in a straightforward narrative, as Shaw's Mrs. Warren tells her daughter about the facts and justification of her past.[5] Mrs. Alving's telling and Pastor Manders' responses are structured rhetorically as a series of small tension-release segments: the poised question, the tantalizing dangling of the as-yet-untold secret, and then – the rhetorical resolution, the shocking new information, the brutal hidden facts revealed. And the newly revealed facts engender another wondering query, another tantalizing as-yet-unspoken secret hanging so to-speak in mid-air; and then – reversal, the heavy, horrible fact dropped at the shocked Pastor Manders' feet. Secret poised, revealed; again and again, poised, revealed. And each revelation is the ground for the next poised, suspenseful, fearful wondering, followed by the thud of the new weighty facts. Listen:

[First Action Sequence: fretfully poised question, anticipating – it knows not what? – followed by the thud of awful realization:]

MRS. ALVING

Well – now, Mr. Manders, now I am going to tell you the truth. I had sworn to myself that you should know it one day – you, and you only!

PASTOR MANDERS

[Poised:] And what may the truth be?

MRS. ALVING

[Thud:] The truth is this, that my husband died just as great a profligate as he had been all his life.

[Second Sequence: shocked queries, each followed by the resolving thud of explanation:]

PASTOR MANDERS (feeling for a chair)

[Poised:] What are you saying?

MRS. ALVING

[Thud:] After nineteen years of married life, just as profligate – in his desires at all events – as he was before you married us.

PASTOR MANDERS

[Poised:] And you can talk of his youthful indiscretions – his irregularities – his excesses, if you like – as a profligate life?

MRS. ALVING

[Thud:] That is what the doctor who attended him called it.

PASTOR MANDERS

[Poised:] I don't understand what you mean.

MRS. ALVING

[Climactic thud: the one that shocked critics and audiences alike – the veiled reference to venereal disease:]

It is not necessary that you should.

PASTOR MANDERS

It makes my brain reel. To think that your marriage – all the years of wedded life you spent with your husband – were nothing but a hidden abyss of misery.

MRS. ALVING

[Finish of thuds for this sequence:] That and nothing else. Now you know.

[Third Sequence:]

PASTOR MANDERS

This – this bewilders me. I can't understand it! I can't grasp it! How in the world is it possible – ? How could such a state of things remain concealed?

MRS. ALVING

That is just what I had to fight for incessantly, day after day. When Oswald was born, I thought I saw a slight improvement. But it didn't last long. And after that I had to fight doubly hard – fight a desperate fight so that no one should know what sort of a man my child's father was. You know quite well what an attractive manner he had; it seemed as if people could believe nothing but good of him. He was one of those men whose mode of life seems to have no effect upon their reputations. But at last, Mr. Manders -

[Fourth Sequence:]

MRS. ALVING (cont.)

-you must hear this too – at last something happened more abominable than everything else.

PASTOR MANDERS

More abominable than what you have told me!

MRS. ALVING

I had borne with it all, though I knew only too well what he indulged in secret, when he was out of the house. But when it came to the point of scandal coming within our four walls –

[Fifth Sequence:]

PASTOR MANDERS

Can you mean it! Here?

MRS. ALVING

Yes, here, in our own home. It was in there in the dining room that I got the first hint of it. I had something to do in there and the door was left standing ajar. I heard our maid come up from the garden with water for the flowers in the conservatory.

PASTER MANDORS

Well – ?

MRS. ALVING

Shortly afterwards I heard my husband com   e in too. I
heard him say something to her in a low voice. And then I
heard – oh, it rings in my ears still, with its mixture of what
is heartbreaking and what is so ridiculous – I heard my
own servant whisper: "Let me go, Mr. Alving! Let me be!"

PASTOR MANDERS

What unseemly levity on his part! But surely nothing more
than levity, Mrs. Alving, believe me.

MRS. ALVING

I soon knew what to believe. My husband had his will of
the girl – and that intimacy had consequences, Mr.
Manders.

PASTOR MANDERS

(as if turned to stone)

And all that in this house! In this house!

Lunging toward play's end

In what has become the conventional realistic play-model, the
dialogue must stay close to the arc of the action which we are,
sometimes very consciously and sometimes relatively
unconsciously, following. Moments come, then, when an
audience, practiced and attuned, can detect better than the author
when the dialogue is not hewing close enough to the line, and it
whispers to itself with moderate impatience, "Is this talk
necessary?" Necessary to what? feeling in its bones the cruel
intent as well as the ultimate sentence under which the play along
with its dialogue must live: maximizing its forward charge to

closure, hurrying its self-immolation, reaching as efficiently as possible its self-destruct.

It's extraordinary how an audience detects that moment when it needs no more, when it holds enough to possess and arrange the sum total of the play's import. In that instant, its attention at once removes itself from the performance. A remarkable and somewhat embarrassing instance occurred at the performance of O'Neill's *A Touch of the Poet* when it first ran on Broadway. The audience detected that the play had ended for them some twenty minutes or so before the final curtain, and during those twenty minutes, it was quietly but determinedly streaming out of the theatre. In cutting a play (one of the most valuable exercises in analysis) one can thoroughly learn how text, though grinding away and saying more and more, may in fact have become functionally motionless.

Parallel dialogue

In the attempt to huddle together two or more functions under the sign of real talk, old-fashioned exposition is seduced into the clumsiness of parallel dialogue. Two speakers tell one another what they both already know, sharing what is inherently a single speech. "Yes, and do you remember…" "Ah, yes, and…!" O'Neill was given to this. In his *A Touch of the Poet*, the play's first act has two scroungers at Con Melody's bar detailing information about Melody they already share – with the slight cover that "the drink" makes it hard for one of them to remember his earlier telling:

> CREGAN: It's like a miracle, me meeting him [Con Melody]again…. Until last night, I'd not seen hide nor hair of him since the war with the French in Spain – after the battle of Salamanca in '12. I was corporal in the Seventh Dragoons and he was major. I got this cut from a saber at Talavera, bad luck to it! – serving under him. He was a Captain then.
>
> MALOY: So you told me last night.
>
> CREGAN: Did I now? I must have said more than my prayers, with the lashings of whiskey in me…. I don't like

sponging. Sure, my credit ought to be good in this shebeen! Ain't I his cousin?

MALOY: You're forgettin' what himself told you last night as he went up to bed. You could have all the whiskey you could pour down you, but not a penny's worth of credit. This house, he axed you to remember, only gives credit to gentlemen.

CREGAN: Divil mend him!

MALOY: (with a chuckle) You kept thinking about his insults after he'd gone out, getting madder and madder....

CREGAN: If I said any wrong about Con Melody –

MALOY: Arah, are you afraid I'll gab what you said to him?

CREGAN: Tell me what I said and I'll tell you if it was lies. [6]

Then Maloy undertakes a lengthy account of Melody's life from birth to this hangover moment with inserted interruptions from Cregan corroborating what he had said in his cups the night before: "There's no lie there," "That's the truth, too," until they catch up to the present, when exposition turns to mutual contribution of more recent facts.

These 'Yes, and moreover...' expositions were instinctively avoided in Greek theatre, in Chinese theatre, in Ben Jonson's Elizabethan theatre, in Plautus' Roman theatre, in which either a Prologue character or a character in the plot itself stepped forward, and frankly and expeditiously cleared up for spectators what was what from the start.

"Two-voice" soliloquy

But within the frame of realism, the deadly task of starting a play with sufficient explicit information for the audience's ease has been more or less solved, infrequently, by the expository speech still intact, and from the mouth of a character who *almost* manages to fit within the frame of the play's attempt at reality. An almost – for some, not quite – successful lunge at this possibility – is in the opening scene of Chekhov's *The Sea Gull*, in which Treplev, the novice writer, recites for us what is the controlling factor in his career throughout the play – his mother's character, and his crippling relation to it. Treplev, talking to his uncle Sorin, recites at length the story of that relation, and provides a portrait of his mother – in effect, a Seventeenth Century *caractere*. It is of course a conventional expository speech aimed at the audience, but provided with context: Treplev and his interlocutor, his uncle who is responding – somewhat demurring, but forgiving – Treplev's confessional. Their talk goes carefully beyond that of merely sharing the telling of an expository catalogue: Sorin adds to it his mild demurrers.

> SORIN: Why is your mother in such low spirits?
>
> TREPLEV: Oh, she's bored. She's jealous. She's already hostile to me and to the whole performance, because it's Nina acting and not she. She hates my play even before she's seen it.
>
> SORIN: (laughing) Well I never! Well I never!
>
> TREPLEV: … She's a psychological curiosity, my mother. A clever and gifted woman, who can cry over a novel, will reel you off all Nekrasov's poems by heart, and is the perfection of a sick nurse; but venture to praise Eleanora Duse before her! Oho! ho! You must praise nobody but her, write about her, shout about her, and go into ecstasies over her wonderful performance in La Dame aux Camelias…. Then, she's superstitious, is afraid of the number thirteen…. She's a miser too. She has seven thousand pounds in the bank at Odessa; I know it for certain. But ask her to lend you anything, and she'll cry.
>
> SORIN: You have got it in your head that she doesn't like your play, and you are nervous and all the rest of it. Set your mind at rest, your mother worships you.
>
> TREPLEV: …. Why should she? She wants to live, to love, to wear pretty frocks; and I, I am twenty-five years old, and a perpetual reminder that she is no longer young.[7]

It's only a slight cover, to be sure. But at the opening of *The Three Sisters*, we're treated to a series of blatantly expository speeches that barely hold within the scene's frame – a considerable challenge for the actor playing Olga, for one, who must embed these speeches in the scene with little help from the playwright.[8] But it is also true that Chekhov's baldly expository speeches can, with considerable actor's and director's ingenuity, be tucked into context with sufficient believability to be persuasive. Loaded with expository facts as they are, these speeches – in effect, monologues – tend to be telling personal confessionals, and so their speakers quickly become our intimates. Still, playwrights now so burdened with information that needs immediate telling, tend either to emulate the Chinese, or let it wait.

Dialogue's three levels

Let's assume that dialogue, whether facing in one, two or any number of directions, is written on three "levels." (Literally, it isn't, but to make clear distinctions among "levels" of speech, it's a simple if crude way of sorting them.) Let's pretend, then, that the notion of "three levels" is in fact the case. First level: "I have a gun, and I'm here to kill you." Blunt. Talks the plot line. Says exactly what the message is and means. Clear, if nothing else. Second level: Texture a little less barren: "Came to visit. Oh yes, I brought you this. Well, it's for one of us. To use. Right." Not a significant improvement, but it leaves a bit of room for innuendo. Third level: Neither the gun nor the killing is referred to, yet the implicit message is that the gentleman is here to kill. Holding the gun, he will chat about his own fear when he was faced with just such a threat, and recall in chilling detail his strategy for outfacing it. Let's look at a classic example, the dialogue from the film, *Pulp Fiction*, at the moment when the killers Vincent and Jules have just burst into a motel room meeting five young men frozen in fear. Jules takes over; his chat is about hamburgers:

> JULES: Hey kids, how you boys doing? (A nervous movement from one of them) Hey, keep chilling. ... You know who we are? We're associates of your business partner, Marcellus. You do remember your business

partner, don't you? .... Looks like me and Vincent caught you guys at breakfast. Sorry about that. What you having?

BRETT (one of the boys) Hamburgers,

JULES: Hamburgers!! The cornerstone of any nutritious breakfast. What kind of hamburgers?

BRETT: Ch-Ch-Cheeseburgers.

JULES: No, no, no. Where'd you get 'em? McDonald's, Wendy's?

BRETT: Um, Big Kahuna Burger.

JULES: Big Kahuna Burger? That's that Hawaiian burger joint. I hear they got some tasty burgers. I ain't never had one myself. How are they?

BRETT: They're good.

JULES: Mind if I try one of yours? .... (does) They're real tasty. ... Me, I can't usually get 'em cause my girlfriend's a vegetarian – which pretty much makes me a vegetarian. But I do love the taste of a good burger. Mmm.[9]

After a mock-polite request for where they have "the shit" hid, Vincent pulls out the briefcase, checks the contents, nods to Jules that everything's there as it should be, they're happy, and Jules asks: "You read the Bible, Brett? Well, there's this passage I got memorized. Sort of fits this occasion." And his recitation from Ezekiel 25:17 about the path of righteousness, rises to a crescendo, at the top of which the two men machine gun all the kids in the room.

What palpably hangs over the entire sequence is the first-level fact. But what is bare of resonance at that level, at the "third" level, becomes nerve-wracking. Still, a caution: Even a third-level dialogue can be rinsed of all irony. Back in the Forties, very high-minded values in American heroes could be taken for granted. A death scene in a football saga avoided all mention of death, focused on talk of the future, and showed how even at such a moment, the dialogue could be a little young:

KNUT: (standing over the dying man's bed) George.

GIPPS: Yes, Mac.

KNUT: George, a telegram just arrived. You been named the quarterback of the All-American team.

GIPPS: You wouldn't kid me, right?

KNUT: No, it's on the level. You're gonna be all right, kid.

GIPPS: I ain't got a complaint in the world, right? I'm not afraid. What's tough about this…. Right. (Pause) Some day when the team's up against it, and the breaks are mean to the boys, ask them to go in there and give it all they've got, and win just one for the Gipper. I don't know where I'll be then, but I'll know about it. And I'll be happy.[10]

Even with dialogue so charged with uplift, a play cannot be written entirely in third level discourse. Shifting from one level to another, it can exploit, for example, sudden contrasts between lightly worn and deeply embedded emotion with powerful impact. An example from Clifford Odets, who was a master of these sudden emotional depth-charges: In *Paradise Lost*, a play about the Great Depression, a young man, an ex-athlete, is reduced to selling children's toys on the street out of a cardboard box. One of the women in the house of the extended family of which he is a part, is barren. We know this merely as a fact, but when the young man arrives after his humiliating day on the street, frustrated and miserable, he mocks her, holding up a toy out of his box, "Hey, Mrs. K, how about buying a couple of toys for your baby?" to which she replies, "If I had a baby, I'd buy him gold toys," and leaves.[11] The suddenness of the leap to a level of intensity nowhere yet touched, her understatement becomes overstatement, a silent yell. Her rejoinder at first level, which might have been, 'How dare you! That's an unfeeling joke at my expense!' would hardly have served. An artful weave of "depth-charge" and alternate "surfacing" of dialogue spares audiences the stint of getting through plays or screenplays written with numbing artlessness of leadenly uniform first-level dialogue throughout. Note:

INT. MIAMI DADE POLICE DEPARTMENT-
INTERROGATION ROOM-DAY

YELINA: Your boyfriend…is in custody for kidnapping.

[Tawny looks over toward her side and sees Pete Keller in handcuffs, being escorted by two Police Officers.]

TAWNY WILLIAMS: Pete did this? Well, I haven't seen Pete in years.
HORATIO: He murders your husband, he kidnaps your stepson and I'm to believe that you haven't seen him in years…Sissy? This is a list of known associates and it appears that you and Pete have been separating people from their money for quite awhile.
YELINA: Usually older, rich men.
TAWNY WILLIAMS: I ripped off rich guys. Okay? I admit it. We picked them out of the Society page in the Herald.
YELINA: Is that how you found your husband?
TAWNY WILLIAMS: Yeah, he…Reed had just been widowed. He was like a prime target. Only this time, it was different. I fell in love with him. Okay? I fell in love with his son. You said I'd been hiding something. That's it. My past. I've been trying to make some changes in my life. People do change.[12]

Sudden "depth charges" are brilliantly used in classical British drama. One of the most memorable is in Webster's Elizabethan tragedy, *The Duchess of Malfi*. The Duke Ferdinand, who has engineered the murder of the Duchess his sister, nowhere in the play openly acknowledges his incestuous attachment to her – the motive behind his motive for condemning her secret marriage. When his hired assassin shows him the dead body of his sister, he stares at it, and instead of the expected formal Elizabethan specchifying over the corpse, he merely mutters a quiet instruction, "Cover her face. Mine eyes dazzle. She died young."[13] Easily one of the greatest understatements in Western drama, while his eyes are dazzled, the entire expression of the Duke's obsessive lust for his sister hardly finds room in the one word, "young."

Sudden revelations, sudden glimpses of emotional depth. We've already described Hedda Gabler's outburst when talking to her friend Thea who exudes admiration and possibly envy for the position Hedda has always held in her eyes even when they were schoolmates, and who doesn't grasp the enormity of Hedda's response: "If you only knew how poor I am!" That sudden glimpse behind Hedda's brittle, contemptuous posture toward little Thea, an open chasm at once closed over, and Hedda's talk immediately resuming its customary mock. Several times over in *Hedda Gabler*, we're treated to the same rupture in the studied sham of her discourse, a sudden "depth-charge" inviting the perception of a despairing Hedda beneath.

Peculiarly adept at such juxtaposition is Chekhov, whose dialogue at first glance appears to be first level with a vengeance, his characters spelling out their stories, reciting their feelings bluntly and out loud. But what is remarkable is that the apparently prosaic dialogue is, as often as not, not what the character is saying at all, or what the scene is "saying." As information, it is first level, in terms of signifying, a complex third. In Act Two of *The Sea Gull*, Nina is asking Trigorin, naively, what it is like to be a famous writer, and Trigorin, in his long and justly famous soliloquy, spells out for her at considerable length his profession's many miseries and tiny pleasures. Not taking into account anything but his tale, one would miss what is apparent, certainly by scene's end, when Nina, in ecstasy, cries, "How beautiful! A dream!" responding to what? – his writer's labors? – no, to the seduction which Trigorin has been successfully conducting with his discourse.

There's another moment in Chekhov when the apparent banality of text is disguising a different story. Vershinin's resumes his editorial in the second act of *The Three Sisters* on the promise of two or three hundred years from now, to which Masha is listening – attentively? Then why does she laugh with delight? Hers is hardly a relevant response to Vershinin's pontificating. It is Nina's response to Trigorin once again, with the difference that it is far from the intelligence of Vershinin's discourse with which Masha is enraptured, but the sheer look and the sound of him, her internal abandon to her love for him, listening or not listening to whatever he's saying.

This is called, of course, "subtext," but let's consider the relation here between text and subtext. The implied subtext is evidenced through dialogue which is, so-to-speak, divorced from the very statement it is in fact making. Chekhov's way of accomplishing "subtext" is clearly to distance as much as possible spoken statement from the unspoken. It can be difficult to know when the "unspoken" is in fact lurking. But when it's recognized that, for example, a gesture, or an action, or a statement, makes no logical connection with what came before, suspicion is properly awakened, and analytic connoitering should begin.

But still, we must make a careful distinction between subtext and dialogue "levels" as described here. By "subtext" in Stanislavsky's sense, we mean the underlying action of the character, of the scene; by third level dialogue, we mean the underlying *statement* of the dialogue.[14]   The difference between the two should be clear, although they are effected by the same device.

Presentational dialogue: the familiar made unfamiliar

If dramatic dialogue can be said to have had a history of its own during the past century, it was the history of its gradually loosening its moorings, even in ostensibly "realistic" plays, from emulating "realistic" talk, and bit by bit returning, with less and less apology, to older, more traditional modes. Before its attempt to sound real, Western drama's dialogue frankly and characteristically faced "out" a great deal more often than it faced "in." Actors spoke dialogue written in presentational style entirely, spoke more to the spectator than to fellow-actors. Dialogue rarely pretended to be intimate speech: it was written and spoken as opera is written and sung – directed far more, whether in colloquy with another performer or not, toward the spectator. It was not essentially felt speech, but emblematic speech, not so much emotion felt as emotion signified. What was "real" was not what was shown; what was shown was what its display referenced, not itself. In Greek tragedy, in medieval drama, in Shakespearean tragedy, in Restoration and in Moliere comedy, dialogue positively fled from the norms of talk, and reordered speech's sentiments into talk wholeheartedly translated into other modes of expression – verse, if possible, at stratospheric distances from talk, or prose, too, but at significant and pleasurable distances. The pride of dialogue was not in its mimicking talk, but in the enormity of its distance from it, taking with it only the *burden* of what was spoken and felt, rarely itself.

But something did come along with that burden: all of the cultural moment's current language's implicit meanings and all its shared echoes of sense. Drama's dialogue soared beyond common usage for the very reason that its incredible trajectory rose *out of* common use. So that even with the model we think we live by – real talk, mirrored talk – dialogue, as always, using shared meanings and shared echoes, still manages, even within the frame of ostensible realism and out of the mutter of apparently ordinary talk, to wrest its uniqueness as dialogue, making as in any age, as Shklovsky put it, the familiar unfamiliar.[15] It escapes from the constraints of realism while taking much of it along.

It escapes in another sense, too: by subverting the unrealistic "realistic" model of four-in-one, loosening those over-familiar harnesses, it buys the leisure to expand its reach into more expressive, more subtle, more startling byways of understanding character and action. These devices and techniques are rarely novel, are lifted generally from the drama of the past, but in the context of contemporary mainstream drama, they usefully subvert.

Soliloquy: the unfamiliar made familiar[16]

Primary case in point: the soliloquy. In it, characters' motives, plans and justifications are recited boldly, baldly, and explicitly, separated from the flow of a scene's dialogue, and stated with a single, insistent purpose. The artifice of the soliloquy is obviously forbidden by "realism," faulted as artistic lapse. But whether or no, soliloquies continue to have enormous vitality, having the very same impact as sudden reversals in the action: he who was entirely in the frame of the play is now suddenly out of it and sharing with us *our* frame of reference – on *our* side of the stage event. We embrace soliloquizers, trust their unguarded testimony as we trust no other, even if they are the villainous Edmund in *Lear*[17] or Aaron in *Titus Andronicus*,[18] Hamm in Beckett's *Endgame*,[19] or the evil brother Franz in Schiller's *The Robbers*.[20]

We've already described one function of soliloquies, their most usual and most useful one: justifications of motive. There are others – some mundane, some deliberately and magnificently irrelevant. The mundane but efficient: exposition. The magnificently irrelevant: irrelevant, that is, to the needs of the plot in bringing it to its closure, but suddenly – as in Harper's airborne reflection on the redemption of human suffering in *Angels in America*[21] – the landscape of the play widens, and suddenly embraces a wealth of meaning that outdistances the normal, the possible, the expected levels of meaning that might bring the play to a sufficient closure – and suddenly, this bonus, this gift from the playwright's mouth breathes a different sort of life into the play's implications that transcends any of our conceivable expectations. Soliloquy at its greatest, the ultimate measure of the playwright's intellect, sensibility, and – probably most telling – his sort of secret internal music emerging as language.

Slighted dialogue, counter-dialogue

Other solutions: some modest, some radical. One (now more standard in film): expository information withheld, let out, deliberately playing games, as in *Strangers on a Train*, with audience comprehension. But even dialogue that is ostensibly explanatory turns out, in Pinter, to be snare and delusion. What sounds like explanation can be either the mad or purposeful inventions of his characters, a record of their mind-set, in no way, apparently, serving the plot. Nevertheless their very obfuscation tends to play a significant role. Whether their natterings are true or not true doesn't matter; what matters is the strategy we suspect they're using and the purpose of that strategy, which remains obscure. The mystery of summary meanings in a Pinter play is intentionally the result of the opacity of such dialogue. There's a great gap between what we hear and what we imagine is transpiring, the connection between the two remaining for us a permanent and disquieting surmise.

In *The Homecoming*, Teddy from California with his wife Ruth is visiting his family – father and brothers – in London; Ruth meets Lenny, one of the brothers, before anyone else is up. Lenny, after chatter, suddenly asks: "Do you mind if I hold your hand?'

> Ruth: Why?
>
> Lenny: Just a touch. (He stands and goes to her.) Just a tickle.
>
> Ruth: Why?
>
> Lenny: (He looks down at her) I'll tell you why. (Slight pause) One night, not too long ago, one night, down by the docks....he begins, and tells a long tale of a woman who approached him there, made a proposal, "but the only trouble was she was falling apart with the pox," so his impulse was "to do away with her," to kill her, but figuring that was too much trouble, he simply "clumped her one," knocked her down, and for good measure, "gave her another belt on the nose and a couple of turns of the boot and sort of left it at that."
>
> Ruth: How did you know she was diseased?
>
> Lenny: How did I know? (Pause) I decided she was. (Silence) You and my brother are newly-weds, are you?[22]

A game of dominance, not unusual in Pinter, seems to have begun with Lenny's "explanation" of why he wants to hold the woman's hand. That might in fact be the case, but it might also not be. The power of his incipient brutality hangs over the scene, we suppose, until we discover much later that the power, even here, is Ruth's.

Pulp Fiction

There's an even more radical example of text wholly countering action in the film *Pulp Fiction*, which opens with two men in a car bandying vapid talk between them, stopping to pull a couple of machine guns out of their car's trunk, walking along a motel corridor to a door while arguing about whether a man doing a foot massage on a woman was reason enough for her husband to throw him over a balcony rail four stories up, coming into a room with five men frozen in terror on seeing them, and chatting with the men for a while before they machinegun all of them. No relation whatever between the deliberately vacuous dialogue preceding the shock of the event. The first sequence, now classic in film dialogue, in the car, on the way to their kill, their talk "preparing" us for nothing:

VINCENT: But you know the funniest thing about Europe is?

JULES: What?

VINCENT: They got the same shit over there they got here. It's just that it's a little different.

JULES: For example.

VINCENT: All right, you can walk into a movie theatre in Amsterdam and buy a beer, and I'm not saying about a paper cup, I'm talking about a glass. And in Paris, you can buy a beer at MacDonald's. And you know what they call a quarter pound of cheese?

JULES: They don't call it a quarter pound of cheese?

VINCENT: They got a metric system, there's no fucking quarter pound of cheese.

JULES: What do they call it?

VINCENT: They call it a Royale with cheese.

JULES: (laughs) A Roy-ale with cheese.

VINCENT: That's right.

JULES: What do they call a Big Mac?

VINCENT: A Big Mac's a Big Mac, but they call it *Le* Big Mac.

JULES: (Imitating) *Le* Big Mac... What do they call a Whopper?

VINCENT: I don't know, I didn't go to Burger King.[23]

Mamet's *Spartan*[24]

David Mamet's dialogue much of the time plays a different game, exploiting no violent contrast between speech and action, but using only speech that is studiedly irrelevant to its buried, never-to-be-excavated emotions. In his film, *Spartan*, a reviewer noticed this difference between Mamet's first-level, standard movie dialogue, and in the same film, authentic Mametese: "The stylized Mamet language is not meant to express a character's thoughts or emotions, but to deflect them. [The actor] Mr. Kilmer's cool, watchful scrutiny turns out to be well suited to Mr. Mamet's approach to language and acting....[He] speaks his jargon with the expected precision, but his face tells another story."

The "story" the film tells: behavior is uniformly robotic, talk is mechanical plot-talk, visible emotion is unrelievedly macho-aggressive; the hint that gentler human emotion is operative beneath emerges twice – in a scene in which a woman confesses, or possibly pretends, that she is the mother of the (plot-object) kidnapped girl, and there's a whiff of visible emotion at the end when Kilmer's woman aide is shot dead. As dehumanized as a computer game, it's a world in which murder is worth no more than an instant's calculation; repetitively, it serves the movie's near-digitalized game's objectives with no residual meaning or value. The flat, colorless dialogue belongs wholly to this dark, frozen, robotic world, and makes, if it makes any at all, a bitterly cruel, unspoken statement.

"Contextual" dialogue

"Contextual" in the sense, that is, of dialogue lost in its own self-involvement. Again: Pinter, but it is very much emulated by other playwrights. It involves evading at least two of dialogue's formal functions, and adhering strictly, although idiosyncratically, only to one. The two evaded are the banalities of plot-expository talk, and the other, dialogue's self-conscious thrusts toward the play's closure. It is dialogue, in fact, that has almost no forward momentum at all. Entirely contextual, it is supporting, in fact is lost, inside the moment-to-moment flow and rhythm of internally-adhered-to thought related to matters that are largely out of sight – a sort of record of the mind's regression – whether in monologue or dialogue – wedded not at all to the play's action's flight but only to its own muffled interiority.   Unlike most soliloquies, Pinter's characters talk not to themselves but to others, who mingle it, if they take it in at all, with their own, similar, private-public rumination.   *The Birthday Party* is very much in this vein, but it also has an alternate, practical function.

The Birthday Party

Goldberg and McCann are waiting for Stanley, their victim, to come down, prepared to take him – we never learn where or why, but certainly for some sinister end.   In his speech, Goldberg's dialogue never touches on the scene's action at all.   It is somewhere else, sardonically ignoring the scene's palpable event and by doing so, creates unbearable tension between the irrelevance of the talk and the reality of what we suspect is happening.   Having more or less already immobilized his victim, and with the terror of what may be anticipated by his next action, Goldberg allows himself, at leisure, to wax expansive:

> GOLDBERG: (to his partner McCann:) You know what? I've never lost a tooth. Not since the day I was born. That's why I reached my position, McCann. Because I've always been as fit as a fiddle. All my life I've said the same. Play up, play up, and play the game. Honor they father and thy mother. All along the line, McCann, and you can't go wrong. What do you think, I'm a self-made man? No! I sat where I was told to sit. I kept my eye on the ball. School? Don't talk to me about school. Top in all subjects. And for why? Because I'm telling you, I'm telling you, follow my line? Follow my mental? Learn by heart. Never write down a thing. And don't go near the water. And you'll find that what I say is true. Because I believe that the world... *Vacant.)*... Because I believe that the world... *(Desperate)*... BECAUSE I BELIEVE THAT THE WORLD... *(Lost)*... *(He sits in chair.)* Sit down, McCann, sit where I can look at you.[25]

There's an overriding irony in Goldberg's non-sequiturs leading him into a verbal trap until he's staring at vacancy, with nowhere for his words to go. But his private panic in no way mitigates the underlying terror of the situation he and McCann are building. While his words are paying no attention to their task, they're readying their quarry Stanley for his paralyzed assent to their abducting him to God knows where.

A Slight Ache

In *A Slight Ache*, the rumination has no intention beyond its own inward gaze; it is closed-off, self-enwrapped. Its "thrust," its plot-relation, at best only meanders toward its objective. A Matchseller, for days, has been standing outside the house of Edward and Flora. Their growing uneasiness, imagining he perhaps has some sort of agenda, moves them to invite him in. But he does not talk, and his perpetual silence in their interviews induces one, then the other, to so-to-speak "create" who he is, and talking to that one, affords each in turn the luxury of increasingly revealing confessionals.

A portion of Flora's:

"…. Tell me, have you a woman? Do you like women?
Do you ever… think about women? [*Pause.*] Have you
ever… stopped a woman? [*Pause.*] I'm sure you must have
been quite attractive once. [*She sits.*] Not any more, of
course. You've got a vile smell. Vile. Quite repellent, in
fact. [*Pause.*] Sex, I suppose, means nothing to you. Does
it ever occur to you that sex is a very vital experience for
other people? Really, I think you'd amuse me if you
weren't so hideous. You're probably quite amusing in your
own way. [*Seductively.*] Tell me all about love. Speak to me
of love. [*Pause.*] God knows what you're saying at this
very moment. It's quite disgusting. Do you know when I
was a girl I loved… I loved… I simply adored… what *have*
you got on, for goodness sake? A jersey? It's clogged.
Have you been rolling in mud? [*Slight pause*] You haven't
been rolling in mud, have you? [*She rises and goes over to him.*]
And what have you got under your jersey? Let's see.
[*Slight pause.*] I'm not tickling you, am I? No. Good…
Lord, is this a vest? That's quite original. Quite original.

[*She sits on the arm of his chair.*] Hmmnn, you're a solid old boy, I must say. Not at all like a jelly. All you need is a bath. A lovely lathery bath. And a good scrub. A lovely lathery scrub. [*Pause.*] Don't you? It will be a pleasure. [*She throw her arms around him.*] I'm going to keep you. I'm going to keep you, you dreadful chap, and call you Barnabas. Isn't it dark, Barnabas? Your eyes, your eyes, your great big eyes. My husband would never have guessed your name. [*She knees at his feet, Whispering.*] It's me you were waiting for, wasn't it? You've been standing waiting for me. You've seen me in the woods, picking daisies, in my apron, my pretty daisy apron, and you came and stood, poor creature, at my gate, till death do us part. Poor Barnabas. I'm going to put you to bed. I'm going to put you to bed and watch over you. But first you must have a good whacking great bath. And I'll buy you pretty little things that will suit you. And little toys to play with. On your deathbed. Why shouldn't you die happy?"[26]

When she leaves, Edward replaces her. He creates a more complicated relation with the silent Matchseller, with sexual undertones like Flora's, but filled with uncertainties, ending, not like hers – with assurance – making the Matchseller her lover-baby-victim, but making him instead a mirror of himself, at the end crying to him in a tortured whisper, "Who are you?"

"Gapped" dialogue

The most radical exploitation of the notion of leaving out more of a play's dialogue than is left in, is certainly Mamet's *A Life in the Theatre*, in which the text of the play's multiple scenes is so truncated that for some of the scenes, little more is left of dialogue than, for example, "Hi. Are you ready? Let's go." This is early Mamet, which, along with *Sexual Perversity in Chicago*[27] and *American Buffalo*, exploits gapping as a technique more thoroughly than anyone has done since Buchner's *Woyzeck*. There's a nugget of text that survives in each of these quickly-vanishing scenes, most suggesting links that might have been significant in the complete telling of the tale, but some so denuded of information as to signify no more, if so much, than that time has passed since the previous scene. What is brilliant in the technique is the degree to which gapped dialogue and equally gapped events conspire to intimate a complete chronicle of a subtly developing relation between two actors, one old and close to finish, the other callow and greedy for place. In effect, the less said and the less shown, then the more rich, the more perceptive and the more knowing becomes the exploration of the tie and rivalry between the two men. The last scene resonates with enormous emotion as Robert, the old actor, left alone in the theater, stands before the empty house performing gracious acceptance of a cheering house's applause, and John, the young actor, comes back to tell him they're locking up. The density of the connection between the two, the shift in their relation over the span of time they've been working in the same theater and sharing the same dressing room, is impacted in this last moment – with no word touching either its meaning or its feeling.

JOHN: You think I might borrow twenty 'til tomorrow?

ROBERT: What, you're short of cash?

JOHN: Yes.

ROBERT: Oh. Oh. (Pause) Of course. (He digs in his pocket, hands money to John)

JOHN: You're sure you won't need it?

ROBERT: No. No, not at all. If I don't know how it is, who does?

JOHN (Pause) Thank you.

ROBERT: Mmm. Goodnight.

JOHN: Goodnight.

ROBERT: You have a nice night.

JOHN: I will.

ROBERT: Goodnight. (John exits. Pause) Ephemeris, ephemeris. (Pause) "An actor's life for me." (Robert composes himself and addresses the empty house) You've been so kind... Thank you, you've really been so kind.

> You know, and I speak, I am sure, not for myself alone, but on behalf of all of us... (composes himself) ... All of us here, when I say that these ... *these* moments make it all ... they make it all worthwhile. (Pause. John quietly reappears.) You know .... (Robert sees John)
>
> JOHN: They're locking up. They'd like us all to leave.
>
> ROBERT: I was just leaving.
>
> JOHN: Yes, I know. (Pause) I'll tell them.
>
> ROBERT: Would you?
>
> JOHN: Yes.
>
> ROBERT: (Pause) Thank you.
>
> JOHN: Goodnight.
>
> ROBERT: Goodnight. (Pause. John exits.) (to himself) The lights dim. Each to his own home. Goodnight. Goodnight. Goodnight.[28]

Nothing makes clearer than Mamet's play the degree to which spectators write the play they're watching. And nothing is more flattering, not to say seducing, than spectators' pleasure in filling the gaps. The art of gapping – not only dialogue but any elements of story – lies in the invitation for spectator to invent, not discover. If it's certain there's nothing there, it's certain it will be provided by the spectator.

Something else is clear: Gapping has the advantage of being able to tell a story, even a conventional one, even a cliché one, without having to pay the price of its clunkiness. There's wit and bravado in the very act of slicing out connections; it has *panache*, it has an attractive air of dismissiveness. It has, on the other hand, the truest feel of time recollected, its swift passage, the past's sad absence. More accurately than tight causal sequence, it submits to inevitability, seeing in retrospect that *it has* happened – however *it* came about, *it has* incontrovertibly happened. The pattern of step by step cause-effect that convincingly arrives at "The End," is, in conviction, as nothing compared to gapping's leaps over time and sequence. Gapping, *because* of its absences, paradoxically assures storytelling its greatest authority.

"Pointless" dialogue

A further virtue of Mamet's way of gapping – one that he shares with some of Pinter's most telling passages – is the mutter of 'Oh yes," "Goodbye" "Of course", "Oh shall we?" and so on – the neutral yammer of social *politesse*. It is not its politeness but its innocuousness that lends poetry and depth to both Mamet's and Pinter's dialogue. Under what passes for aimless palaver, the unspoken dialogue is going on which is made heavily evident by its absence, and the statements emerging from that absence are complex and fascinating. We, out of necessity moved by our struggle with this unrelenting first-level chatter, rework and reinterpret. The talk gives little hint of motive, intention, action, or anything at all, and so we, imputing increasingly human, increasingly intentional, increasingly emotional scenarios in our reordering and translating, provide continuous "third-level discourse" for the scene.

TRADITIONAL "BOILERPLATE"

Remote from the deflected and gapped dialogue of so much contemporary playwriting are the formally structured texts built into the story-telling tradition of Western drama. Nothing reflects so much the stability of that tradition than the reappearance of the same speeches in the same sanctioned positions performing precisely the same functions and saying very much the same things for the same traditional reasons in the plays of the past twenty-five hundred years. Invariably, they occur on those occasions when traditional drama is most itself, telling its tale plainly and familiarly. These are the texts which serve the most formal and necessary functions of conventional dramatic story-telling, and in drama from the Greeks to the Nineteenth Century, hardly a play was written ignoring them. Following the signposts along the way of traditional dramatic structure, let's give some of the most notable of them the names of their functions: the speech of "Exposition," "Justification," "Persuasion," "Accusation," "Confession," "Reconciliation." There are more, but these will serve for illustration.   Since traditionally, the forward propulsion of stage dramas depended primarily on language, the major moments of drama, the ones that had most resonance, were precisely those moments when speeches such as these served as the great hinges of the "action," moving the drama forward in its stately story-telling grooves, serving too as the drama's arias, the occasions when drama rose to its genuinely primal function – the elevation of ordinary human feeling, motive and expression to their potential grandeur.

The resort to such texts was universal and perfunctory.   But since over these centuries the very greatest as well as the most mediocre playwrights resorted to them, their strategies were very often not perfunctory, and   when the appropriate moment came for such passages to be harnessed, Western dramatists could rise to great occasion, and produce memorable variants for their stereotypical functions.

The rhetoricians and grammarians of Byzantium during the Fourth Century A.D. excised and anthologized such passages from the texts of ancient Greek tragedies, and the Romans taught the art of oratory – most especially the speeches of "persuasion" – for the instruction of students being groomed for public office, on the understanding that the essence of winning public office – as it still is – is the ability to persuade.   *Rhetoric* – Aristotle's treatise and others – was the rule book; tragedy's speeches – Euripides' in particular – were the models for students to imitate.   The rhetorical structure of the speeches, so carefully studied and anatomized, survived in the formal tragedies of the Renaissance and Seventeenth Century; the habit of them lingered into the Nineteenth.   But even though no formal attention is paid to them now, the function of those speeches is hardly lost, even in current drama that knows nothing of their origin or tradition.

The Romans, as noted, studied those texts for their lessons in persuasion – as before a crowd or in a court of law: the rhetoric of argument.   But speeches from the texts of Greek tragedies also responded to dramatic strategy as opposed to merely logical persuasion, and so there developed out of those texts the most genuine kind of character specificity, revealing itself through the character's twists of feeling and turns of intention, unique feeling and intention particularizing those speeches in the course of fulfilling their bare function. And mirroring human emotion and intention in all their nuance and rapidity of change, dramatic speech, over and above its allegiances to formal logic and cultural imperatives, also reflected much of the wordless knowledge that constitutes the real sagacity of humans' understanding of one another. To put it simply, when we listen to Medea, through the formality of her logic's coherence and the forest of her cultural fixities, still, even now, we get it. The inherent strategy of dramatic expression itself, together with each playwright's own strategies, guides and at the same time can divert the simple function of these speeches for the purpose of saying more than that function in itself intended or imagined. A sampling of some of the greatest and most subtly crafted of these speeches' strategies:

The speech of exposition

Aeschylus' Agamemnon

We've said enough about exposition when it's in the service of "realism," or tries desperately to accommodate to it. Here is an example when it's unhindered by the obligation to seem what it's not. In one of the greatest of expository sequences, the opening of Aeschylus's *Agamemnon*, a single character, a Watchman, standing on the roof of the scene-building (the story's palace building) is suffering. He's been all night shivering with cold while waiting, as he has for many nights, for a beacon signal, and in a larger way, he's miserable for his city's situation. In the course of the recitation of his misery, we learn – not the entire "argument" of the coming trilogy, but what is far more valuable for the tragedy's initial lure – that there are secrets about this house that cannot be spoken: "An ox sits on my tongue." Exposition is suspended; for revelation, we must wait – not just to share the secrets, but their terrifying gravity as well. And just as the pattern of light that governs the time-span of the play gradually moves from darkness to brilliance, so the revelation of the house's dark secrets will be exposed gradually, but at the tragedy's climax with blinding clarity.[29]

The beginning of slow revelation comes with the chorus of old men whose entrance follows. Their recollection of the events of the last ten years – our "back story" – is told tremblingly: what do those terrible events portend – the evil beginning of the war, the decision of Agamemnon to sacrifice his daughter Iphigenia that the war might continue, the decision of Zeus which has already, certainly, determined the end – which it is best, the trembling old men conclude, not to know before that end.[30]

The context, in other words, in which this hesitant, only half-revealing expository opening is couched, is fear – specifically, the fear that the future will come about at all. By the device of failing its ostensible function, the opening accomplishes a great deal more, suffusing emotionally the tragedy's entire action with an atmosphere of dread, and propelling the spectator forward toward the knowledge the Watchman is loath to tell, and the Old Men are loath to discover.

Oscar Wilde's *Lady Windermere's Fan*

At the opposite end of the possibilities of dramatic discourse is Oscar Wilde's brilliantly conceived expository speech, satisfying the whole of its plot function in, so to speak, one breath. The Duchess of Berwick is visiting Lady Windermere for Oscar Wilde's sole purpose of burdening her with the plot's initial exposition: her husband, she's to inform Lady Windermere, is having an affair with a Mrs. Erlynne. But the seriousness of her message is carefully suffocated by her vapidly meaningless, wonderfully irrelevant prattle outside the matter at hand. The barnacles of irrelevance suspended from the Duchess' warning are in fact the essence of Wilde's meaning: at one and the same time in which Lady Windermere's dilemma is to be seen and understood as threatening – that scandal is social death – it is also understood to be paper thin: with a bit of wifely legerdemain, no one will really care, and everyone will agree not to notice. The plot's values, we're told from the start, are melodramatically Victorian; the posture toward them, we're cued by Wilde to assume, is cynically bemused. The Duchess has arrived with her daughter Agatha.

DUCHESS: Agatha, darling! Will you go and look over the photograph album that I see there? Dear girl! She is so fond of photographs of Switzerland. Such a pure taste, I think. But I really am so sorry for you, Margaret, on account of that horrid woman. She dresses so well, too, which makes it much worse, sets such a dreadful example. Augustus – you know, my disreputable brother – such a trial to us all – well, Augustus is completely infatuated with her. It is quite scandalous, for she is absolutely inadmissible into society. Many a woman has a past, but I am told she has at least a dozen, and they all fit. About Mrs. Erlynne. Agatha, darling! Will you go out on the terrace and look at the sunset? Sweet girl, so devoted to sunsets! Shows such refinement of feeling, does it not? After all, there is nothing like Nature, is there? I assure you we're all so distressed about it.... He goes to see her continually, and stops for hours at a time, and while he is there she is not at home to anyone. Not that many call on her, dear, but she has a great many disreputable men friends – my own brother particularly, as I told you – and that is what makes it so dreadful about Windermere. We looked upon *him* as being such a model husband, but I am afraid there is no doubt about it. My dear nieces – you know the Saville girls, don't you? – such nice domestic creatures – plain, dreadfully plain, – but so good – well, they're always at the window doing fancy work, and making ugly things for the poor, which I think so useful of them in these dreadful socialistic days, and this terrible woman has taken a house in Curzon Street, right opposite them.... And they tell me that Windermere goes there four or five times a week – they *see* him.... It's quite true, my dear. The whole of London knows it. That is why I felt it was better to come and talk to you, and advise you to take Windermere away at once to Homburg or to Aix, where he'll have something to amuse him, and where you can watch him all day long. And now, my dear child, I must go, as we are dining out. And mind you, don't take this little aberration of Windermere's too much to heart. Just take him abroad, and he'll come back to you aright.[31]

Speeches of justification

In the great dramas of the Seventeenth Century – Elizabethan, French and Spanish – it is the speech of justification that gives them their deepest moments of psychological and philosophic reflection, that raises the level of the meaning of human acts to their fullest potential. We've explained the speech's plot function before; its larger function must be spelled out now.

The degree to which such leisurely articulation, such moments of detailed deliberation of plan and justification, are exploited in drama, is precisely the degree to which it finds its depth and wisdom.   Although the speech of justification is obviously secondary to the action itself, it becomes the most significant component in the spectator's judgment of character. The moral significance of the raw motive: 'I want,' 'I want to kill him,' 'I want to win the battle," I want to seize the throne,' is first subjected to the audience's rough, tentative judgment, but the subsequent spelling-out in soliloquy of its 'Because' is decisive. Its articulation glimpses not only the depth and richness of the play's ethical texture, but also the subtlety, the nuance, of its characters' texture. It makes for the difference between comic-book hero and Hamlet. Since all heroes do the same things – they revenge, they sack cities, they kill enemies, they kill their lovers, they kill themselves, they marry – it spells out the difference between innocuously determined behavior and profoundly determined behavior.   It opens the window on the playwright's human terrain. It becomes, in Corneille and Racine, for example, the most important speech of all.   As quickly as possible, their scenes devolve on the consideration of decisions, the justifying of motive, the weighing of the proprieties of the rigid code of Honor against the urgings of the ego-driven Will (in Corneille) or against the doom-ridden affliction of Love (in Racine) as opposed to the practical possibilities of a forthcoming plan of action, and they are weighed at almost infinite length in preparation for the moment of confrontation, the moment of plan-carried-out. And as a result of these scrupulous, pained deliberations, what is at stake in the scenes of action that follow, moves far beyond the momentary anxiety of the plot, and also beyond the character's momentary dilemma, but in effect, the consequence to the play's largest extension of its moral weight and meanings. Examples: Here are four characters answering the question: What shall I do? Is it appropriate? Is it just?

Corneille's *Cinna*

The Emperor Augustus in Corneille's drama debates with himself on the wisdom of keeping or surrendering his office. His speech is a kind of summary of the vanity of human wishes in which ethical, not practical considerations weigh most heavily. As he struggles toward his dilemma's resolution, with his intention fixed on arriving at an ethically justifiable decision, his manner, his sagacity, his reasonableness, enlarge the moral stature of the man. He counters the examples of the "barbarous" Sulla who during the days of the Republic retired from public office and died beloved, and the "gentle" Julius Caesar, his own father, who stayed in public office and was assassinated. "One beckons me to follow, one breeds fear." But examples in themselves, he reasons, can be deceptive, since "What destroys one man preserves another." And so his decision whether to remain as Emperor or resign and leave Rome a Republic once more will wait, he concludes, on the advice of his trusted advisors.[32]

This conclusion is characteristic of French Classical debates of self-justification; their reasoned conclusion is subsequently mocked by their plot consequence. The very "friends" on whom Augustus will rely for loyal advice are secretly the leaders of the conspiracy to assassinate him. When he discovers this fact, he enters on a second speech of justification, one of the most remarkable of Western tragedy's deliberations on human motive, justification, and act.

He begins, instinctively, by responding to the news of their betrayal by forgiving them in advance: "There is no crime against me that repentance will not erase." And he prejudges the fault to be not theirs, but his. Consequently, he undergoes his dark night of the soul: self-accusing, castigating the crimes of his past, denigrating his kingly "omnipotence," and judging his treasonous subjects to be just. Enraged against himself, he suffers ultimate self-betrayal by abandoning himself to "passion." "Ah, how my reason fails me in my need," he cries, and it fails him utterly. His decision flails between murdering his subjects and murdering himself; finding revenge by dying, and so cheating his assassins of their revenge, and taking a tyrant's total revenge against the Rome that "hates us." Recovering, he looks back on his momentary derangement, and mourns his helplessness to overcome "the awful battle of a wavering heart." At the end, the battle remains unresolved: he prays for "some command," some counsel to tell him what to "follow, what avoid, and either let me die, or let me reign."[33] He's undergone the torment of a man of conscience looking implacably into himself, but still ends with his total bafflement altogether unresolved. The speech is the great demonstration of the functioning of the tripartite division of human motive in French Classicism: reason battling strenuously to overcome passion by strength of will.

Le Cid

Unlike Augustus, Rodrigue in Corneille's *Le Cid*, argues his justification rationally, neatly. His articulated argument remains uncluttered by the emotional substratum of his dilemma: he considers his pro and con, on the one hand, on the other hand. But Rodrigue can come to no neat conclusion: his quandary is mired in conflicting absolutes. To the code of honor, he has absolute obligation to revenge his father's insult, and equally absolute obligation to his love for Chimene, whose father is, unhappily, the object of his revenge. Dilemma is doubly compounded: not accomplishing his revenge, he loses his honor, the essential virtue without which he is unworthy of Chimene's love. But in his speech of justification, as in Hamlet's, the emotional power of his dilemma doesn't touch the clarity of his reasoning. Line by line, *pro* is balanced against *con*, the symmetry of argument reflecting precisely the symmetry of his rational dilemma.[34]

Euripides' *Medea*

In another world of "justification" altogether is Euripides' Medea. In justifying the murder of her children, rationality is devastated by emotional eruptions. Justifications for their murder? She enumerates: her revenge against Jason, matching cruelty for cruelty. But the arguments against revenge are not rational arguments; the sight of her children banishes argument. The progress of her justification is profoundly diverted again and again by the degree to which the presence of her children – whether put aside or standing before her – looms in her mind. The speech's progress is a complex interchange between the arguments reason can muster and the non-arguments that well up to subvert them altogether. Medea's suffering is at the center of her "reasoning," not implicit, but its controlling substance. The sight of her children wins out; at the end of her tormenting considerations, she banishes the thought of murder.[35] (Later, overwhelmed once again by the thought of Jason and his crimes against her, she murders them in his sight.)

Buchner's *Danton's Death*

Perhaps unique among speeches of justification is Danton's, in Buchner's *Danton's Death*. The speech's strategy doesn't so much pursue argument as avoid it. There's on the one hand the argument for leaving Paris with dispatch to avoid Robespierre's guillotine, and on the other Danton's total indifference to the question itself. Here, the complexity of contraries, rather than their neat division, makes a tangle of reason, and so a tangle of the speech's structure. Danton reverts to the question of fleeing under the urgency of his followers who are desperate to get him moving, but he falls away from the question to, for him, more significant ones. In his unhurried rumination while dressing, he quashes distinctions between life-defining causes ("Why must men fight one another? We should sit down and be at peace together.") and what material difference there is between one kind of dying (by guillotine while in health) and another (by feverish old age,) or between a large, ambitious, empty life, and a tiny, but tasteful one. And he concludes, finally, that in either case, life isn't worth the effort.[36]

But there's a note in his "speech of justification" rarely if ever struck in any other. Beside the emptiness and despair Danton professes, there's a redeeming posture that goes with it: the pleasure of the rumination itself, the pleasure of winning a victory over the "committed" Robespierres that passes their understanding. Danton, in this meditation, wins that victory of the resigned skeptic's restraint over the headlong brutality of the grim believer. It's a victory belonging to the private self alone; one that's otherwise meaningless, not credited or even noticed by anybody else.

The Seventeenth Century's way of sorting logical quagmires – both in English and in French drama – by neat articulation of their contraries, gives place here to the Nineteenth Century's disillusioned anti-Romantics like Buchner to the vagaries of the immediate, the irrelevant, the negation of, rather than the reverence for values, the dismissal of logically balanced constructs altogether, all of which distorts and minimizes the formality of speeches of justification. But their function remains implicit even in the heart of such distortion.

Speeches of persuasion

This, the most studied of all the forms of formal address, in drama or out, the speech of persuasion automatically exploits the most implicit and most cherished values of its cultural moment. When appealing to the judgment of highest authority – father, husband, the fair one, prince, judge, the mob – they are usually updated versions of the value systems derived from history's precedent – honor, fealty, sexual purity, godly piety, the laws of love, and, later, Christian charity and democratic egalitarianism. In these renovated versions, the values may be noble, or noble but cynically exploited. Whatever their efficacy in themselves – their nobility or ignobility – beyond their being artful, wise, accurate in their aim, more to the point, they are dramatically – not always, but more often than not – studies in self-betrayal. The pleader in his every word is giving himself away – sometimes to us alone, sometimes also to his interlocutor. But very rarely to himself. Dramatically, the speech of persuasion at its most ironic is a study in self-blindness. While the playwright registers the character's passionate conviction, marshaling his proofs and arguments, he's demonstrating at the same time the character's limit in his understanding of the real task of persuasion at hand, or the fictive image of himself, or his blatant substitution of private yearning for moral justification.

Shakespeare's *The Winter's Tale;* Racine's *Britannicus*

Innocent Hermione defends herself, in *The Winter's Tale*, before the King her husband, Leontes, who has condemned her to death for adultery. She pleads her case with utter conviction. The values to which she appeals are as upright as herself – we esteem her for the directness and the trust with which she advances them in her defense: her integrity; her chaste and loyal life; her noble station – being a great king's daughter, a king's wife, and mother of a royal prince. And fittingly for so noble a queen, she discounts life altogether rather than live under such accusation and shame. Point by point she argues her innocence, her claim on justice, and on Leontes' own knowledge of her virtue. But Leontes is proof against persuasion: he is suddenly, unaccountably, mad with jealousy, and is blind to appeal. Her rightness is incontestable, but it has no purchase against the imprisonment of his madness.[37]

Similarly, in Racine's tragedy, Agrippina, mother of Nero, pleads for Nero to restore his confidence in her, so that she might once again assume her rightful place in his counsels. Although Agrippina's is no match for the innocence of Hermione, her plea has the same forthrightness, the same marshalling of all the good she can muster for her argument. But that her appeal is, like herself, corrupt is plain on the face of it, and plain in her litany of "favors" to her son – the path of blood and treachery through which she waded to bring him to the throne; the gratitude toward her which is "spent" because of the treacherous minions with whom he's now surrounded and who betray her; his destruction of the allies she's placed around him, and their threat to destroy her as well – instead of winning the trust of her son, all betray the treachery of her motives in this appeal for peaceful reconciliation. Apparently having achieved it, she leaves after Nero's conciliatory embrace, but in contrast to the blindness of Leontes, with the very clear-mindedness of Nero's guile which is superior to her own, he turns to his confidant and orders, "Free me from Agrippina's fury."[38] Both fail abjectly. In one case, the virtuous plea falls on a madman's deaf ears, and he hears nothing; in the other, the vicious plea is heard by ears wide open. Astute and vicious, they hear everything.

Euripides' *Hippolytus*

Agrippina openly pleads the evil she did for her son's good, and so betrays herself. Hippolytus, pleading what appear to be impeccable virtues, betrays himself just as thoroughly. For his defense before his father Theseus of the monstrous charge of incest with his stepmother Phaedra, he confidently recites the catalogue of those virtues. But the right-minded speech put into the young man's mouth is a study in self-condemnation. Within the forthright honesty, substantial logic and self-congratulation of his arguments is the inadvertent revelation of his hopeless ineptitude.   Every word he utters, every one of them true, condemns him in the eyes of his father as a weak, effeminate, immoral coward, one precisely capable of the crime for which he's charged.   How does so much virtue accomplish such vicious retribution? First, the temper and style of his self-defense. For all his swearing "by earth and sea" to his innocence, he recites his defense with an astonishing coolness. It's the consequence of his certainty of his own innocence, but fatal to his father's fixed assumption of the revolting criminal nature of his guilt. Among his doltish arguments, is Hippolytus' proud assertion of his spending all his time training at the gymnasium, and so has never had time or inclination for a thought about sex at all. Given his father's warrior's machismo, that's less than convincing proof of his never having thoughts of sex at all.[39]

In all three instances, the pleaders' very natures take false measure of their judges; their speeches serve as revelation of themselves as they battle blindly against a wall of judgment they misapprehend.

Shakespeare's *Mark Antony*

Not so Mark Antony's speech of persuasion over the body of the murdered Caesar, addressing the Roman mob. Totally cynical and totally accurate, he is, among these four, the example of the cunning argumentation of which the Sophists were accused in ancient Athens, distrusted for their supposedly studied, calculated guile in argument. The speech demonstrates the rules of persuasion absent conscience, the guide for its structure not logic but the absence of logic, assuming little or none in the subjects wooed. Instead, Antony's persuasion is guided by his assumptions of human logical fallibility, human emotional instability, human greed, and finally the human capacity for moral frenzy. That the speech's arrow in shooting for its mark is accurate, is a tribute to Mark Antony's sagacious cunning, the perfection of demagoguery, admirable, as the other three are inept, in its measurement of the capacities of the "judges" to be persuaded. But – what is more usual than not in Shakespeare – there's a doubleness in the moral "character" that emerges: the gross means to his end are matched in the portrait of Mark Antony by the profound moral fervor of his loyalty to his Caesar, and the equally profound outrage of his reaction to Caesar's assassination. Both "natures" are predictive of the rest of his actions.[40]

Accusation and denunciation

Shakespeare's *King Lear;* Sophocles' *Oedipus at Colonus*

The two most towering denunciations uttered in Western drama are certainly Lear's denunciation of his daughters Goneril and Regan, and Oedipus' of his sons Polyneices and Eteocles. Apart from the height of their fury, the contrast between them is enormous. Lear, new to ingratitude, shocked by its excess, moves in the course of his outburst to the verge of madness.[41] Oedipus, inured to twenty years of betrayal, exile and homelessness, hearing the appeal for help from his now-beleaguered son, is moved to wrath, and capping that, to prophecy.[42] But the greatest contrast between them is the power of Oedipus's curse and the impotence of Lear's.

First, one daughter, then the other, curtails Lear's authority, dismisses his shocked protestations as mere senility claiming more than its due. Lear suffers a series of attempts to suppress his incipient rage, but when he can bear no more, it bursts from him torrentially. But it goes – nowhere. Despite the fact that he utters possibly the greatest poetry in English drama attempting to match his language to his rage, it ends in a sputter – "I will have such revenges on you both / That all the world shall – I will do such things – what they are yet, I know not; but they shall be / The terrors of the earth!" And reduced to the proud plea that he will not be reduced to tears before his daughters, and with nothing more terrible with which to punish them, his impotent frustration opens the door to the only avenue left to him: "Oh fool, I shall go mad!" Denunciation is derailed, for want of the authority to punish, the very authority which he had voluntarily abandoned.

On the other hand, Oedipus, already beggared, outcast, a wandering pariah for some twenty years, retains immense authority. His gods, who've been paying close attention – unlike Lear's equivalent Olympians, who "kill us for their sport" – have granted great holiness to his great suffering, and further, through oracle, have given him the power to bestow blessing on the land that will grant him sanctuary. Approached by his son who once rejected him, begging his father's blessing against defeat in battle and death, Oedipus has the spiritual wherewithal to muster wrath like Yahweh's, and certain of its efficacy, condemns his son – in fact, both rival sons – to their mutual destruction. "Now go! I abominate and disown you," he thunders, and the curse Lear mouths with empty words, Oedipus accomplishes wholly, with words that bear sanctioned weight.

Sophocles' *Philoctetes*

The rhetoric of accusation can be querulous as well as thunderous; and Philoctetes, as victimized as the foregoing thunderers, defines himself – as they defined themselves – by the emotional measure of his complaint. Once again, the ironic juxtapositions of Greek portraiture: Philoctetes, betrayed twice over by the Greeks, once when abandoned on a barren island because of the horrible odor of the suppurating wound he had sustained, and now tricked by Neoptolemus into surrendering the bow whose magic will win his despised Greeks their war, and whose life-preserving value for himself in his exile will be lost. His denunciation is double: from the height of his rage, he cries anathema on his betrayer

Neoptolemus; and on his knees, he fawns, begs, appeals to the "true self" of the same Neoptolemus for succor. He is alternately the powerful one and the helpless one, the proud, the cringing. And another opposition: on the one hand hoarsely whispering to the silent Neoptolemus, on the other crying aloud like Lear to the caverns and crags and headlands of his landscape, the familiar great auditors of his griefs, who are also silent.[43]   Once again, denunciation is derailed by his every other word betraying the fact of his impotence.

Confession

In confessional speeches, there's unavoidable self-abasement; but whether the confession exhibits upright nobility, punishing self-condemnation or even shameless groveling, what is universally the case: the essence of selfhood, *amour propre*, is never lost.   Hidden yet supporting the words of the villain, the beggar, the witch, the confessed traitor, the shamed adulteress, is the inner pride of self-display. Whatever it is, no matter how abject or proud, it's that posture that is being positively celebrated in its speech.   In the moment of its dramatic statement, against its ostensible purpose, it is fundamentally pleading to be esteemed. The pride of confession is in its courage to speak at all, and in the great confessional speeches in Western drama, it's that particular note that informs them all, and no matter what is being confessed, they share in that fundamental distinction.

What is there to confess?   Nothing, unless acknowledging a code that is more or less inflexible. The confessor recites his sin, and judges himself a sinner in that precise light; otherwise, there is no sin. Rigidity of code is everything; without it, the sin – whether lying, murder, theft or copulation – is fun. It is the key to the pride of confession: the sinner wholeheartedly acknowledging the rule-book. It is, therefore, the double note repeated universally in speeches of confession: the self-scourging for the sin, the proud burden of acceding to the code.

Rojas' *Celestina;* Heywood's *A Woman Killed with Kindness*

One of the most affecting confessions is Melibea's in the Spanish novel-as-play, *Celestina,* whose clandestine love affair with young

Calisto had been, unknown to Melibea, enmeshed in a world of sordid maneuverings, and had ended tragically and shockingly with her witnessing her lover's fall to his death. The Catholic creed by which Melibea acknowledges her sin allowed as well, in Sixteenth Century Spain, for a downright confrontation with the world's realities, a confrontation unknown to the more morally transfixed Protestant drama in the North. Having suffered the death of Calisto, and recognized the trail of greed, lies, cunning and cynical contempt of the army of procurers and cheats who profited in bringing about the lovers' meetings and serving their "delightful error of love," she confesses to her father the whole of her sin. She describes frankly the surrendering of "the flower of my virginity;" the whole of the sordid career that attended the month of that love, and then – another code – the demand of genuine love that she share the doom of her lover, and in the same way. The confession ends with her farewell to her father, and then, almost matter-of-factly, with her leap to her death.[44]　What gives especial dignity to Melibea's confession is the sense of utter appropriateness she accedes to concerning each of the necessary steps to be undertaken: the full confession of all the facts, then the leap to death.

English Anne Frankford, taken by her husband *in flagrante delicto*, exhibits no such dignity: she wallows at once. "When do you spurn me like a dog? When tread me under your feet? When drag me by the hair?" Does she beg for pardon? "Oh! I am so far from hoping such sweet grace, as Lucifer from Heaven.... I would I had no tongue, no ears, no eyes, no apprehension, no capacity." I want, she is praying, to become physically what I now am morally: nothing.[45]　But unlike Melibea's, her speech does not issue from herself, or from *a* self, but from a paradigm: the text, the hysteria, the groveling, is written not so much to be real as illustrative, the fit speech and action for the parable of temptation and sin, and as parable, to be shown at its exemplary extreme. She is not the first and not the last of drama's Puritanical English adulterers who, once discovered, enter at once into the proper behavioral mechanisms for exhibiting absolute self-loathing and hysterical self-negation. The difference between the two confessions is the difference between Spanish Catholic and

English Puritan sensibility in dramas involving religion and sex: one keeps its feet fairly firmly on the ground; the other is characteristically sermon-in-motion, model illustration for Holy Scripture.

Guess Who's Coming to Dinner?

In perfect contrast to both, in the film *Guess Who's Coming to Dinner*, paterfamilias Spenser Tracy is adamant against admitting a black man to his table, let alone to an alliance with his daughter. By the end of the film, he sees the light. What light? In one of the longest passages of monologue in film, he abjectly, and with his new insight proudly, acknowledges the code of democratic egalitarianism, and does so with all the wrenching abnegation becoming to his former sin, and with all the piety owing to his new-discovered creed. But this code is redolent of sentimental, not Puritan or Catholic piety, and so instead of leaping to his death or suffering prayer and fasting for the same end, his incipiently good heart is rewarded by his enlightenment, and like Scrooge in Dickens' Christmas story, the new man is suffused with terminal benignity.[46]

Code governs speeches of confession. Depending on the code, white lies may weigh as heavily as rape or murder. The power of the code, not the slightness or the gravity of the sin, determines the dramatic power of the confession.

Reconciliation

The speech of reconciliation in traditional drama is characteristically the last step before closure: once it's spoken, we're on the verge of universal forgiveness, or at least tolerance for what remains unresolved or unforgiven. Order – particularly in classical comedy and in Shakespearean comedy, tragedy and history – is happily rescued from disorder. Prose comedy intent on symmetry and neatness for its finish, might even resort to rhyme. Formally, and delightfully, all the cast is gathered for the end, and after reconciliation all around, smiling, comedy sometimes ends with a full-cast dance.

More gravely, the speech of reconciliation might go beyond its formal plot function, and signify something considerably more than   smooth hands-around: it might, as it does in some of the mightiest of dramas, reconcile a great endeavor, in the body of the play's action, to a final understanding, a final assent to what was hard-won, what is finally known and embraced as what is so. These are, naturally, exceptional moments in drama, and very often drama's normal parameters can't accommodate them; they tend to soar beyond limit, or to its edge. The short final chorus in *Oedipus at Colonus*,[47] the final speech in Milton's *Samson Agonistes*,[48] the exodus of the magician Prospero in *The Tempest*:[49] in all of these, there's a summing-up, a huge ingathering of human experience – and whether the conclusion is sweet or bitter, the implied act of reconciliation figures as more than the closure of the drama itself; it figures as a long and hard-won assent – and sometimes, for the poet-dramatist, the summing-up of a lifetime. In moments of such intentional reach, it's as though the implicit sham of dramatic representation is exploded, and shows what it's been confining.

DIALOGUE AS MUSIC

With the loosening of the moorings of the prosaic Ibsenian model for dialogue now more or less accomplished, the exploitation of language's eloquence among contemporary writers of very wide difference is their most distinguishing, and certainly most beautiful, common trait.   In the Seventeenth Century, speeches were structured either in formal, even stanzaic, verse or in traditional rhetorical shapes, largely exploiting the potential of language for its own sake. But whether dramatic language exploits Baroque delight in language's display, or exhibits the spare, tight-lipped mutter of our contemporary masters of language, great dialogue, then and now, is closer to song than to speech. In the Seventeenth Century, nothing could have been clearer than that ambition to emulate the expressiveness of music in drama's language: Lear's condemnation of his daughters, and later in his madness, his howling at the storm (perhaps the greatest spoken music of all);[50]   the interrupted double sonnet Romeo and Juliet,[51] at first meeting, recite to one another, his lips, like pilgrims, going to hers and from hers, back again; Henry's harangue to his soldiers before their coming battle,[52] "Tomorrow is St. Crispian;" Sophocles great Chorus in *Antigone* on the truncated greatness of man; all these speeches, ostensibly directed toward others, are flagrantly separated from the give and take of the dialogue's flow, and granted enormous independence to accomplish aria or chant or monody, entirely above and beyond their utility.   Memorable in our own drama are these same parentheses, these same arias and chants, within and yet outside the flow of talk, bearing the same essentially musical burden. Tennessee Williams, a master of soliloquy whether spoken solo or in dialogue with others, writes speeches as arias, almost prose-poems, with the self-consciousness of language signifying its poetic intent: Blanche recounting the suicide of her homosexual friend, the bang of his gunshot echoing repetitively in her head;[53] Amanda Wingate soliciting subscriptions on the telephone, and registering her triumph;[54] Catherine's account of the cannibalistic murder of her sexually abandoned cousin on the beach in Italy;[55] Big Daddy telling the funny story about the elephant's penis in the zoo;[56] and probably most incredible of all, Hannah's recitation of her experience with an embarrassed but insistent salesman in a rowboat asking for indelicate favors that her deeply human kindness could not deny[57] – told with the rhythm and rhetoric of poetic discourse, not merely to add to our stores of information, but to our stores of sensuous response, many levels of response invited, as in Seventeenth Century poetic drama, from the listener's ear, their value displacing and exceeding altogether their functional value in the telling of the tale.

In periods of drama when such practice is rampant, there is a valid separation of intentions on the part of playwrights: the tale is told for the sake of the tale told, but a rhetorical/poetic vaudeville is generated for the sake of the other but concurrent pleasure. In the last century, the first master of this gamesmanship was Bernard Shaw, who revived brilliantly the rhythms and harmonies of the Eighteenth Century's rhetoric of Reason, and joined to it stylistic echoes of The King James Version of the Bible. In American drama, there are a number of contemporary playwrights the sheer dazzle of whose language, the tones and colors that seep into their lines from the familiar traditions of rhetoric as well as from the originality of their own distinctive voices – even on occasion in invented language – persuades and even thrills as much as does the matter of their plays. Four examples of many – from August Wilson, Sam Shepard, David Mamet, Tony Kushner – of this remarkable, sometimes even breathtaking, resurgence of American theatrical language that touches rhythms and tempi and aural harmonies as nuanced as their equivalents in musical expression.

In each instance, it's the phenomenal ear of a genuine master of dialogue that catches the rhythm, the sound, the insistent melodic repetition of the voice – the writer's genuine, most intimate knowledge of his character, its unmistakable signature. It's that heard voice that is – far from being reproduced – refracted into formal composition. Four examples quoted here, not so much for the sake of imitation, but for the recognition of the lunge of contemporary writing toward a language of extreme sensibility, which even though made directly out of the language of ordinary usage, aspires to a precision of expression, and an aural resonance, as eloquent as poetry and as sensuous as music.

David Mamet's *Glengarry Glen Ross*

Levene, after the thrill of closing a huge real estate deal, is back at the office, and he is passing along to Roma the story – already legend in his mind – of the prowess, the push, the sure footedness, with which he put the finish on the deal, how he, the kind of man who had learned his salesman's lessons perfectly way back, "did it:" Overriding the speech celebrating his prowess is the inherent song of his euphoria: his long riff, his glee, his attack, his grip of his quarry between his teeth, his pounding finish.

> LEVENE: "Bruce, Harriet, the kitchen, blah: they got their money in *government* bonds.... I say *fuck* it, we're going to go the whole route. I plat it out eight units. Eighty-two grand, I tell them. "This is now. This is that *thing* that you've been dreaming of, you're going to find that suitcase on the train, the guy comes in the door, the bag that's full of money. This is it, *Harriet, Bruce*.... "I don't want to fuck around with you, you have to look back on this. I do, too. I came here to do good for you and me. For *both* of us. Why take an interim position? *The only arrangement I'll accept* is full investment. Period. The whole eight units. I know that you're saying 'be safe,' I know

what you're saying. I know if I left you to yourselves, you'd say 'come back tomorrow,' and when I walked out the door, you'd make a cup of *coffee*.... You'd sit *down*.... And you'd think 'let's be safe....' And not to disappoint me you'd go *one* unit or maybe two, because you'd become scared because you'd met possi*bili*ty. But this won't do, and that's not the subject...." Listen to this, I actually said this. "That's not the subject of our *evening* together. Now I handed them the pen. I held it in my hand. I turned the contract, eight units eighty-two grand. "Now I want you to sign." (Pause) I sat there. Five minutes. Then I sat there, Ricky, *twenty-two minutes* by the kitchen *clock*. (Pause) Twenty-two minutes by the kitchen clock. Not a *word*, not a *motion*. What am I thinking? "My arm's getting tired?" No. I *did* it. I *did* it. Like in the *old* days, Ricky. Like I was taught.... Like, like, like I *used* to do.... I did it."[58]

Sam Shepard's *The Tooth of Crime*

Hoss mistook his enemy: "... still playing the Sixties. That's where I thought you were. Earlier. I figured you for Beach Boys, in fact." The battle between the two generations – Hoss's and Crow's – is played out entirely in terms of the metaphor of Hoss's dying Sixties music and Crow's now – Seventies – sound. Like heroic figures out of Homeric myth, they meet in a "battlefield" confrontation, their weapons: the music and text of one decade fighting the music and text of the other. Music, in fact, is part of Shepard's text in the fight scenes, the prose hitting rhythms that play into the score, but not fitting the words to the notes. In Round One, Crow's battle text begins:

> CROW: "Pants down. The moon show. Ass out the window. Belt lash. Whip lash. Side lash to the kid with the lisp. The dumb kid. The loser. The runt. The mutt. The shame kid. Kid on his belly. Belly to the blacktop. Slide on the rooftop. Slide through the parkin' lot. Slide kid. Shame kid. Slide. Slide."
>
> BOSS (*counters:*) Never catch me with beer in my hand. Never caught me with my pecker out. Never get caught. Never once. Never, never. Fast on the roof. Fast on the

roof. Fast through the still night. Faster than the headlight. Fast to the move."[59]

Crow's "body blows" – his guesses at the pubescent and adolescent "shameful sins" of Hoss's generation, wins the round, according to the referee's scoring, by keeping Hoss on the defensive. Shepard's directions for the playing:

"They each pick up microphones. They begin their assaults just talking the words in rhythmic patterns, sometimes going with the music, sometimes counterpointing it. As the round progresses, the music builds…. Their voices build so that sometimes they sing the words or shout. The words remain as intelligible as possible, like a sort of talking opera."

Words doing battle: Crow's "blows," short phrases, generally two beats each, against Hoss's slighter, longer riffs, do all the work in their fight.

August Wilson's *Ma Rayney's Black Bottom*

Sitting in the back room waiting with the other musicians to start recording with vocalist Ma Rainey, Levee's rage has been building, his emotional revulsion about to spill over against the white man's brutality and the black man's genuflecting to God instead of giving back the brutality he gets. Enraged at Cutler's talking God and defending the black man's scared prayer, Levee, brandishing a knife, ready to kill Cutler – he eventually does – answers him with a roar. His text is incantatory, and *literally turns into speech song*.

> LEVEE: That's your God, huh? That's your God, huh? Is that right? Your God, huh? All right. I'm gonna give your God a chance. I'm gonna give your God a chance. I'm gonna give him a chance to save your black ass.
> (Levee circles Cutler with his knife. Cutler picks up a chair to protect himself.)
>
> TOLEDO: Come on, Levee… put the knife up!
>
> LEVEE: Stay out of this, Toledo! (Levee alternately swipes at Cutler during the following:) I'm calling Cutler's God! I'm talking to Cutler's God! You hear me? Cutler's

God! I'm calling Cutler's God! Come on and save this nigger! Strike me down before I cut his throat!

SLOW DRAG: Watch him, Cutler! Put that knife up, Levee!

LEVEE: (to Cutler) I'm calling your God! I'm gonna give him a chance to save you! I'm calling your God! We gonna find out whose God he is!

CUTLER: You gonna burn in hell, nigger!

LEVEE: Cutler's God! Come on and save this nigger! Come on and save him like you did my mama! Save him like you did my mama! I heard her when she called you! I heard her when she said, "Lord, have mercy! Jesus, help me! Please, God, have mercy on me, Lord Jesus, help me!" And did you turn your back? Did you turn your back, motherfucker? Did you turn your back?

(Levee becomes so caught up in his dialogue with God that he forgets about Cutler and begins to stab upward in the air, trying to reach God.)

Come on! Come and turn your back on me! Turn your back on me! Come on! Where is you? Come on and turn your back on me! Turn your back on me, motherfucker! I'll cut your heart out! Come on, turn your back on me! Come on! What's the matter? Where is you? Come on and turn your back on me! Come on, what you scared of? Turn your back on me! Come on! Coward, motherfucker! (Levee folds his knife and stands triumphantly) Your God ain't shit, Cutler.[60]

Tony Kushner's *Angels in America*

Counter to the gross power and percussive beat of Levee's and Crow's and Levene's texts, Harper, while her plane is moving up to thirty-five thousand feet toward the ozone layer during her jet flight to San Francisco, has a vision. Looking down at the broken shards of human suffering rising in air to "join hands and clasp ankles," she invokes, at least in metaphor, both secular and canonical literature's endlessly revived promise and affirmation of dead souls, flying up, being "repaired." Her text reaches a quietly controlled, and enraptured, lyricism.

> HARPER: When we hit thirty-five thousand feet, we'll reach the tropopause. The great belt of calm air. As close as I'll ever get to the ozone. I dreamed we were there. The plane leaped the tropopause, the safe air, and attained the outer rim, the ozone, which was ragged and torn, patches of it threadbare as old cheesecloth, and that was frightening. But I saw something only I could see, because of my astonishing ability to see such things. Souls were rising, from the earth far below, souls of the dead, of people who had perished, from famine, from war, from the plague, and they floated up, like skydivers in reverse, limbs all akimbo, wheeling and spinning. And the souls of these departed joined hands, clasped ankles, and formed a web, a great net of souls, and the souls were three-atom oxygen molecules, of the stuff of ozone, and the outer rim absorbed them, and was repaired. Nothing's lost forever. In this world, there is a kind of painful progress. Longing for what we've left behind, and dreaming ahead. At least I think that's so.[61]

***

CHAPTER 10

"PACKAGING" MEANING

Leaving concern with the making of plays, we turn in this last chapter to the business of audiences and particularly critics — concerned with the translation of plays into structured meaning. The translation can hardly be thought of as self-evident or direct. It involves complications in the mind as it settles on meanings congenial to its own sense of – what? Logic? Questionable. The mind taking in drama may have deeper satisfactions in *its* mind than mere logic. But it does still cohere to patterns of thinking that it *calls* logical, and though they may or may not be, those patterns may well be more congenial, more familiar, and even more persuasive. To look into them, and to note how they shape conceptual designs of plays, we must take a bit of a detour to note how thought itself – thought as such – frequently makes its way to its most confident conclusions.

Nietzsche generously reassures us about the value of thought: "Thought," he writes, "is the most persistently exercised function in all stages of life – and also in every aspect of perception or apparent appearance! Obviously, it soon becomes the *mightiest* and the most *exacting* of all functions, and in time tyrannizes over other powers. Ultimately it becomes a 'passion in itself.'"[1] We'll explore the nature of its tyranny and especially its possible presence as "a passion in itself," for good or ill, in drama. How can it do harm? we ask. How can it be for ill?

There are two kinds of thinking, we may safely assume: proper and improper. Proper thinking is rational; it follows the rules of logic, and applied to the drama, it produces – as we've seen in earlier chapters – structures that make for a single overall dramatic "statement" which is analogous to a complete sentence, that is, a complete thought. Improper thinking, mocked by linguists and philologists, is non-rational – or, better, para-rational – and consists of a "flow" of thoughts which willy-nilly add up sometimes only to random reflections, sometimes to purposive reflections, and more often than not to conclusions more powerfully and unyieldingly held than those which logic aims to prove.

First and foremost: It assumes that thinking is *thinking in images*. This makes considerable sense, since there is no other way to think. Anything that is not immediately present, to be thought of at all, needs first to be thought, that is, represented, as image. Whether the thought is of an object, an event or a concept, it must first be imagined, and can only *be* imagined, as image. Victor Shklovsky denies this. He makes fun of the notion advanced by the philologist Alexander Potybna, that "Art is thinking in images." Potybna further compounded his sin: "Without imagery there is no art." We will compound it even further, as Shklovsky inadvertently does himself. He's describing a device in the novel, *Tristram Shandy:*

> "If we visualize the digressions [the principal device in Sterne's novel] schematically, they will appear as cones representing an event, with the apex representing the causes. In an ordinary novel such a cone is joined to the main story line at its apex; in *Tristram Shandy* the base of the cone is joined to the main story line, so that all at once we fall into a swarm of allusions."[2]

The acrobatic zeal Shklovsky would need to demonstrate this legerdemain he wisely leaves to imagining.

THINKING OBJECTS

"My keys! Where did I put my keys?" Thinking of possible places, candidates occur one after the other, sometimes in sequence, sometimes in a jumble. To put the question in words at all means first seeing them in image, and the sequence of "thoughts" that follows will be expressed in words, to be sure, but in various stages of accuracy and completeness with respect to the images that have leaped to mind. And if you want help in finding the keys, you begin a sort of *verbal pointing* at the images in your head in a series of passes at describing the possible places where the keys are hiding ("You know, when I left them in the... in the what? The desk file drawer, don't you remember?... No, in the box on the..." – and so on.) And meanwhile, you in your need to get someone to find the damn keys are struggling to *say* the pictures in your mind, even though, as you *know* them in your mind, they take considerable adjusting to reach some semblance of formality of discourse before anyone can take up the challenge. It is not merely a question of "expressing" what you have in your head, but *reducing* what you have in your head to accommodate a possible form of expression needed for, and available to, mutually intelligible discourse. And this, of course, is the sentence, known universally as a complete unit of thought. But is it?

A SENTENCE - A UNIT OF THOUGHT?

The sentence in reality may or may *not* be a complete thought; what is certain is only that it is a unit of its *expression*. The difference is of course profound. Let's allow for a moment that thought is not consonant with single sentences, that with respect to the characteristic shape of thought, its confinement within sentence structure is arbitrary, that the stringency of the sentence structure of subject and predicate confines the activity of thought, pretending its real nature, pretending, that is, that the way in which thought normally flows can be replicated in strings of single sentences, or that thought can originate in them, and in them find itself perfectly realized, and to the extent that it cannot, it is dismissible as thought.

But thought's flow is subversive, and crams itself into the confinement of sentences out of harsh necessity alone. Its life is in the flow of its images which may have "logical" sequence or may be irrelevant to logic. It truncates its independent flow only when it needs the services of sentences. In the instance of getting help in finding your keys, the utterance finally achieved of a whole sentence is achieved by ejaculating words aiming toward, thrusting toward, those images, then trying another tack, and so on, to encompass in adequately intelligible words the images in your mind. And for the practical purposes of getting someone to move on the task, the finally organized, completed sentence put together, says all that is needed to be *said*. But how much of the imagery in the mind – the thought – which encompassed all the possible locations in which the keys were successively intuited to be hiding, did that simple final sentence ("It's in the fridge, for God's sake!") itself encompass? A wee bit, no more. The comprehensible sentence grasps what it *needs* of the thought to accomplish its purpose, but it can hardly be said to comprehend the whole of the referenced "thought."

But in Chomsky,[3] in early Wittgenstein,[4] the pursuit of meaning assumes the congenial accord of one sentence and one thought, so that meaningful statement is studied within their common parameters. It assumes that the expression of thought *within* sentences, and further, the linking of sentences one with the other, accurately replicates sequential thinking. The bridge from sentence to sentence, as it scrutinizes facts and follows the rules of logic, should demonstrate Thought itself, then, sitting for its ideal portrait.

That thought relates back to image is as absurd to them as it is to Shklovsky. Its absurdity is easily demonstrated by that much abused sentence: "There is no elephant in the room!" The negative, the argument goes, eliminates the possibility of the sentence replicating, or mirroring, an image: after all, how can there be an image of *absence*? But in order to absent the elephant, it must be apprehended first – and that apprehension is in the form of an image, and that image is the underlying thought itself. The sentence, to be sure, neatly eliminates the image of the elephant from its place in the room, but though it is abandoned by the sense of the sentence, the elephant hovers forever in the originally apprehended image, and is permanently domesticated in the thought – a little, perhaps, outside the room.

THINKING EVENTS

If the nature of thought and the process of logic were one, they should, and would, lead by the same avenue to the same conclusions. In contemplating history, for example, the logic of argument and the sequence of thought should, and would, follow the same route. Let's follow a sequence of thought about an event.

Historical events in themselves are stable, each belonging inextricably to a time and place, but they're rarely "stable" in the mind. The mind calls up an event – let us say, the French Revolution. To "call it up" is to imagine it. But a colossal event such as the French Revolution cannot be "imagined," that is, *seen*, at a glance. A single image, for starters, will do for reference: heads lopped by the guillotine; Robespierre in his study ruminating darkly, consigning enemies to perdition; the Assembly in wild confusion, the parties shouting at one another. But as with objects such as keys, images of events tend to be called up to some purpose. Intending to remember the Revolution – let us say, *fondly*, – image instantly shifts; that is to say, another image or images intrude on those first dark ones: enlightened citizens storming the Bastille in a blow for freedom, Tom Payne holding up a sheet of paper on which is printed: Liberte, Egalite, Fraternite; effete aristocrats wheeled through the streets of Paris in tumbrils, ending oppression. In other words, an overlay of qualifying images countering the dark implications of the first set. An even more difficult circumstance: describing in an essay, say, the "nature" or the "meaning" of the Revolution, or the historical event as such. Instantly, a weird process begins aimed at rational discourse. In the interest of objectivity, "statements" accrue which try like the devil to ingraft newly-gathering multiple images on already-ingested multiple images. In language, that results in hastily inserted corrective expressions such as: "… but that is not to say…," and "naturally, we must take into account…," and "but of course, that's hardly the whole story, there's also the important consideration…," each of these demurrers and qualifiers occasioned in the mind by a newly intruding image or images, and as the images of the Revolution slip and slide, and as the objective point of view is threatening to derail, necessitating the beating down of some and the "foregrounding" (as we say now) of friendlier ones, a synthetic semblance of the history of the Revolution emerges. Even more frightening for Reason is the situation of two interlocutors disagreeing – each in turn grabbing the tails of quickly-resurrected images floating by, each image in turn quickly dismembered or buried by newly-remembered, newly-intruding counter-images. Their "argument," which on the face of it will more than likely pass for well-informed, enlightened and "rational," is in point of fact triggered point by point by images coming to the momentary rescue of each interlocutor. And characteristically, as argument moves closer to the forbidding moment of defeat or victory, image-selection automatically hardens, and each contender ends with a definite portrait in his own head of the completeness – given his file of increasingly and stubbornly and carefully sequenced images – of his private victory. The hardening of that sequence of images is what we call a point of view.

THINKING CONCEPTS

And so the separation of the processes of thought from the structure of sentences may possibly be a legitimate way of studying the problem of how meaning actually manages to get caught in language. Sometimes. Because it is not the case that words, sentences, paragraphs or whole treatises faithfully correspond to the image-thinking from which they derive; they only try to. Words, sentences, etc., make their endless attempt to *approximate* images in the mind, and do so – depending on the arsenals of language available to hand – with varying success. But judge the terrible task of language when it is confronted by the usual nature of what we call "abstract thoughts" whenever it is attempting to fix them definitively in words! Unlike objects such as keys, unlike events such as the French Revolution, the image/thoughts it is aiming at have themselves little or no stability, but leap and dodge, self-correct and self-expand, multiply and contract, in the very moments when language needs most that they stand still – a condition we've almost detected in the plight of the two debaters trying to best one another in their "discussion" of the French

Revolution. Those thought/images from moment to moment are shape-changing and ephemeral, altering even as we stare at them, so that however "expression" may yearn for their stability, their essentially fleeting character irresponsibly eludes it. The drama of the mind struggling to do what it sometimes treasures most – the forming of large, abstract and summary concepts – is at perpetual disadvantage in its battle to best the mercurial nature of thinking itself.

TRANSCENDING

How does the struggle to form such concepts overcome this barrier? It transcends it. By aggressive leaps, it formulates concepts long before it knows their reasons. It can be taken as a rule: in concept-formation, conclusion precedes its justification, not by a process of logical argument, but by one of visualization. It arranges and rearranges bits of mental imagery into the pleasing shapes it needs to support whatever suppositions it holds dear. The pieces are adjusted and readjusted in mental diagrams, and their final pleasing arrangement is taken for the concept's truth.

Diagrams? Literally. An elementary example: A "concept" weighing positives and negatives sets them out mentally to the right and to the left, for example, on either side of an imaginary line. Slightly more complex: an historical concept demonstrating some sort of "force" moving forward or backward, and seen too as moving slowly or quickly, "sees" it in a large reductive image representing both direction and mobility. And with a greater complexity of factors intruding on simple diagrams, the picture then becomes seriously dimensional, extending in two, three, or in one notable case, four dimensions.

Relatively simple concepts go no further. They make do with diagrams of up/down, right/left, in/out, fast/slow – in other words, the mind's normal stock of images for dimension, direction and mobility. But the complexity of diagrammatic pictures depends wholly on the ingenuity of the mind that draws or paints them in its private mental space. For truly ambitious, stunningly complex conceptual diagramming, mentally or on paper, Einstein and Freud offer notable testimony:

"Einstein once said… that when he thought about science, he thought visually, he thought in pictures, and this appears to be the case with Freud…. [Freud's] first purely psychoanalytic drawing [was done in a style] reminiscent of [his] earlier [anatomical] sketches – looping lines connecting nodes – but the nodes now represent[ed] psychological processes like memory, not physical locations in the brain. A few years later, the diagrams become much more abstract: a sketch from 1900 illustrating mental processes involved in dreaming looks like a bar graph. A diagram completed in 1898 [of] 'the psychical mechanism of forgetfulness' resembles the schematic for an air-conditioning system, complete with arrows and boxes."[5]

However the complexity and oddity of "concept" images so carpentered, the language describing them – whether in ordinary words or in the signs and symbols of mathematics or geometry or symbolic logic or any other – each word, each sign, each symbol means nothing until it is translated into private diagrammatic representation, and it is *that representation* which is the mind's – anyone's mind – resource for making sense.

But "thought," said Nietzsche, "tyrannizes over other powers," and eventually "becomes a passion in itself." It is the ingenuity of complex conceptualization playing games with its substitute diagrams, that *is* "the passion in itself," and while it can produce "thought" of sound value, it can also produce catastrophic delusion, and play havoc with the value of intellectual enterprise. There is a wonderfully telling passage in one of Gertrude Stein's *Notebooks* describing the process of "thought" through which her much admired, intellectually gifted brother passed on the way to one of his largest conclusions. It is a paradigm of the nature of *important thinking,* the nature – to put it more formally – of "concept formation." Her brother was Leo, and his concept had to do with "binocular vision and its relation to attention," a concept that came to him after thirty days of fasting – Leo was subject to severe digestive illnesses, and strenuous fasting was one of his periodic therapies:

"Eyes turn in, [writes Stein] in those not having wealth of experience or having no capacity for wealth of experience. Great thinkers eyes do not turn in, they get blank or turn out to keep themselves from being disturbed. It is only sentimentalists or unexperiencing thinkers whose eyes turn in. Those having wealth of experience turn out or are quiet in meditation and repose.

"This pragmatic idealism [the ultimate consequence of Leo's new concept] is a perfectly natural result, bound to come as [Herbert] Spencer's cosmic philosophy sprang out of evolution and in the present creator's case the field was quite ripe.... [T]he fanaticism of fasting made it already [likely] and the concept of binocular vision and its possible relation to attention fired the brain and la voila a pragmatic idealism which is... a contradiction in terms. They used to universalize consciousness [*crossed out:* that at least had some excuse] now they universalize attention....

"The idea yes that is imagination in a sense, a logical imagination if one can call it so, but which like all logical processes not reinforced by experience is short and never sustained, which has been, is, and will be characteristic. It is because of this that most apparently logical people are so illogical because rationality means you have to be rational about something.... Most people who are noted for logic have the quality of non-appeal to experience. Sometimes it is very good if well started, it can never run long. It is impossible that it should, it either becomes logic chopping, ideistic conceptions, mania or it don't go on long. *Real thinking is conceptions aiming and aiming again and again always getting fuller, that is the difference between real thinking and theorizing.*" [Italics added.][6]

The gap between what we commonly know and what, out of need, we claim to know is universal, permanent and huge, and no modesty of intent nor vows of intellectual caution can ever narrow that gap, sustained as it is by one of the deepest of human longings: to live in an environment of cosmic certainties. The leap for Leo from "unexperienced" thinking to a formal system of "pragmatic idealism" took thirty days, but it can be contracted to a mere instant by practiced fashioners of "concepts." And that moment of "leap" from its sources in experience, however rich or however barren, characteristically shuts the door on modest knowing, and enters into that world in which – as Stein puts it – "eyes turn in" away from reality's tangibles, and settle into the supremely comfortable world of "concepts," a world in which, when it has lost experiential substance, words talk knowingly to words.

Painful though it may be to suggest that this intellectual atavism operates well beyond the fanaticism of Leo's fasting, we find it fully embraced in every realm of thought that takes any measure of liberty from the constraints of what Stein calls "experience." Absent that constraint, "Leo's leap" operates with abandon in all of them – philosophy, theology, psychology, the social sciences, and in most of contemporary literary theorizing. Bertrand Russell notes one glaring case in point to which we shall return: Hegel.

> "That world history repeats the transitions of the dialectic… is the thesis [Hegel] developed in his *Philosophy of History*. Like other historical theories, it required, if it was to be made plausible , some distortion of facts and considerable ignorance. Hegel, like Marx and Spengler after him, possessed both these qualifications."[7]

PYRAMIDING

Without dwelling on further embarrassing examples – multiple leap to mind – we pass to the further characteristic of "concept formation" similarly embedded in apparently rational thinking: pyramiding layers of abstraction. This habit is at the heart of Stein's critique of intellectual "eyes turning in" – the habit of "concepts" after their first tentative formulation flying, like arrows to their mark, toward the ultimate reach of abstract formulation. As Stein exemplifies it, it is what happened to Herbert Spencer in structuring what he called his "synthetic" philosophy.[8] Spencer is indeed paradigmatic. Having absorbed the idea of evolution even before Darwin's *Origin of Species*, he was one of the first to elaborate – one might say, elasticize – the idea toward a fully fleshed philosophic system embracing whatever disciplines could be shown to conform to an "evolutionary" pattern. And in this "fleshing out" of a summary abstraction lies the particular labor that, following "Leo's leap," turns problematical guesses into confident "proofs," that is, playing – to steal from Wittgenstein's coinage of "language games"[9] – "concept-games," playing with their rearrangement and reordering. Such games are sufficiently removed from tangible realities to allow their object to be not "proof" in the ordinary sense, but a different order of proof, one that finds verification in the concept when it achieves in imagination   the two objectives that stand in for "proof:" comprehensiveness and coherence. That's the ideal of an ultimate "system:" all-embracing comprehensiveness, all its elements internally cohering. Patience and ingenuity, sometimes lasting over a lifetime, have produced such over-arching systems, some with hardly noticeable flaws.

That the process is delusional may or may not be the case. It is possible that the ultimate formulation is miraculously in touch with fact and experience. It's the singular distinction, for example, of the exact sciences that they hold these formulations at arm's length and regard them as tentative until, braced by fact and logic, they come into their own as proven. But it is not given to run-of-the-mill formulators to run backwards over the path they might have tracked to make sure. In these disciplines, and in casual thinking (in which concept-formation flourishes mightily) that process is rare. Concepts so born have the freedom to elevate from level to level of abstraction until, unassailable in such airy reaches, they become, and remain, lifelong conviction. Luckily, among dinner table "logicians," they don't, as Stein notes, last long – possibly during the time of dinner. Unluckily, for the most of humanity who are in terrible need of sustained and unchanging conceptual sustenance, once its allegiance is fixed, it prefers death or murder to their loss..

What is the difference then between what Stein calls "real thinking" or "creative thinking" which rarely knows these easy resolves, and this kind of "theorizing" thinking which goes like an arrow to its mark? What does she mean by "real thinking aiming and aiming again and again?" It is based on the feeling, widely shared by the *avant garde* at the turn of the century, of the collapse of stable structure that carried over into language, thought, meaning and representation. It was a shared need for, in every way, beginning again. There are no ready paths but those to be cut or discovered for the first time. Its authenticity lies precisely in its avoidance of mental sallies toward abstract summary; it remains close to what it knows experientially and intimately rather than theoretically (as Stein once put it, "Do you know because I tell you so, or do you know, do you know")[10] and from that vantage, "aims and aims again and again" at conclusive certainties. *But* it allows that the realization of that goal is not its ultimate object. Instead, its object is the accumulation of residues of meaning, of suggestion, of insight along the way, never "transcending" or muting the reality and authenticity of its private knowing. Its aim was not the building of cosmic structures in which it had little faith, but in building privately, modestly and consequently authentically structures that intellectual conscience could support. In other words, "real thinking."

HOW DOES DRAMA THINK? HOW IS IT THOUGHT?

To come at last to the relevance of all this to our subject: drama. How, in itself, does drama "think?" And how is drama "thought" by its spectators, its readers, its critics? To answer in a word: Conventional dramatic structure is obedient to the predictability and banality of logical thinking; but, paradoxically, insofar as drama's audience can escape from logical constraints, it offers the exhilaration, unpredictability and irrationality of "improper" thinking, and in those states of alogical bliss, finds drama's visceral, emotional and intellectual rewards – as well as its intellectual fantasies. First, its banality:

DRAMA'S LOGIC

Let's recall for a moment what was outlined at the beginning of this book: the logical framework of the traditional play, and the collaboration of action and thematic structure in reaching a play's closure. Like the sentence, drama's traditional and most basic model is made up of a subject (the protagonist), and a predicate (his action.) Insofar as they're serving the play's logic, they are indistinguishable from one another, as the protagonist, armed with his initial motive, clambers through his obstacles, his conflicts, his detours, until he reaches final victory or defeat. And, to recall further, the connection between beginning and end reconfirms moral stability after it had been threatened by the temporary instabilities of the play's interim action. Additionally, the logic of the play's *thematic structure* guarantees that the play, as a *statement*, ends up as, presumably, a wise lesson.

LOGICAL ANALYSIS

To put it grossly, then, the logic of dramatic structure is made up of a parable and its homily. To get at the *logic* of the play, dramatic analysis roots out that basic parable, and then enlarges – usually considerably – on its homily. Why, it is right to ask, is this double labor, although accurate, also banal? Because of its uniformity, its repetition, and its coercion. Insistently, uniformly and inevitably, for twenty five centuries, traditional Western drama has replicated in its very form the same implicit sermon of cosmic reassurance, and the same virtuous lessons to be derived from humanity's lapses from that reassurance. Characteristically, critical analysis labors to elevate these humble homilies to lofty insights – particular favorites: man inevitably submitting to destiny, and even more brow-furrowing, free will battling with its mortal enemy, determinism – and other inflations which are little more than the same wind blown uniformly from the similar structures of the lightest, silliest farces to the most devastating tragedies. A notch above these vaporous summings-up are the lessons scratched from the plays of playwrights genuinely engaged with difficult moral, cultural and political dilemmas, who expend their intellectual energies resolving, or at least testing, powerful resolutions of such questions. But when their techniques remain more or less within drama's conventional framework, that very framework tempts and teases a tiny, residual, summary statement out of even such a play's "meaning." No damage is so serious to such plays as to mistake the particular bend and richness of their thought for the tired implications of the dramatic form itself. They either beat against and challenge its restraints, or, *faux de mieux,* make a virtue of them. Either way, the critical lapse lies in missing the difference between the particularity and expanse of such statement and the residual banality of dramatic form's inherent statement.

As to that terminal statement: the lesson, the *bromide*. Luckily, intelligent drama makes a point of sidestepping the conclusion that waits dumbly for its moment until the end. It avoids the summary statement that follows from the story it tells, and when it doesn't avoid it, the mark of its banality is stamped even more damningly on the play's forehead: "And so, dear audience, being a true friend leads to lasting friendship, and selfishness leads to loneliness." Or, even more uplifting, "Great love will face any challenge, just as great love of country will face even death." In both great plays and stupid plays, the mere logic underlying their story may say no more; but when that summarizing rubric is revealed explicitly and read as the play's burden of meaning, it shrinks both levels of plays to the same tiny dimension. It is the fault of neither the great nor the stupid play; their thematic structure has no alternative but to ride smoothly to the accurately summarizing platitude that marks their mutually terminal intellectual death.

Let's avoid noting or quoting the classical playwrights who stooped to explicitness at the end of their plays – plays that had, in their telling, cleverly managed to hide the platitude of their "lesson." Note how dismissively wise and careful Shakespeare mocked thematic "summing-up" in one of his tragedies: "And never was there such a tale of woe/ As this of Juliet and her Romeo." And even more beside the point is the summary couplet concluding *King Lear*: "The oldest have borne most: we that are young/ Shall never see so much, nor live so long," which, being pointless and gratuitous, skirts the deadliness of a "lesson's" *finis*.

Granted, not all closure statements are deadly. We've already paid tribute to closure in Milton, in Sophocles, in Shakespeare, that deliberately flies from the banality of summary meaning by meaning incomparably more. It leaps from thematic summary, as we've noted, to statement that awakens possibilities of "meaning" beyond the scope of the play itself, and in their final verses reaches for a kind of visionary wisdom rather than the logical step that links its story's parable to its QED.

ILLOGICAL ANALYSIS

We turn to the "illogical" or "improper" way of thinking about drama that's governed by random reflections, or sometimes by purposive reflections, and frequently by unyieldingly assured reflections that become fixed in the mind as strongly as though they were born out of logic itself.

RANDOM FLOW OF THOUGHT

One of the joys of wallowing in fiction is that there is no need to accommodate the randomness of one's thinking to the demands of communication – no real need even to reduce it to words and sentences. Since it has no practical purpose to fulfill, its randomness provides a series of speculative holidays spread out during, for example, a drama's unfolding. It's one of the deepest pleasures of reading or watching plays that one need not bend that random flow to any purpose, but let it flow freely in a state of mind midway between dream and attention.

What interferes with this holiday from reason is that the events of the play, its plot and so on, are not strung together in a similarly willy-nilly way, but are controlled – at the least – by the progression of the plot. And that progression, far from being self-contained and self-justifying, is deeply concerned with engaging the drifting spectator into palpitating interest in itself. It diverts the inattentive mind by accurately administered seductions – seductions we've specified some pages back: fearful anxiety, moral outrage, and/or breathless curiosity. Once harnessed to these basic atavisms, the spectator's randomness is successfully engaged, even utterly coopted, until the play's resolution satisfies and releases those awakened visceral appetites. But meanwhile, those appetites are wonderfully served. The moments are thrilling when the spectator's yearning and the plot's events are rolling along in perfect accord. There is euphoria, even glee, at surrendering the self to those strong, controlling seductions.

But utterly coopted? Well, no. Another process begins unbidden, one which eventually leads to what we like to think of as rational criticism. The spectator, exercising a moderating will of his own, makes an implicit demand: that the pace and intensity of the flow of events conform to the rate and degree of his seduced interest. If it does not, a division occurs between the rhythm of performance and the rhythm of the spectator's need for gratification. And further: rarely is seduction so enthralling that the spectator will lose his sense of ordinary likelihoods – likelihoods which, once violated, make his bonding with the play hard to recover: things taken for granted, familiar settings, ways, known over a lifetime, of speaking, behaving, thinking, feeling, hardly noted until they're shown a bit inaccurately or actually distorted, violating the spectator's deep certainties of the way things are. And should he fall out of sync with the pace and intensity of the telling, or with its reasonable connection with what he normally knows as so, then the very first and most automatic level of responses – disbelief, dissatisfaction, annoyance, boredom, etc – combine to distance him, "alienate" him, from the fiction.

There is on the one hand the thrill of total surrender, and on the other, the intrusive disharmony that separates the spectator's response from the drama's own solicitations. "Alienated," he watches, or reads, with a colder eye. And with this one small step toward objectivity, the mind begins the giant step toward transforming plays into objects that mean wholly and only what it wants them to mean: critical analysis. The beginning:

There are – as we watch or read or simply contemplate a play – two in each of us: a public and a private self. The public one is of course Kaspar, the character in Handke's play who is entirely indoctrinated into knowing and thinking what everyone else in his world thinks and knows. And this one weeps, sings along, claps his hands at the play's communally embedded signals should there be any – and few are the plays that have none – and they win his deepest gratification. But even joiners are not altogether Kaspars, and in the very act of waving the party's flag at the Tea Party's public meeting, or the nation's flag at the national convention, he can still distance himself from rah-rah and recognize that the self that is doing this is not entirely himself. Inwardly, silently, he demurs. While genuflecting with the crowd, he thinks: This is embarrassing, this is stupid. Smiling and applauding the candidate's babe-in-arms, he thinks: I hate babies. Clenching his jaw and snarling at the politically incorrect, he lets himself think: Who cares?

Criticism begins as the private self's protective act of defiance against total cooptation. Once it begins, it can hold to that knowledge with unshakable integrity, and silently withstand any and all public, even publicly moral, even publicly ideological, assault. No matter how far its wisdom may have traveled since its inarticulate nonage, these forever-privately-accumulated certainties remain stubborn, silent and secure. There is, in fact, nothing else that so reliably separates the self from the blur of everybody else, that defines so precisely the self's uniqueness. And it remains so, the spectator's privately funneled vision, as he enlarges into the Critic.

THE CRITIC AND THE IRRATIONAL

If we recall how the debaters of the French Revolution arrived at their point of view, and how Leo leaped to his firmed-up concept, we can follow now the same process: scrambling for resonating images from the play's stores, the hardening of a sequence of those images to support a "point of view," the leap to formulating the play's summary meaning – its "concept." Just as when the mind deals with a multiplicity of historical facts, or with the many variables in class or race or sex, or with the endless variations of human behavior, the schematics of analysis displace the tangibilities of dramatic experience, and smoothly transition to the fixed notional demands of the spectator-critic.

It's an irresistible process: the absorption of the object – the play as an event in time – into new formulation, and the impossibility of the spectator-as-critic recognizing that formulation as anything but the object's own reality. Critical analysis at its most complete and its most complex is an independent exercise in concept gamesmanship that bears no necessary relation to the play as an event. The question then returns: how spurious or how relevant can these structured concepts be for mirroring the experience of a play? Let's look at a few widely differing examples of analyses attached to a single play, some with a modest sense of trepidation, some with none: three brilliant, influential studies of Ibsen – in this instance, of his *Rosmersholm* – in which constructs lie in wait for the play to realize them.

Freud's *Rosmershom*[11]

Freud's analysis of Ibsen's play is focused primarily on its central character, Rebecca West. The analysis is stretched to fit over a conceptual frame for which a crucial item of evidence had to be "discovered" to fulfill its pattern. In his essay, "Those Wrecked by Success," Freud summarizes his premise: "Psychoanalytic work has furnished us with the thesis that people fall ill of a neurosis as the result of a frustration." The libido, Freud explains, is prohibited from fulfilling its wishes because of the intervention of the morally-directed ego, which blocks the lunge of the libido's amoral wish. But when it gets through anyhow, the psyche is "made ill by [its] success," because of the more punishing superego. Embedded in the superego's punishment is another level of guilt than the one against which the ego contended. That second, "unconscious" level, prevents the wish's "success" from being realized as pleasure, and causes the otherwise unexplainable frustration and neurosis.

Freud's analysis of Rebecca follows this pattern. When she came to Rosmersholm, she unconsciously recapitulated the family romance of her childhood, when her stepfather, Doctor West, had become the object of her passion, and by becoming his mistress, obliterated her rival, her mother. "She stood under the domination of the Oedipus complex, even though she did not know that this universal phantasy had in her case become a reality. When she came to Rosmersholm, the inner force of this first experience drove her into bringing about, by vigorous action, the same situation which had been realized in the original instance." This repetition was accomplished by Rebecca's campaign to bring about Rosmer's wife's suicide, and winning Rosmer's subsequent proposal of marriage.

It's Freud's reading of the play's ending that's critical for his analysis. In order to bring Rebecca's psychological career into line with the idea of the double guilt of "those wrecked by success," he introduces the play's secret factor: incest. Rebecca, having succeeded in winning Rosmer after doing away with his wife, refuses Rosmer's proposal. Why? To clear her conscience, she must confess to her "murder" of Beata – so she is a criminal and unfit for reward. But, Freud adds, she's confronted by, but cannot confess, her deeper guilt – that she was not only the mistress of her step-father, Doctor West, but his biological daughter. She "fails," then, to relish her success because of her deeper, unconscious guilt in duplicating the incestuous arrangement with a replica father-figure. It is a three-level diagram, in other words, in which its descriptive elements are each given volitional force, thus creating a dynamic battle scene fought internally and, remote from both audience and character, "unconsciously."

So emotionally fraught is the play's secret that, Freud explains, it had to be deliberately "concealed... from the easy perception of the spectator or reader," whose "serious resistances, based on the most distressing emotions, would have arisen, which might have imperiled the effect of the drama."[12] Ibsen, in other words, took the precaution of concealing the outcome of his drama, lest the audience discover it to the peril of the play's success.

The reading is ingenious and close: Freud tracks the dialogue in the two passages critical to his thesis, underscores in the first Rebecca's confession of her conscious guilt and refusal of Rosmer, and then reads in the second passage, in Rebecca's outburst of denial, the deeper secret she has concealed from herself, and knowing it now, conceals from the others. It's Freud's "discovery" that the pattern of Rebecca's psychological career replicates the pattern of his psychoanalytic "thesis." It is made possible by his further discovery that what remains unrevealed at the play's end, the underlying guilt of incest, follows "logically" from the pattern of Rebecca's responses. Ibsen, with his "wealth of the knowledge of the mind," understood Rebecca in this way too, but thanks to his care for his audience's sensibilities, revealed it to no one else.

Shaw's *Rosmersholm*[13]

Freud is not the first to recognize the intimate accord between his thinking and that of an author. Shaw too revels in his tight intellectual companionship with Ibsen; the two think as one in his *Quintessence of Ibsenism,* to the exclusion of all the critic-fools who read Ibsen in the light of their own moral prejudices. But Shaw, proselytizing for Ibsen's morality, bends Ibsen's so far in the direction of his own that agreeing with him requires forgetting half or more of Ibsen's text. Nevertheless, for the time in which he wrote it, when Ibsen was first being introduced to a shocked England, his polemic is on the mark and brilliantly ingenious.

Shaw's premise in a nutshell: the Idealist, even, and especially, the votary of Ibsen's "ideals," is the prime Ibsenian moral villain, worse than the worst Philistine; it is left to the lone Realist in a million to understand precisely the original moral posture of the dramatist. Shaw explains and exemplifies that Realist. And he does it for all of Ibsen's major plays up till the time of the writing of *The Quintessence*, illustrating in each the tragicomedy of Idealism – whether the Puritanical or the Ibsenian kind – and its failure to apprehend the novelty of Ibsen's moral thought.

Shaw, a late bloomer, was relatively young when he wrote *The Quintessence* (he was 34), and his Realist's skill in moral argument was to wait for later enrichment. At the time, it was this: Morality evolves. The evolution of its precepts was essentially the devolution of its most subversive but principle ideal: Duty. He writes:

> "What, during all these overthrowings of things sacred and infallible, has been happening to that pre-eminently sanctified thing, Duty?.... First there was man's duty to God, with the priest as assessor. That was repudiated; and then came Man's duty to his neighbor, with Society as the assessor. Will that too be repudiated, and be succeeded by Man's duty to himself, assessed by himself? If so, what will be the effect on Duty in the abstract? ....
> [When] the emancipated slave of God falls under the dominion of Society, which, having just reached a phase in which all the love is ground out of it by the

competitive struggle for money, remorselessly crushes him until, in due course of the further growth of his spirit or will, a sense at last arises in him of duty to himself. And when this sense is fully grown, which it hardly is yet, the tyranny of duty is broken; for when the man's God is himself; he, self-satisfied at last, ceases to be selfish. The evangelist of this last step must therefore preach the repudiation of duty. This, to the unprepared of his generation, is indeed the wanton masterpiece of paradox."[14]

Though the story Shaw tracks in detail is the same as Freud's, given the intent of his polemic, nothing in the two readings of *Rosmersholm* retains a vestige of common understanding; they make, at the least, two wildly different plays. It is a story, according to Shaw, "of the priest [Rosmers] who regards the ennobling of mankind as a sort of rare process of which his cloth gives him a monopoly, and the clever woman [Rebecca] who pictures a noble career for the man she loves, and devotes herself to help him achieve it." Rebecca, "an unpropertied orphan," a Radical and Freethinker, is at first an interloper in the staid precincts of Rosmersholm, and calculates (as in Freud's version) the demise of Mrs. Rosmers and the capture of Rosmer's love. But here is the wide parting between Freud and Shaw: after the death of Mrs. Rosmers, Rebecca's "low passion" for Rosmers undergoes a rapid elevation to a higher plane, in which her ambition is no longer centered on herself but on him alone, urging him to become a man of action, a Radical and a Freethinker. But this sudden about face from his respectably vapid program of "ennobling mankind" in general, provokes his conservative community to change tack from merely whispering about his relation to Rebecca, to threats of blackmail against this traitor to their party. Under accusation, Rosmers realizes the truth: his love for Rebecca, and his psychic complicity in his wife's suicide. To expiate his "crimes," he offers marriage to Rebecca, which she, "knowing the guilt is hers," refuses. Now Shaw takes Freud's liberties in reading the meanings of both Rosmer's and Rebecca's words in the play's last pages. Rosmer's demand that Rebecca make Beata's sacrifice — to commit suicide — to prove her ennobled love is answered cryptically by

Rebecca's: "I am under the power of the Rosmersholm view of life *now* [Shaw underscoring the word *now* to claim his own reading.] What I have sinned, it is fitting I should expiate."[15]

For Shaw, the significance of the play is in the ultimate contrast between Rosmer's "monstrousness" in "asking the woman to kill herself in order to restore the man's good opinion of himself," which is a lapse into "the *old fatal ideal* of expiation through sacrifice," and Rebecca's "higher light," in which "the woman's soul is free of this to the end." In a questionable reading, Shaw understands her uttering the single word *now* to be "a protest against the Rosmersholm view of life." And in her "expiation," Shaw grants her the very "virtue" he regularly scoffed at in all "womanly women:" in their double suicide, Shaw says, she "goes to her death *out of fellowship* with the man who is driven thither by the superstition which has destroyed his will." Shaw's already explained in his Preface that when men and women become equals, the woman gains the right to turn her back on womanly "duty" and be governed by her own will alone. And so, stretching the matter of the play to fit his frame, he posits for Rebecca a sacrificial deed "out of fellowship," which is precisely the one his "womanly women" were benighted enough to succumb to "out of duty."

A debased Rosmer and a transcendent Rebecca fit Shaw's moral scheme precisely, but Freud's discovering Rebecca's incest at the final moment of revelation, and Shaw's discovering her keen moral insight at the same moment, strain Freud's supposition that the play exemplifies transparent "logic."

Johnston's *Rosmersholm*[16]

More deeply explored and more intellectually consequential than either of these is Brian Johnston's analysis of *Rosmersholm,* which occupies a long and prominent section in his three-volume study of Ibsen's prose plays. In it, priority is given to one analytic approach alone: what we've called its "thematic structure;" in Johnston, its "Idea." "While watching an Ibsen play," he writes, "we are aware of a logic and a purpose driving the events, shaping its structure, and *the gradual unfolding of an idea, inherent at the beginning, which the total action is bringing to light.*"[17] Psychology in Freud's terms and morality in Shaw's are altogether put aside for a study of Ibsen's drama that subsumes both psychology and morality under the larger concern for the "Idea" that informs not only *Rosmersholm* but the entire "cycle" of Ibsen's last twelve prose plays. Johnston writes:

> "The psychology of *Rosmersholm,* for all its fascination at the realistic level, [is there] for the purpose of directing our attention through the particulars of the act to the wide-ranging universals. For this reason, Freud's famous study of Rebckka [*sic*], assuming in the fictional character the same unconscious drives as in the actual human being, must be viewed as an example of misdirected insights, for it relates the action and the speeches of the character to an inner psychological structure when these details, demonstrably, contribute to an objective esthetic and ideological structure. We must look at the politics of the play in exactly the same way as we look at the psychological; both indicate spiritual forces that have taken on a particular local habitation but which are, in their universal aspects, independent of local historical circumstances."[18]

The construction of the twelve plays as a single work is governed by that single overarching "idea," an "idea" in precise consonance with Hegel's analysis of history's dialectic. Very, *very* briefly, history in Hegel is the history of *Geist,* or Spirit, as it struggles through its historical stages of dialectical conflict to achieve a progressive "evolution of consciousness" which will inevitably eventuate in "Freedom." (Ibsen's very similar formulation is a progressively evolving program for "a nobility of character, of will, of spirit" "to make us free.") Not to put too negative a reading on this formulation, it advanced the ideals of Eighteenth Century Enlightenment which burgeoned throughout the Nineteenth Century, and in one guise or another provided for every late Nineteenth Century belief, without exception, a teleological notion of history's movement upward toward a variety of nebulous Absolutes. "Freedom," from Schiller to Ibsen, was one of them.

The stages along the way are described in Hegel's *Phenomenology of Spirit* as historical or "universal" dialectical struggles in each of the (separable) "periods" of European history from the Greek city-states to Hegel's own time.   In each of them, there is an interplay of forces in Spirit's struggle upward between barbarity and civilization, for example, or oppression and freedom, or tradition and enlightenment, their "dialectic" particular to each age.[19] Ibsen, in Johnston's reading, dramatizes the dialectical flux of these world-historical forces as they manifest themselves within the confines of the present "age," in late Nineteenth Century's domestic settings.   But it's Hegel's idea that the structure of the mind consists within itself of all its prior phases of existence.   And so, echoing the drama of Spirit's evolution, Ibsen's characters also contain the Past's residue *within* the Present.   In the process of recapitulating that Past, the contemporary world and its characters both struggle to go forward, and at the same time are held back by, the ideologies of the past.   Ibsen's focus, then, is on the *archetypal conflicts beneath* the apparent drama and disorder of his characters' everyday lives.

Dramatically, the consequence of all this is first in the *"design"* of Ibsen's characters.   They are set in "dialectical balance," each representing more than a personal self — each also a counter, a propositional "meaning," within the dialectic.   But their humanity, insists Johnston, is far from lost in serving their function; the very essence of the dialectic is *struggle,* and the positioning of these "signifying" characters is in terms of the struggle they undergo, both with their opposites and within themselves.   Consequently, in Johnston's understanding, the play is composed of a "latticework" of characters, whose *self*-relations and *inter*-relations impinge on and repeat one another.   In a more abstract sense, all the characters in the play equal *one* character, since the composite of all of them is that "character" struggling to overreach the Present and at the same time hold allegiance to the Past.

In *Rosmersholm*, the play Johnston considers "one of the most perfect of Ibsen's dramatic structures," the balance of characters pits Rebecca, the enlightener, "the combater of oppressive ghosts," against Rosmer and Rosmersholm, with their "civilization" and old tradition. But the "negative" of Rebecca is initially her impure motives, her still-inadequate emancipation, and the "negative" of Rosmer's world is its oppression and superstition. And so "Rebekka and Rosmer, like the protagonists of Greek tragedy, [are] both the vehicles and the victims of universal forces." Aligned with Rebecca's "enlightenment" are two secondary characters who represent the inadequate and failed versions of enlightenment, Ulrich Brendel and Mortensgaard; and with Rosmer, the oppression of Dr. Kroll, the superstition of Mrs. Helseth, and the "ghost of the past" of Beata.

The studied symmetry of all this is reinforced by Johnston's depiction of the "Idea's" progression through the play (the stages of the struggle of the forces of "Tradition" and "Enlightenment") and the detailed hints – the symbolic guides – connecting the play's current world-historical struggle with its forbears – in this case, the period of Enlightenment preceding the French Revolution, and further back, the barbaric Germanic hordes besieging traditional Roman civilization. The freight of meaning is borne *in part* by the present-tense action, but it's these stores of details and subtly significant moments in the action that reflect the wide scope of the "world-historical" drama of which this current drama is one stage and one instance.

"The grave closing moments of the play," concludes Johnston, "round out the great themes of its argument… Though each no longer can rejoin the stream of life,… they can between them affirm the reality of the potent spiritual union of their disparate traditions."[20] It is a mutual transformation: Rebekka's "ruthless will," the negative of her "enlightenment," is transformed by the spirit of Rosmersholm; Rosmer's "ability to articulate" his demand for her sacrifice [that she commit suicide for him] "reveals to what an extent he, too, has absorbed her courageous will." The end of the drama is transcendent and Wagnerian, concluding this "stage" of the Spirit's struggle – but it is only a way-station in the Cycle: "death is the dialectical consummation of a particular spiritual form that will remain incomplete, and therefore invalid, until it is consummated… Rosmer and Rebekka are given the dignity of spiritual forces raised to such a level that they alone can pass judgment on themselves." Remote from the psychological and political/ethical readings in Freud and Shaw, Johnston's

Rosmer and Rebecca, themselves their only worthy judges, "consummate" – in their "assent to death" – their spiritual affirmation.

The scrutiny in depth of each of Ibsen's prose plays as it is fitted into its place in the *uber-drama's* sequence, is impressive in precision and detail, and, given the attribution to Ibsen's cycle of Hegel's thesis, the pursuit of paradigmatic associations in the plays to world-historical movements, must be recognized as more than mere intellectual ingenuity. It's an instructive example of a technique of analysis that, in ambition, breaks the bounds of what ordinarily passes for "contextual" analysis. It's geared to opening up an avenue of understanding of drama that goes far beyond – as Johnston himself is proud to point out – the usual parameters of dramatic analysis. Johnston's analytic perspective in exploring Ibsen opens the door to world history, to world literature, to world myth, and most particularly, to the world of thought itself as it is woven into the understanding of a single work, so that that work may be understood within the framework of its largest conceivable intellectual context.

That is his ambition, and his analysis of Ibsen is his demonstration of its efficacy. In his reading of Ibsen in the light of Hegel, how large is that context? Putting aside the rhetorical afflatus of Hegelian terms and regarding his analysis in skeletal reduction to its sense, it is not, as Johnston claims, an expansion of meaning and relevance, but in fact its severe reduction and simplification, not different in kind from Freud's and Shaw's. Why not?

The attempt to carve out a drama's "statement" from a reassembling of its explicit facts is not different from the attempt to conceive of the French Revolution's meaning from an assemblage of *its* explicit facts. Both harness themselves at once to a different process altogether: in both cases, the reading of its meaning is accomplished by a *displacement* of the object – the play or the Revolution – to a clean and quiet place where it can be reconstituted in metaphoric recollection and representation, where selectivity and omission are automatically harnessed to a higher purpose. As we've already pointed out, in that clean and quiet place, a conceptual framework waits, within which no discovery is ever made – only corroboration of its givens and its certainties. In each of our three critical essayists, that "ideological" or "ethical" or "psychological" framework is emblazoned on and in the process of thinking, of imagining, of concluding. The three "analyses" cannot contradict or qualify one another; they can only shy away from one another. Given the same dramatic "facts," given the same ostensible connections between events, they are three remotely different seers and hearers and processors that can only regard the others as looking at and listening to something else.

Whether in Freud, in Shaw, or in Johnston, whether the "concept" is flimsily exemplified as in Shaw or more solidly as in Johnston, the "fit" of the analysis to the waiting frame is guaranteed – no matter what the "structure" and no matter what the object of analysis. Conceive for a moment that *Rosmersholm* is drawn to the measure of Kieregaard or Jansenism or Islam or Maimonides. Perfect fit. Given any object of analytic potential, there is no problem of relevance, no drama's text that cannot be illuminated in all its secret meanings, within the folds of any fixed construct pictured in any mind. Every detail fits, every one that doesn't is a counter-example, every one that's baffling is holding its secret for only the time it takes for ingenuity to ferret it out. They are, in a way, like the conventional construct of the dramatic form itself – but a new instance, each one, of the possibility of the stability of meaning. Like the drama's inherent construct, the analytic construct is a design, and it is compelling or not exactly as a drama is – if one is still seeking in fictional forms for such happy reassurance: it envisions the *idea* of summary certainty. Implicit in Freud and in Shaw is the same fulfillment of diagram as Johnston makes explicit. Implicit in both is the ultimate completion toward which the single analysis of a play hopes.

"RANDOM" FLOW OF THOUGHT

But there are those for whom the zeal in that hope is either dampened or gone, who see these constructs as so many castles in air, and done, they think, with that kind of innocence, don't even need shoring up against their ruins. For their sake, let's go back by way of conclusion to that picture of the patron watching a play or a film somewhere between dreaming and paying attention. Let's suppose he is not at all seduced by drama's initial seductions, that he agrees that single sentences do not necessarily hold single thoughts, and that whether they do or not, it's of no concern to him. In other words, divested of the ambition to reverence "constructs," he surrenders to a different way of "thinking" drama altogether. He is therefore in a position to note the flow of words and sentences more than the apparatus of "constructs," and has resigned himself to a kind of drama – the best of contemporary drama, that is – which no longer speaks as traditional drama usually did: in whole sentences meaning them to be uttering whole thoughts. Belief systems run, as we know, very deep. The assurance that the words and sentences were saying it all meant that listening for the whole sense of the drama, as well as the whole of its life, was in what was being *uttered*, and not in what was being withheld. And there remains the deep and lasting pleasure of hearing that Seventeenth Century text that needed no subtext, and its sentences and words that needed no additions to their sensuousness and opulence; and there is, one must suppose, a sense of loss that that assurance of the fullness of words and sentences can't be trusted any more, and so a new and very different kind of *saying* of meaning, profound and subtle meaning, is borne by our contemporary modes of dramatic discourse. And it's based on this understanding:

That the deadliest, dullest dialogue now is dialogue that speaks in single sentences, each of which bears the burden of a single thought. Why has it become such bad dialogue? Why is it so bereft of meaning now – the kind of meaning once so rich, so alive? It has, of course, still the great value of clarity, but it also has now the great defect of being detachable from the speaker, and of betraying the more significant value of dialogue, which is – more than its statements of facts or of logical propositions – the revelation of the speaker's person. That there is such a person speaking now, is in the evidence of the flow of thought *behind* his speech, but also the evidence of its inexpressibility – that it cannot be fit into words. *Belief*, after all, in words saying everything is now as much in question as is solid structure and abiding meaning.

Both these evidences – of thought going on behind speech, and that that thought can never be put into speech, exists only in dialogue in which something is missing, in which something is clearly not being said. This has everything to do with what, from moment to moment, we're listening *for*.

Let's go back for a moment to our missing keys: "Look in the fridge, for God's sake." The essential difference between that demand in real talk and in dramatic talk is that the practical reason for its being said in a drama is hardly listened to because of our deeper concern with who is saying it – and to get from that saying the imputation of a living being. The spectator's assumption that there *is* such a living being inside the character is that his command about the keys is only a partial expression, or possibly a substitute expression, or even the equivalent of a "silence" that substitutes *for* an expression, as the character *aims toward, or thrusts toward,* the possible thoughts he could be signifying of those running in his head, and that he's jabbing at one or another of the possible ways of saying it. In profoundly crafted modern dialogue – in Mamet, in Pinter, in Shepard – almost nothing is spoken of what is in fact being said, leaving us wide windows of opportunity *around* the lines of dialogue to infer that richness, or that jumble of thoughts, lying behind spoken words.

It is not "subtext." As we've already said, unspoken "subtext" is merely the controlling logic of the play's action, in other words, the plot, and its function is wholly wedded to that plot. The "surround-sound" of the imaged thoughts out of which the actual lines of dialogue are spoken, on the other hand, is made up of the freight of random insights, interim, fleeting recognitions, off-center, out-of-the-loop comments in the head that no dialogue, no matter how explicit or how dense in its telling, can possibly cram into words if it is to be intelligible as talk to other characters in the play, or to us. And yet it is precisely that flow of thought, above and behind, which in fact defines the human activity of thinking and supposing and imagining and inventing in that continuous flow with which we may be privately familiar in ourselves, but for which we have no avenue, and expect no avenue, for its total expression from others. Were the presence of that "flow" lost to the language of the drama, its characters would present themselves to us as effigies carved in wood.

THE ACTOR AS PLAYWRIGHT II

We return, then, for salvation to the function of the actor as playwright. It is the most critical function of all for the life of the play, and it relates most entirely to the spectator long before he becomes the critic, the spectator in the guise in which he wins his deepest and most lasting experience of the play, in, once again, random, unstructured passivity.

That spectator, we may recall, responded to a different sense of experience altogether.   It consisted of gleaning largely disconnected bits of insight from the drama's moments, and being indifferent to the labor of analysis, it derived its pleasure and profit from passive absorption, catching with neither critical intent nor analytic anxiety unstructured intimacies of recognition and private moments of discovery if and as such pleasures offer themselves. His own connection, then, the spectator discovers, is less with the play as play than with actor as person.   It is he who is the generator of revealing and subtle insights, and contributes to the "statements" that insinuate themselves from the play as a succession of independent moments, rather than as a whole design.

But no more than the playwright can the actor "express," that is, recite or even "indicate," that wealth of the mind's activity. But if one watches closely the performance of great, or even greatly intelligent actors, one is overpowered by its silent presence. It is, in fact, the supremely distinguishing mark of the richly endowed actor, that he says fully without saying what can't in any case be said.   In deep rapport with his interior life, he intimates its presence.

And oddly, it is the unconscious bond with that interior life that is the bridge between drama and spectator, the silent conversation entered into while the actor is acting. Some pages back, we called it "follow through" on the actor's part.[21] More than that, it's the sign of his humanity – beyond type, beyond kind, beyond "character," beyond plot function, beyond subtext, it is the subtle evidence of his interior life that the spectator is privileged to share.

If dialogue is the inadequate filter for the statement that means to say it all, the revelation of acting is in the discovery, and the recovery, of that other statement for which the words are either an intentional miss or a substitute. And it's in that process that the play's thought is genuinely glanced at – the thought that is memorable, that is gleaned from the actor's saying. And it's this plane of "meaning" that exceeds by far the blandness and the neatness of the play's ostensible statement – particularly the one that is shrinkable to the length of a sentence, the one that has been packaged before the play was written, the one that is so hoary as to be dismissible as sermon. And that, paradoxically, is where the play's genuinely lasting, genuinely cherished meanings lie if they lie anywhere, not formally structured, not even necessarily coherent, and not certainly divorced from the play as a temporal event, but fleeting, quickly emerging and quickly dying, caught by the spectator's sympathetic resonance, for a moment, then another moment, on the fly.

***

AFTERWORD

There is a story, a true story, of the Kansas City slaughterhouse that sends an army of pigs through a declining ramp fitted with sets of barrier-locks preventing the pigs from backing up and losing ground. Once in a lock, they're committed; lock after lock they're committed more and more and can't retreat. But now and then there's pig that gets close to the last barrier, hears the terrified squealing of his brothers who are being slaughtered *en masse*, and decides, no. Turning around, hunching his way through the oncoming pack, slipping and sliding through the whips of the cattle-hands along the route, he gets close to the end of the run. But not out. Every once in a great while, there is one like that, and when the rest of the pigs are all in the slaughterhouse, the cattle-hands come back and take this one back alone, lock by barrier-lock. Either way, he ends up dead, but the hands, for all their trouble, acknowledge and remember the courage of this one, a hero among the pigs.[1] They're our real and only hope: the pigs who say no, and run for dear life the other way.

***

APPENDIX
ON PURGATION

In Aristotle's view, the perfection of tragedy is achieved when at its end, moral and emotional response are fused, fall into lockstep, and bring about the spectator's moral, ideological and emotional ease. This is accomplished by *Purgation* – the most famous, but the most ambiguous term in the *Poetics*. How is it said to function? By a "purging" of pity and/or fear and similar emotions. Nietzsche called this a "medicinal" theory of tragedy – excreting, so to speak, the pity and fear which the spectator accumulates until the last moments of the tragedy, when terminal judgment is visited on the protagonist as he succeeds or fails, and the spectators' bowels, so to speak, which held that emotional cargo, drop their load. But Nietzsche's mockery of the notion need not be entirely shared; a more generous view of *Purgation* might be wrested from several passages in which the notion is clarified:

In a passage blaming the tragedian Agathon for failing to stay within the limit of a story's "proper magnitude," (i.e., its proper scale and length,) Aristotle praises him, on the other hand, for "his marvelous skill in [his] effort to hit the popular taste" by producing "a tragic effect that satisfies the moral sense." But how does Agathon hit this "popular taste?" By doing the very opposite of what Aristotle recommends elsewhere as the proper way to produce the tragic effect: "This effect," he writes, "is produced [by Agathon] when the clever rogue... is outwitted, or the brave villain defeated." Agathon is flattering the "popular," or vulgar, taste by his tragedy's overcoming the "cleverness" of the rogue and the "bravery" of the villain, and despite those potential appeals, still punishing their vice – with audience approval – an easy, and easily satisfying, fantasy. The spectator wishes that such a thing should always happen, and Agathon provides him with illusory instances of it – an insipid way, Aristotle implies, of providing gratification at play's end.

A more genuine "moral sense" that must be satisfied is not so easily assuaged. The ordinary norms of expectation and belief – good rewarded, evil punished – subvert the complex experience that Aristotle predicates for tragedy, which involves (1) a profound and complex emotional response, (2) a confirmation of moral propriety, and at the same time, (3) *the shock of surprise* at how the revelation of moral propriety comes about.

If all this is to come about through the perfect collusion of morality and emotion, it's useful to ask: Which morality? Which emotion?   Certainly not the simple "fitting reward, fitting punishment" of Agathon and his insipid audience.   It takes an apparent *imbalance* between the protagonist's initial deed and its final judgment to bring about the peculiar emotional charge proper to tragedy, and at the same time the revelation of the ultimate moral composition to which tragedy subscribes.   To wit: the representation of a protagonist preeminently good, who through a "fatal flaw" of character or possibly through the "flaw" of ignorance, is destroyed by a punishment far beyond the deserving of that "flaw."   Because of that non-relation between moral expectation and final punishment, the spectator experiences shock – the shock of a perceived imbalance in moral propriety.   And to increase that experience, there's that mandatory moment of Reversal when the likely outcome had seemed to be, or might have been, the reward of his virtue, or at least his escape from the consequences of his "flaw," but which by *surprise* turns out – suddenly – to be the opposite.   Aristotle explains its logic in this way:

> Tragedy is an imitation not only of a complete action, but of events inspiring fear or pity.   Such an effect is best produced *when events come on us by surprise;* and the effect is heightened when, *at the same time, they follow as cause and effect.*   The tragic *wonder* will then be greater than if they happened of themselves or by accident; *for even coincidences are most striking when they have an air of design.* [Italics added] (Butcher translation, Chapter 9.)

"An air of design." In other words, an intimation of an underlying design of cause-effect transcending unlikelihood. What greater reassurance can one have of inherent order than unlikelihood, no matter how astonishing, turning out to be, or rather *surfacing as* the connective tissue of what at first seemed to be ill-fitting and non-sequential. The sudden recognition of that apparently hidden design – the suggestion, if not the revelation, of cosmic coherence – has the reassuring force of religion or superstition. We can go to bed not superficially but deeply reassured.

It is precisely that reassurance of the stability of cause-effect undergirding events that solaces pity and/or fear – the pity and fear that constitute the human reactions to the protagonist's apparently undeserved punishment. And so moral disjuncture elicits our emotional terror and/or pity, but the concurrent glimpse of *inherent* design becomes its emotional assuaging –that is, the surrender of those emotions. The "pity and terror" experienced at this ending, together with their deep assuaging, "produces," in Aristotle's formulation, "a tragic effect that satisfies the moral sense."

And so conventional structure, along with its ostensibly simple sequence of cause–and-effect, carries heavy freight that bears with it fixed prescriptions as to inherent beliefs, so strongly powered by custom that they traditionally succeed in eradicating all other options – options that answer more to the purpose of particular times, particular places, and to the many exigencies of human experience. For human experience hardly bears out, with the uniformity dramatic practice demands that it do, the firmly set stabilities that more or less invisibly underpin the structural demands of the familiar design of plotted action.

***

ENDNOTES

1. PLOT STRUCTURE

1. *"peripeteia [reversal]...anagnorisis [recognition]:"* Aristotle's definitions: "Reversal of the Situation is a change by which the action veers round to its opposite, subject always to our rule of probability or necessity. Thus, in the Oedipus, the messenger comes to cheer Oedipus and free him from his alarms about his mother, but by revealing who he is, he produces the opposite effect.... "Recognition, as the name indicates, is a change from ignorance to knowledge, producing love or hate between the persons destined by the poet for good or bad fortune. *The best form of recognition is coincident with a Reversal of Situation,* as in the Oedipus.... [W]e may recognize or discover whether a person has done a thing or not. But the recognition which is the most intimately connected with the plot and action is, as we have said, recognition of persons. This recognition, combined with Reversal, will produce either pity or fear; and actions producing these effects are those which, by our definition, Tragedy represents. Moreover, it is upon such situations that the issues of good or bad fortune will depend. Recognition, then, being between persons, it may happen that one person only is recognized by the other – when the latter is already known – or it may be necessary that the recognition be on both sides...." [Italics added] [*The Poetics,* tr. S.H. Butcher, Chapter 11]

2. "The criminal you are seeking:" W.B. Yeats translation, in The Collected Works of W.B. Yeats: Volume 1, The Plays, NY, Scribner, 2001, p.375, line 213.

3. *"Action Structure:" "Activity"* should not be confused with *"Action,"* – though sometimes it's more attractive and agreeable. Although it can provide pleasure and relief for spectators, it is not really essential to the functioning of a scene, or of a play. But its presentation is usually elaborate, sometimes monopolizing much of the play's time, protracting its time for the sake of its own display, and though accomplishing only a little for the ongoing action, is frequently the most attractive ingredient of the entertainment. A classic example: in performances of *Romeo and Juliet* and *Hamlet* in Western mining towns in the Nineteenth Century, it was the duels between Romeo and Tybalt, and between Hamlet and Laertes, that made the evening for the miners. And the travelling actors – some of the most famous of their time – protracted those moments with

brilliant displays of swordsmanship, exploiting what was easier and more popular to exploit than story or text. But note: the longer the duel went on, the longer the action proper marked time. What the actual "action" was breathlessly waiting for was for the duel to be over and done with so it could get to its result, which result (the win or loss) was the next step needed to propel the next unit of action. It seems almost a shame to call these displays merely delays or downright irrelevances. Though their distension is an unwelcome intermission from the action proper (the whole ten rounds played out in fight films; the extended mayhem of the shoot-outs in cop movies; the battles and car-or horse- or plane-contests or races on land, sea or air which coopt most of the screen time in war or chase movies just as they coopted most of the stage time in Nineteenth-Century nautical or steeplechase melodramas) the case is easily made that like the Western miners watching Shakespeare, the audience for the fight or battle or horserace is there more for the sake of that irrelevance than for the main menu. There is no period in the history of the drama when room was not made, or palpitating anxiety not given, even when only the severest action-structures were tolerated as art, to these, in the strictest sense, excrescences. But the distinction is still in itself absolute: activity is not action, no matter how physically strenuous, how dazzling, how brilliantly executed, how positively thrilling it may be. We really ought to defer here to Aristotle: what may be removed from the action, he says, without injury to the plot, is not needed; still, the plays and movies that better understand audience's paranoias and anxieties think it is.

4. *"Plot is the soul of tragedy:"* "Plot, then, is the first principle, and as it were, the soul of tragedy." Aristotle (384-322BC), *Poetics*, Ch.6, *tr.* S.H. Butcher, in J.H. Smith and E.W. Parks, eds, *The Great Critics,* NY, Norton, 1932, p.10.

5. *Strindberg's Road to Damascus:* in Part Three of the trilogy (1900-01), Act III, sc.1. The "Tempter," conducting the defense of the accused, searches for the actual initiator of the crime, and finally brings to witness "The Serpent" in the Garden of Eden, whose answer to his question, "Now, Serpent, who was it that beguiled you?" is choked off by the trial's participants, who are outraged by the question and its anticipated answer. [tr. Graham Rawson, NY, Grove Press, 1960]

6: *"Montagues and Capulets:"* In *Romeo and Juliet,* Act 1, sc.1, the two rival "households," "from ancient grudge," as the Prologue tells us (though we never learn the cause of their quarrel) are fighting in the streets of Verona. Because of their division, the "pair of star-crossed lovers" from "the fatal loins of these two foes" ultimately take their lives, and out of mutual sorrow (and possible chagrin), the quarreling families are at last reconciled.

7. *"Macbeth fighting rebellion:"* In *Macbeth,* Act 1, sc.2, a soldier reports to King Duncan Macbeth's battle victory over rebels against the crown. Grateful Duncan at once rewards his faithful officer with a new title – Thane of Cawdor.

8. *"Children of Cadmus:"* At play's opening, King Oedipus is surrounded by beseeching citizens whom he addresses: "Children, descendants of old Cadmus, why do you carry the branches of suppliants?" (tr. W.B. Yeats, *op.cit.,* lines 1-5)

9. *Kafka's Metamorphosis:* Franz Kafka's (1883-1924) novella, 1916. [*The Metamorphosis and Other Writings,* ed. Helmut Kiesel, NY, Continuum, 2002]

10. *"Cassius awakens Brutus' inherent moral hostility:"* Julius Caesar, Act 1, sc.2., lines 55-121, in which Cassius, discerning in the "veiled look" of Brutus his unspoken fears concerning Caesar's ambition, makes them explicit.

11. *"implanted by witches and wife:"* Macbeth, Act I, sc.3, lines 47-50, in which the witches on "the blasted heath" unsettle Macbeth by predicting his becoming "King hereafter;" followed by Act I, sc.5, lines 55-74, in which Lady Macbeth suggests that Duncan at his arrival should be murdered.

12. *"It must be by his death:"* Julius Caesar, Act II, sc.1, lines 10-34: Brutus's reasoning begins with his conclusion, to which he gradually persuades himself: "It must be by his death," he says, and then goes on to justify his already-formed decision. The speech is a brilliant study of an easily deluded mind's self-persuasion made up of fanciful metaphors trumping his repeated recollections of fact by verbal fiction: "[F]or my part, I know no personal cause to spurn him," he admits, nor can he recollect a single instance in which Caesar exhibited any of the overweening ambition of which Cassius has accused him. And yet, "'tis common proof that lowliness is young ambition's ladder." And so, the better part of wisdom, he concludes, is to "think him as a serpent's egg, / Which hatched,

would as his kind grow mischievous, /And kill him in the shell." This, Brutus's first speech of justification, captures the ongoing fantasy of metaphors always percolating in his mind that will later govern all his reasonings and all his decisions.

13. *"Conspirators meet, Brutus:" Julius Caesar,* Act II, sc. 1, lines 86-229, in which the success of the plan for taking power after the assassination of Caesar is undercut at its birth by Brutus's insistence that Cicero not be joined to the conspiracy, and that Anthony not be assassinated together with Caesar.

14. "Portia's remonstrance:" Julius Caesar, Act II, sc.1, lines 233-309, in which Portia urges her husband Brutus to share his secret plans with her; he tempers, and doesn't.

15. "Macbeth's interior debate:" Macbeth, Act I, sc.3, lines 127-142:

"Two truths are told

As happy prologue to the swelling act

Of the imperial theme...

This supernatural soliciting cannot be ill, cannot be good. If ill,

Why hath it given me earnest of success,

Commencing me truth? I am Thane of Cawdor.

If good, why do I yield to that suggestion

Whose horrid image doth unfix my hair

And make my seated heart knock at my ribs

Against the use of nature?"

16. "Battle of Agincourt": *Henry V,* Act IV, scenes 3-6.

17. "To be thus is nothing.... fears in Banquo": *Macbeth,* Act III, sc. 1, lines 49-52.

18. "Tomorrow and tomorrow": *Macbeth,* Act V, sc. 5, lines 17-26.

19. "Arm, arm, and out!": *Macbeth,* Act 5, sc. 5, lines 45-51.

20. "Macbeth murdering Duncan:" Act II, sc. 1&2.

21.   Clarissa Harlowe: *Clarissa, or the history of a young lady (1748)*, Samuel
      Richardson's epistolary novel in seven volumes and one million
      words – certainly the longest and possibly the greatest of English
      novels, the triumphant climax of sentimental   literature in the
      eighteenth century.   It follows in excruciating detail the "anatomy
      of the female heart," recounting Clarissa's "fatal misstep" eloping
      with the libertine Lovelace,   and the subsequent miseries she
      endures during her smitten conscience's long journey to death. [ed.
      Angus Ross, NY, Penguin Books, 1985.]

22.   *de Sade's Justine:* (1791) J. V. Girouard; (1953) Olympia Press

23.   "Plato rails and Aristotle mollifies:" See Endnote p.165, below

24.   *Lady Windermere's Fan:* (1892) The play's critical moment occurs in
      Act III when Lady Windermere is on the verge of being
      compromised by the fan she accidently left in Lord Darlington's
      drawing room. Lady Windermere fled to Lord Darlington from the
      ball at her home when she suspected that her husband's new
      mistress was his invited guest. She is rescued from discovery when
      Mrs. Erlynne, her suspected rival but in reality her own mother,
      steps out of hiding and claims the fan for her own, compromising
      her own already tarnished reputation to spare Lady Windermere's.
      The tension mounts during the excruciatingly long chitchat among
      the visiting gentlemen while the fan, on the carpet, waits to be
      noticed. [Oscar Wilde, *Plays, Prose Writings and Poems,* NY, Dutton,
      1962.]

25.   *Strindberg's Miss Julie:* (1888), tr. Edwyn Bjorkman, NY, Dover
      Publications, 1992.

26.   Therese Racquin (1873): tr., Kathleen Boutall, in Seeds of Modern
      Drama, (1963), Vol. III of Norris Houghton, ed., Laurel
      Masterpieces of Continental Drama.

2. MANIPULATING STRUCTURE

1.   "Open City:" (1945). Italian film directed by Roberto Rossellini,
      produced by Minerva Films, SA, screenplay by Sergio Amidei and
      Roberto Rossellini.

2.   *Ibsen's Rosmersholm,* (1887). Henrik Ibsen (1828-1906), *Rosmersholm,*
      in tr. and ed., Rolf Fjelde, *Ibsen, The Complete Major Prose Plays,* NY,
      Penguin, 1978.

3. Schnitzler's "The Duel" (1901). Arthur Schnitzler (1862-1931), [in *Lieutenant Gusti*, tr. Richard L. Simon, St. Paul, MN, Green Integer, 2003]

4. *L'Avventura:* (1960. Italian film directed by Michelangelo Antonioni, produced by Cino del Duca, screenplay by Antonioni and Elio Bartolini.

5. *Poirot:* Hercule Poirot, the fictional detective in thirty of Agatha Christie's novels. He shares with the other iconic detectives the distance between his single-minded devotion to sleuthing – his "logic," his "order and method" – and singularities of person and style: his military, upward-climbing moustache, his dyed hair, his limp, his scrupulous, vain tidiness, his dandified but out-of-fashion clothes, his dodge in manner and speech in order to be mistaken professionally for a simpleminded charlatan. [Agatha Christie, *Hercule Poirot's Casebook,* Putnam Publ. Group 2004.]

6. *Chekhov's The Three Sisters:* (1901), Anton Chekhov (1860-1904), *Plays,* tr. Michael Frayn, Methuen, 1988.]

7. *"stories… Maupassant… Schnitzler."* Guy de Maupassant (1850-1893), regarded as the greatest of French short story writers, shared with the Viennese Schnitzler mordant analysis of bourgeois life in late nineteenth and turn-of-the-century Europe. Olga Knipper, Chekhov's actress wife, while playing in *The Three Sisters* in Moscow, wrote to the ailing Chekhov in Yalta an extravagant compliment: "You are my great genius. You are the Russian Maupassant." For Olga Knipper, they shared the same uplifting pessimism.

8. *Martin Esslin: The Theatre of the Absurd,* 3rd. edition, NY, Random House, 2004, pp.75-76.

   Waiting for Godot: (1952) Samuel Beckett (1906-89), *Waiting for Godot,* NY, Grove Press, 1954.

   Endgame: (1955-57), NY, Grove Press, 1958.

9. *"Stein… landscape:"* Gertrude Stein (1874-1946): "If a play was exactly like a landscape then there would be no difficulty about the emotion of the person looking on at the play being behind or ahead of the play because the landscape does not have to make acquaintance…. [I]t is there and so the play being written the relation between you at any time is so exactly that that it is of no importance unless you look at it…. I did write Four Saints [in Three Acts]… it made a landscape and the movement in it was like

a movement in and out with which anybody looking on can keep in time."

("*In and out*," that is to say, *forward and back*, avoiding progressive time.)

["Plays," in *Lectures in America*, NY, Modern Library, Inc., 1935, pp.122; 131.]

[*Four Saints in Three Acts* (1934), an opera, score by Virgil Thomson, in Gertrude Stein, *Last Operas and Plays*, ed. Carl van Vechten, NY, Rinehart, 1949.]

10. *"Arlecchino... trip to the moon:"* a *lazzo* (comic bit interrupting the action) of the seventeenth-century Parisian commedia dell'arte actor Domenico Biancolelli who played the masked character of Arlecchino. In his monologue, he describes in detail his fantastic journey to the moon. [In Pierre Louis Duchartre, *The Italian Comedy*, NY, Dover, 1969, pp. 143-144.]

11. *Grabbe*: Christian Dietrich Grabbe (1801-1836) German "anti-Romantic" playwright, had, like his like-minded contemporary Buchner, turned with despair from all "idealist" notions of structure and causality. In his play, *Jest, Satire, Irony and Deeper Meaning*, he goes so far as to destroy the "illusion" of the plot by stepping into the action in his own person. [NY, Ungar, 1979.]

12. *Buster Keaton* (1895-1966). In one of his silent films, fleeing from the Keystone Kops, he runs into a movie theatre and onto the screen, joins in the film's action, and temporarily escapes.

13. *The Importance of Being Earnest:* (1895), Oscar Wilde (1854-1900), Orchesis Press Reprint ed, 1990. The most sagacious and the most – as he himself claimed – "advanced" critic of the 1890's, Bernard Shaw, who was himself at the same time tracking new paths in comedy, missed entirely the cunning of Wilde's mock:

"The play has a plot – a gross anachronism; there is a scene between the two girls in the second act quite in the literary style of Mr.[W.S.] Gilbert, and almost inhuman enough to have been conceived by him; the humor is adulterated by stock mechanical fun to an extent that absolutely scandalizes one in a play with such an author's name to it.... [T]he general effect is that of a farcical comedy dating from the [eighteen] seventies.... brought up to date as far as possible by Mr. Wilde in his now completely formed style. Such is the impression left by the play on me. But I find other critics, equally entitled to respect, declaring that The Importance of Being Earnest is a strained effort of Mr. Wilde's ultra-modernity, and that it could never have been written but for the opening up of entirely new paths in drama last year by [my own] Arms and the Man. At which I confess to chuckle.... In The Importance of Being Earnest, there is plenty of this rib-tickling: for instance, the lies, the deceptions, the cross-purposes, the sham mourning, the christening of two grown men, the muffin eating, and so forth. These could only have been raised from the farcical plane by making them occur to characters who had, like Don Quixote, convinced us of their reality and obtained some hold on our sympathy. But the unfortunate moment of Gilbertism breaks our belief in the humanity of the play."

14. "Wedekind's Lulu plays": Benjamin Franklin Wedekind (1864-1918), [The Lulu Plays: Earth Spirit, Pandora's Box, tr. Carl Mueller, Greenwich, CN, Fawcett Publications, 1967.]

3. RETROGRESSIVE ACTION

1. "*the question of Oedipus' 'tragic flaw':*" The relevant passages in the *Poetics* that bear on the idea of the "tragic flaw" are these: 1) "A perfect tragedy should... imitate actions which excite pity and fear, this being the distinctive mark of tragic imitation. It follows plainly, in the first place, that the change of fortune presented must not be the spectacle of a virtuous man brought from prosperity to adversity: for this moves neither pity nor fear; it merely shocks us. Nor, again, that of a bad man passing from adversity to prosperity: for nothing can be more alien to the spirit of Tragedy; it possesses no single tragic quality; it neither satisfies the moral sense nor calls forth pity or fear. Nor, again, should the downfall of the utter villain be exhibited. A plot of this kind would, doubtless, satisfy the moral sense, but it would inspire neither pity nor fear; for pity is aroused by unmerited misfortune, fear by the misfortune of a man like ourselves. Such an event, therefore, will be neither pitiful nor terrible. There remains then the character between these two extremes – that of a man who is not eminently good and just, yet whose misfortune is brought about *not by vice or depravity, but by some error or frailty*. He must be one who is highly renowned and prosperous – a personage like Oedipus, Thyestes, or other illustrious men of such families." [Italics added] [*Poetics*, S.H. Butcher, tr., Chapter 13]

2. *Citizen Kane:* (1941). Directed by Orson Welles, produced by RKO Radio Pictures and Mercury Productions, screenplay by Herman J. Mankiewicz and Orson Welles.

3. *"air of design"*: Poetics, Ch. XI: "But again, Tragedy is an imitation not only of a complete action, but of events inspiring fear or pity. Such an effect is best produced when the events come on us by sunrise; and the effect is heightened when, at the same time, they follow as cause and effect. The tragic wonder will thee be greater than if they happened of themselves or by accident; for even coincidences are most striking when they have an air of design."

4. *Chinatown:* (1974). Directed by Roman Polanski, produced by Paramount Pictures, screenplay by Robert Towne.

5. *Sherlock Holmes:* Conan Doyle's exploitation of his detective ran through four novels and fifty-six short stories (written from 1883 to 1914) to become one of the most famous names in world fiction: the quixotic Victorian solver of crimes with miraculous powers of deduction based on the merest slivers of evidence.

6. *Philip Marlow:* Raymond Chandler's hard-boiled detective of the Twenties, a cynical private eye with a vestige of idealism and – unaccountable irrelevance – a liking for chess, poetry and quiet reflection. Raymond Chandler, *Collected Stories*, Everyman's Library, 2002

7. *Memento:* (2000). Directed by Christopher Nolan, produced by I Remember Productions, Newmarket Capital Group LLC, screenplay by Christopher and Jonathan Nolan.

8. *La Moustache:* (2005). Directed by Emmanuel Carrere, produced by Les Films des Tournelles, Pathe Renn Productions, France 3 Cinema, screenplay by Jerome Beaujour from the novel by Emmanuel Carrere.

9. *Ionesco, Bald Soprano:* (1950), Eugene Ionesco (1909 – 1994), *The Bald Soprano and Other Plays*, NY, Grove Press, 1950.

10. Strindberg's *Road to Damascus*: See Endnote for, Ch. 1, #5.

11. *The Father:* (1887), August Strindberg, *The Father*, tr. Michael Meyer, London, Methuen, 1976.

12. *The Dream Play* (1901;1906) in *Six Plays of Strindberg*, tr. E. Sprigge, Doubleday, 1955.

4. DOUBLE PROTAGONISTS AND CONFLICT

1. *"The Law of Conflict:"* Robert McKee, *Story*, NY, Harper-Collins, 1997, pp.210-211.

2: *"Hegel...on drama :"* "Dramatic action, however, is not confined to the simple and undisturbed execution of a definite purpose, but depends throughout *on conditions of collision*, human passion and characters, and leads therefore to actions and reactions, which in their turn call for some further resolution of conflict and disruption. What we have consequently before us are definite ends individualized in living personalities and situations pregnant with conflict... the final result presupposed... which has none the less to work out its tranquil resolution." [Italics added] [*The Philosophy of Fine Art*, tr. F.P.B. Osmaston, London, 1920, vol. IV, p.249.]

3. *"Hegel...on Sophocles' Antigone:"* (On the contradiction of ethical positions achieving tragic harmony at closure:) "The most complete form of this development is possible when the individuals engaged in conflict... stand fundamentally under the power of that against which they battle and consequently infringe that which (for their safety) they ought to respect. Antigone, for example, lives under the political authority of Creon... so that her obedience to the royal prerogative is an obligation. But Creon also... is under obligation to respect the sacred ties of relationship, and only by breach of this can give an order that is in conflict with such a sense. In consequence of this we find immanent in the life of both that which each respectively combats, and they are seized and broken by that very bond which is rooted in the compass of their own existence.... Among all the fine creations of the ancient and modern world... the 'Antigone' of Sophocles is from this point of view in my judgment the most excellent and satisfying work of art.:" [ibid, p. 318.]

4. *"Preparation, Complication and Resolution:* The origin of this breakdown is to be found in *The Poetics*, although Aristotle delineates only two of the terms, not three: "Every tragedy falls into two parts – Complication and Unraveling or Denouement.   Incidents extraneous to the action are frequently combined with a portion of the action proper, to form the Complication; the rest is the Unraveling. By the Complication I mean all that extends from the beginning of the action to the part which marks the turning-point to good or bad fortune. The Unraveling is that which extends from

the beginning of the change [the major plot Reversal] to the end."
[*Poetics,* Chapter 18]

The 17th century Spanish playwright, Lope de Vega, in his *"The New Art of Writing Plays in this Age,"* follows Aristotle's breakdown of the plot into two major parts, but – being the consummate popular playwright of his time, so much so that all plays in Spain became popularly known as "Lopes" – added a codicil to Aristotle to guarantee the audiences' breathless attention up to the last moment. He advised the novice playwright: Divide the matter of your play "into two parts, [and] see to the connection from the beginning until the action runs down; but do not permit the untying of the plot until reaching the last scene; for the crowd, knowing what the end is, will turn its face to the door."

But in explaining the breakdown of the three-act structure in which he wrote his eighteen hundred or so plays, he specifies the three parts which became the practical standard in Europe – whether for a three-act or a five-act play – from the seventeenth century on: "In the first act, set forth the case. In the second weave together the events, in such wise that until the middle of the third act one may hardly guess the outcome. Always trick expectancy; and hence it may come to pass that something quite far from what is promised may be left to the understanding." "Setting forth the case" became part one, the Preparation. Noticeably, in neoclassical tradition, the leisurely "setting forth" of part one delayed "weaving together the events" so considerably as to make one wonder at the patience of, for example, English Restoration audiences undergoing an act or so of enforced dramatic leisure until evidence of Complication could finally be sighted.   [Lope da Vega (1569-1635), *op.cit.,* in B.H. Clark and H. Popkin, eds., *European Theories of the Drama,* NY, Crown, Rev. Ed., 1965, p.66.]

5. *Machiavelli's Mandragola:* (1520), Niccolo Machiavelli (1469-1527), *Mandragola,* tr. A. and H. Paolucci, NY, Prentice Hall, 1957.

6. *"Scribe's Glass of Water:"* Eugene Scribe (1791-1661), *The Glass of Water,* tr. D. Bodeen, in *Camille and other Plays,* ed. Stephen Stanton, NY, Hill and Wang, 1957.

7. *"Dumas fils, Le Demi Monde:"* Alexandre Dumas (1824-1893), *Le Demi Monde* (1855), in Barrett Clark, ed. *World Drama, Vol. II,* Dover Publications, 1933.

8. "Albee, Who's Afraid of Virginia Woolf?" (1962). Edward Albee (b.1928), Who's Afraid of Virginia Woolf?(paperback) Signet Books, New American Library, 1983.

9. *In the Jungle of Cities:* (1923), Bertolt Brecht (1898-1956), *In the Jungle of Cities and Other Plays,* ed. and tr., Eric Bentley, NY, Grove Press, 1966.

10. "Scribe.... pointlessness": Dumas fils, a disciple who adopted in his own plays and at the same time rejected the Scribian formula, recognized the deeper source of his dominance in the theatre during the comfortable mid-century of burgeoning bourgeois prosperity: "Still, the drama owes one real innovation to him.... M. Scribe thought to add [to the Romantic's story of love and marriage] a good three percent income.... And so well did M. Scribe's ideal coincide with that of his public, that the public recognized him at once as its representative; and during a third of a century the high priest of this bourgeois religion celebrated mass every night at the altar of the half-crown."

[Alexandre Dumas *fils,* "Preface to *A Prodigal Father,"* (1868), in B.H. Clark and H. Popkin, *op. cit.,* p. 375.]

11. *Strangers on a Train:* (1951), directed by Alfred Hitchcock, produced by Warner Brothers Pictures, screenplay by Whitford Cook and Patricial Highsmith, from the novel by Highsmith.

12. *Laurel and Hardy:* Stain Laurel (1890-1965) and Oliver Hardy (1892-1957), the immensely popular team of slapstick comedians, from their silent short films beginning in 1919 through their transition to sound feature films in the Thirties to their retirement in 1950. Wikipedia on the Internet has a description of their signature routine, this time involving a third actor:

"A famous routine the team often performed was a bizarre kind of 'tit-for-tat' fight with an opponent. In the basic scenario, the pair would begin the fight by damaging something that the opponent valued, while the opponent did not defend himself. However, when the pair were finished, the opponent would then calmly retaliate by damaging something that Laurel and Hardy valued, while the pair strangely refrained from defending themselves. The pair then dispassionately retaliated with an escalating act of vandalism and so on, until both sides were simultaneously destroying property in front of each other. An early example is Laurel and Hardy's silent classic, Big Business."

13. *Schiller's Mary Stuart:* (1800), Friedrich von Schiller (1759-1805), *Mary Stuart,* tr. Walter Herderer, Continuum, 1990.

14. *The Father:* See Endnote Ch. 3, #11.

15. *"Hegel... conflict:"* Passage quoted in Endnote, Ch. 4, #3.

16: Arthur Miller's The Crucible (1953) : Arthur Miller (1915-   ), in Arthur Miller's Collected Plays, NY, Viking Press, 1957.

17. "Doctor Stockmann:" in Enemy of the People (1883), in Rolfe Fjelde, Ibsen, Prose Plays.

18. "latter-day Hegelian saints:"

"Rostand's Cyrano:" Edmond Rostand (1868-1918), *Cyrano de Bergerac* (1897). Cyrano, beggared and held in contempt by the enemies he's accumulated by his stubborn integrity, when he's at last murdered in the street, dies flaunting his pride in his *"panache."* [C.B. Johnson, series ed, NY, Pocket, 2004.]

Buchner's Danton:" Georg Buchner (1813-1837), *Danton's Death* (1835), Danton, defeated in his struggle with Robespierre's Reign of Terror, goes to his death with the wisdom of the resigned epicurean indifferentist over the political passions he has learned to despise. [in Buchner, *Danton's Death, Leance and Lena, Woyzeck,* Oxford UP, 1999.]

Musset's Lorenzacchio (1834) :" Alfred de Musset (1810-1857). Lorenzacchio recognizes the ultimate pointlessness of his determination to assassinate the Florentine tyrant, and the pointlessness of his own death which will inevitably follow, but in the face of their avowed absurdity, knows that nothing else gives meaning to his life. [in Musset, *Seven Plays,* ed, Peter Meyer, Oberon, 2006.] –

Byron's Manfred:" George Gordon Byron (1788-1824), *Manfred* (1817). Guilt-ridden and desperate, rescued from the suicide he contemplates while wandering in the Alps, confronted at the moment of his death by "Spirits" from below contending with an "Abbott" for his soul, he rejects both, claiming the priority of his "mind" alone to know and judge and bear the burden of his crimes eternally. [in *Byron Poetical Works,* eds, F. Page and J. Jump, Oxford UP, 1970, pp.390-406.]

"Ibsen's Brand (1866):" Pastor Brand, having surpassed the capability of his flock to live up to his demand for "All or Nothing," serene

and radiant, has accomplished the journey to the mountain's top, but when there, is buried in an avalanche. Ambiguous response from Above when he begs for judgment: "God is Love." [in Henrik Ibsen, *Brand and Peer Gynt,* eds and trs, J. Kirkup, J.M. Walter, C. Fry, Oxford UP, 1972.]

"Shaw's Marchbanks:" Bernard Shaw, *Candida* (1895), Act III: The final line is Shaw's stage direction, after the poet Marchbanks is rejected by Candida for her bourgeois husband: "But they do not know the secret in the poet's heart." [in *The Complete Plays of Bernard Shaw,*London, Paul Hamlyn, 1965, p.152.]

"Caesar:" Shaw, *Caesar and Cleopatra* (1899),*"* Act IV: When Caesar's argument for the practicality of rejecting revenge is in turn rejected by everyone, he concludes: "If one man in the world can be found, now and forever, to know that you did wrong, that man will have either to conquer the world as I have, or be crucified by it." [*Ibid.,* p.291.]

"Saint Joan (1923):*"* Shaw. In the Epilogue, Joan, returning to earth after her sanctification in 1920, is nevertheless invited by her closest supporters not to stay, so asks: "Oh God, who madest this beautiful earth, when will it be ready to receive thy saints? How long, O Lord, how long?" [*Ibid.,* p.1009.]

5. MULTIPLE PLOTS

1. *Countess of Pembroke/ Sir Philip Sidney circle:* The ambition of Sidney (1554-1586), poet and statesman, in his "Art of Poetry," was to establish the "regularity" of classical tradition in English theatre. Seneca's tragedy was his model for that "regularity," and the playwrights in their circle, Greville, Daniel and Alexander, wrote English tragedies in the Sixteen Eighties modeled on what was presumably the propriety and decorum of the Roman plays. But Seneca's tragedies were taken in the popular theatre as models for melodrama, bombast, and abandonment of classical restraint. T.S. Eliot describes the Pembroke circle's "Senecal" drama mournfully:

    "It was after Sidney's death that his sister, the Countess of Pembroke, tried to assemble a body of wits to compose drama in the proper Senecan style, to make head against the popular melodrama of the time.... [T]he shy recluses of Lady Pembroke's circle were bound to fail.... Senecal tragedy in its final form, in the work of Greville, Daniel and Alexander... were written after any real hope of altering or reforming the English Stage had disappeared.... Deaths there are [in their tragedies], of course, but there is none of these tragedies that is not restrained, far more discreet and sober, not only than the Tragedy of Blood, but than Seneca himself. Characters die so decently, so remote from the stage, and the report of their deaths is wrapped up in such long speeches of messengers stuffed with so many moral maxims, that we may read on unaware than any one concerned in the play had died at all."

[T.S. Eliot (1888-1965), "Seneca in Elizabethan Translation," *Essays in Elizabethan Drama*, NY, Harcourt, Brace, 1956, pp.39; 41-42.]

2.   Heywood's A Woman Killed with Kindness: (1603), Thomas Heywood (1574-1641), A Woman Killed with Kindness, in E.C. Dunn, ed., Eight Famous Elizabethan Plays, NY, Modern Library, 1950.

3.   *Plautus and Terence:* Plautus (c.254-184BC), whose comedy derived as much from native Roman sources (as an actor, he had performed in the popular Atellan farces) as from his "contaminations" of Greek New Comedy, was celebrated in antiquity and in the Renaissance for the wildness, but also mastery, of farcical and even serious comic plotting, and for the brilliant originality and metrical variety of his dialogue. Terence (c.195-159BC), whose comedy was given to more "thoughtful laughter" than Plautus's, endeared itself to cultivated Romans, and far less, apparently, to popular audiences. Hundreds of plays are attributed to Plautus, of which perhaps two dozen are authentically his. Terence wrote only six, all extant, having died on an expedition to Greece, possibly to procure more comedies of Menander for adaptation.

4.   *The Brothers:* in *Anthology of Roman Drama*, ed. P.W. Harsh, NY, Rinehart, 1960.

5.   Mash, Rosanne, Cheers, Golden Girls:

Mash: (1972-1983) Twentieth Century Fox TV; Korean War medical unit;

Rosanne: (1988-1997) Carsey-Warner Company; Midwest blue collar family;

Cheers: (1982-1993) Paramount Television, Charles/Burrows Productions; Bartender, staff and patrons in Boston bar.

Golden Girls: (Middle-aged women sharing Miami house)

6. *Middleton and Rowley's The Changeling:* (1622) Thomas Middleton (1570-1627), William Rowley, 1585-1642), *The Changeling,* in D. Bevington, ed, *English Renaissance Drama,* NY, Norton, 2002.

7. Doll House (1879), in Rolfe Fjelde, Ibsen, Prose Plays.

8. "Ibsen's Love's Comedy.....:" Love's Comedy (1862), Wild Duck (1884), Brand (1866), Master Builder (1892), John Gabriel Borkman (1896). All but Brand and Love's Comedy are in Rolf Fjelde, Ibsen, Prose Plays.. Brand, in verse, is in Brand, tr. Hill, NY, Doubleday, 2000. Love's Comedy, in verse, is in Ibsen, Lady Inger...., Everyman's Library, ed. Ernest Rhys, Doubleday reprint, 1925.

9. *Commedia dell'arte:* The first commedia company on record was formed in 1550; the companies reached the height of their popularity both in Italy and on tour throughout Europe in the mid-Seventeenth Century, but its considerable influence on dramatic practice and performance lasted into the Twentieth Century. The legends of its prowess in performance, particularly in its "improvisatory" skills, gradually exceeded fact, but its central place in the image and idea of "theatre" remains alive.

10. Allardyce Nicoll, *The World of Harlequin,* Cambridge, Cambridge UP, 1963.

11. in The Three Sisters, Act 4

12. *Bartholomew Fair* (1614), Ben Jonson, in D. Bevington, ed., *English Renaissance Drama,* NY, Norton, 2002

13. *"field full of folk":* In *Barthomew Fair's* fashioning of a "field full of folk," Jonson is as much in the medieval tradition of cosmic social satire as in the classical tradition of a less universalizing moral satire. The democratization of a mass of characters, whether being depicted as multitudes equally sharing worldly pleasures or deadly fate, belongs to the medieval imagery of the mordant leveling of human kind. The dance of death, for example, "democratized"the human horde in one fell swoop; there was sinning humankind en masse in the flames of hell; of blessed humankind ranged in heaven; or on earth and among the living, the more moderate ups and downs of life in "a field full of folk." In *Piers Plowman,* the poet Langland dreams of such a field, and ruminates on mankind's condition as though all of it were gathered in one field, every class and kind as they "worked and wandered," the poet allegorically

fulminating against the classes of the nobility, the church, the merchants, the monastics, the guildsmen, all oppressing and exploiting those on the lowest rung, the plowmen, all violating the rule of Christ. Jonson's play, on the face of it a Breugel canvas of brisk revelers, resembles more in its pervasive tone and mockery Langland's bitter dream. [William Langland (c.1332-c.1400), *The Vision of William Concerning Piers the Plowman*, (c.1377), tr. E.T. Donaldson, NY, Norton, 2006.]

14. *Alchemist* (1619), *Volpone:* (1609), Ben Jonson, in D. Bevington, *English Renaissance Drama*,NY, Norton, 2002.

15. *Nashville:* (1973), Directed by Robert Altman, produced by Paramount Pictures, screen play by Joan Tewksbury.

6. ACTION'S FOUR ALTERNATIVES

1. *The Long Christmas Dinner:* (1931), Thornton Wilder, (1897-1975), in *The Long Christmas Dinner and Other Plays in One Act,* University Press, Coward-McCann, 1931.

2. David Storey, The Changing Room: (1972), David Storey (1933-), in The Changing Room, Home, The Contractor, Avon, 1972.

3. *The Contractor:* (1971), ibid.

4. *Strange Interlude:* (1928), Eugene O'Neill (1888-1953), in *Nine Plays by Eugene O'Neill,* NY, Modern Library, 1932.

5. *"moment in King Lear:"* Act IV, sc. 6, lines 11-23.

6. *The Thirty-Nine Steps:* (1935), directed by Alfred Hitchcock, produced by Gaumont British Picture Corp., screenplay by Charles Bennett from the novel by John Buchan.

7. *Camus' The Stranger:* (1942), Albert Camus (1913-1960), *The Stranger,* NY, Vintage, 1946.

8. *deposition scene: Richard II*, Act IV, sc.1, in which Richard maneuvers a series of delays in the completion of the ceremony;

   wedding scene: Much Ado About Nothing, Act IV, sc.1, in which Claudio brutally cuts short his wedding with Hero, accusing her of whoredom;

graveyard scene: Hamlet, Act V, sc.1, in which Hamlet, during burial ceremony, leaps into Ophelia's grave to counter Laertes' show of mourning.

9. On the stage and in film, courtroom dramas, making much of the technicalities of the law but at the same time exploiting violent dramatic coups, indulged in its earlier days of the Twentieth Century in tearful melodrama, a little later in the thrill of shocking plot-reversal, and toward the end, more soberly and more quietly, in moral virtue and social good.

    Madame X, a hugely popular courtroom melodrama filmed a half dozen times between 1920 and the 1990's, in which a young trial lawyer defends a woman accused of murder, but is unaware that she is his mother. Intent on not shaming him and ruining his career, she refuses to be known as other than Madame X. [The first film version (1920), directed by Frank Lloyd, produced by Goldwyn Pictures, screenplay by J.E. Nash from the play by Alexander Bisson.]

    The Night of January 16 (1935), a courtroom drama by Ayn Rand for which each night a jury was selected from the audience, and at the end of the play, delivered its verdict. There was an overpoweringly aggressive character in it who, in the play's many productions, became a hero for followers of Rand's "Objectivity philosophy." Ayn Rand, *Night of January 16,* Plume Reprint, 1971.

    The Paradine Case (1947), a courtroom drama in which a lawyer defends a woman accused of poisoning her old, blind husband; the trial lawyer complicates his case by falling in love with his client. [Directed by Alfred Hitchcock, produced by Vanguard Films, screenplay by Alma Reville, from the novel by Robert Hitchens.]

    Witness for the Prosecution (1957). The defendant's wife unexpectedly becomes a witness for the prosecution, leading to a scramble of plot reversals. [Directed by Billy Wilder, produced by Edward Small Production, screenplay by Larry Marcus from a short story by Agatha Christie.]

    Inherit the Wind (1960), a courtroom drama which revisited the 1925 Scopes (or "monkey") trial in which the defendant was convicted in Tennessee for teaching "Darwinism" instead of "Creationism." The play became a classic during the period when the controversy appeared to have had a clear winner – "Darwinism" – and been left forever. [Directed by Stanley Kramer, produced by Lomitas

Productions, screenplay by H.J. Smith from the play by Jerome Lawrence and Robert E. Lee.]

Owen Marshall, Counselor at Law (1971-74), a TV drama series produced by Universal TV, in which a California small-town attorney defended his clients with great compassion for his defendants and for morality. [Produced by Universal TV.]

10. *In the Matter of J. Robert Oppenheimer:* (1964), Heinar Kipphardt (1922-1982), Oppenheimer, the director of the building of the first atomic bomb in Los Alamos, subsequently under investigation (simulating courtroom trial) by Atomic Energy Commission accused of subsequently delaying the building of hydrogen bomb.   The underlying argument of the play moves to the question of Oppenheimer's deepest guilt, the making of the bomb at all. [NY, Hill and Wang, 1968.]

11. *Are You Now or Have You Ever Been? The Investigations of Show-Business by the Un-American Activities Committee, 1947-58:* (1972), Eric Bentley (1916-   ), McCarthy Senate hearings investigating Communist influence in the entertainment industry. The text is almost entirely from transcripts of the hearings. [NY, Harper, 1972.]

12. *Gross Indecency: The Three Trials of Oscar Wilde,* (1997): Moises Kaufman (dates), text from court transcripts, letters, memoirs, biographies and Wilde's writings, which builds the case of Wilde as victim of "a shared public hypocrisy." [NY, Vintage, 1998.

13. *The Godfather* (1972). [Directed by Francis Ford Coppola, produced by Paramount Pictures, screenplay by Coppola and Mario Puzo, from the novel by Puzo.]

14. *The Deerhunter:* (1978), Working class kids from a tight Polish-American community are transformed by the Vietnam War. [Directed by Michael Cimino, produced by Universal Pictures, EMI Films, Ltd., screenplay by Cimino and Deric Washburn.]

15. *'Dionysian/Apollonian:* The dichotomy, the basis of Nietzsche's theory of tragedy, describes these contrasting deities as unified in tragedy.   Reference to the concept is rampant throughout Nietzsche's "The Birth of Tragedy." The first passage, introducing the concept:

"Through Apollo and Dionysus, the two art-deities of the Greeks, we come to recognize that in the Greek world there existed a sharp opposition, in origin and aims, between the Apollonian art of sculpture, and the non-plastic, Dionysian, art of music. These two distinct tendencies run parallel to each other, for the most part openly at variance; and they continually incite each other to new and more powerful births, which perpetuate an antagonism, only superficially reconciled by the common term "Art;" till at last, by a metaphysical miracle of the Hellenic will, they appear coupled with each other, and through this coupling, eventually generate the art-product, equally Dionysian and Apollonian, of Attic tragedy. In order to grasp these two tendencies, let us first conceive of them as the separate art-worlds of *dreams* and *drunkenness*." ["The Birth of Tragedy," p.167.]

But it is passages like the following that inspired and reinforced the pursuit of the myth-origins of modern cultures, giving an almost religious zeal to the felt need for their anthropological resurrection. Ironically, it was Nietzsche, who was later to pronounce the death of God, who here in his first work provided the justification for something similar to substitute.

"Without myth, however, every culture loses its healthy creative natural power: it is only a horizon encompassed with myth that rounds off to unity a social movement. It is only myth that frees all the powers of the imagination and of the Apollonian dream from their aimless   wanderings. The mythical figures have to be the unnoticed omnipresent genii, under whose care the young soul grows to maturity by the signs of which the man gives meaning to his life and struggles: and the state itself knows no more powerful unwritten law than the mythical foundation which vouches for its connection with religion and its growth from mythical ideas." ["The Birth of Tragedy," p.327.]

James Frazer: (1854-1941). *The Golden Bough, A Study in Comparative Religion,* (originally in two volumes and subsequently expanded to twelve), is based on the thesis that cultural and intellectual evolution evolved from a universal psychic impulse manifested in primitive myth, then subsequently ritualized. At the beginning, a false causality appears to exist between rituals and natural events, but the rituals persist after their origin is forgotten, and they are reinterpreted and given new meaning by later cultures. The evolution proceeds in stages: from magic and ritual, to religion, to science. But a universal ritual pattern persists: the sacrificial killing of the year god by his successor in a perpetual ritual of renewal and resurrection.

James George Frazer, *The Golden Bough, a Study in Magic and Religion,* Abridged Edition, Macmillan, 1951.

Gilbert Murray: (1866-1957), following Frazer, posited that the origin of Greek Tragedy lay in the ritual seasonal killings of the *eniautos daimon,* the year god. Though he is identified presumably with many Greek gods, the ritual is understood to be particularly related to Dionysus and "the original Dionysian mystery." Murray sketched the sequence of events that underlay the performance of this "mystery," a sequence, he affirmed, still operative in 5th century tragedy: "Agon – Messenger/Sparagmos – Threnos – Anagnorisis - Theophany," or, translated, "Contest – Messenger/a Tearing to pieces –Lamentation – Discovery/Recognition – Resurrection." When it was suggested to Murray that few Greek tragedies in fact followed this pattern (just as it was demonstrated by later anthropology that variation in cultural and intellectual evolution is far greater than Frazer supposed) he modified his thesis. ["Excursus on the Ritual Forms Preserved in Greek Tragedy," in Jane E. Harrison, *Themis,* Cambridge, Cambridge U.P., 1912.]

Carl Gustav Jung: (1875-1961). The "primitive psychic impulse" in Frazer is replicated by Jung in his concept of the "collective unconscious." In Jung, it is involved in a process of "individuation," a harmonious synthesis achieved by the individual when the abiding elements retained by the collective unconscious – "archetypes" – are "integrated" in a psychotherapeutic process with the demands of the conscious personality. That the unconscious is "collective," universal, and abiding is evidenced (similar to Frazer's "evidence" of universal primitive myth/rituals) by the fact that the same symbols appear in dreams, myths and works of art from cultures in any time or place. [*The Basic Writings of C/G. Jung,* ed. V.S. de Laszlo, NY, 1959.]

Joseph Campbell (1904-1987). Following in this tradition, Campbell writes: "The symbols of mythology are not manufactured; they cannot be ordered, invented or permanently suppressed.... Freud, Jung and their followers have demonstrated irrefutably that the logic, the heroes, and the deeds of myth survive into modern time." And like Jung, he invokes these buried psychic treasures in dreams and myths for the "integrative" therapy they provide for the conscious self: "[T]hey carry keys that open the whole realm of the desired and feared adventure of the discovery of the self. Destruction of the world which we have built and in which we live, and of ourselves within it; but then a wonderful reconstruction of the bolder, cleaner, more spacious, and fully human life – that is the lure, the promise and terror of these disturbing night visitants from the mythological realm that we carry within."

And, again, like Frazer's naming of his basic myth-ritual, the Scapegoat-God's annual assassination, Campbell names and fully elaborates the "monomyth" that stocks his notion of the collective unconscious – the monomyth that appears piecemeal and somewhat disguised, in story-telling, dreaming and cultural myth constructs. In barest outline: "*A hero ventures forth from the world of common day into a region of supernatural wonder: fabulous forces are there encountered and a decisive victory is won: the hero comes back from this mysterious adventure with the power to bestow boons on his fellow man.*"

[*The Hero with the Thousand Faces*, Princeton U.P., 1949, pp4; 8; 30.]

16. *"only aesthetically:"* "[O]nly as an aesthetic phenomenon may existence and the world appear justified; and in this sense it is precisely the function of tragic myth to convince us that even the ugly and unharmonious is an artistic game which the will plays with itself in the eternal fullness of its joy…. The joy aroused by the tragic myth has the same origin as the joyful sensation of dissonance in music. The Dionysian, with its primordial joy experienced in pain itself, is the common source of music and tragic myth" ["The Birth of Tragedy," *op.cit.*p.336.]

17. *"Euripides' telling…. "* Euripides (480-406BC), *The Bacchae:* (406BC), [ed. David Franklin, Cambridge, UP, 2000.]

18. *"Campbell's Frog King:"* From the story of the frog king in Grimm's Fairy Tales, Campbell extrapolates the frog king's significance: as "Herald," or initiator of the symbolic journey/adventure.

Once the frog king has recovered the Princess's golden ball, she forgets her promise to reward him. But just such a "blunder – apparently the merest chance – reveals an unsuspected world, and the individual is drawn into a relationship with forces that are not rightly understood…. As a preliminary manifestation of the powers that are breaking into play, the frog, coming up as it were by miracle, can be termed the 'herald;' the crisis of his appearance is the 'call to adventure'…. The call rings up the curtain, always, on a mystery of transfiguration – a rite, or moment, of spiritual passage, which, when complete, amounts to a dying and a birth." [*op. cit.*, p. 51.]

19. *Joyce, Ulysses*: (1922), James Joyce (1882-1941), *Ulysses*. [NY Random House, 1934.]

20. *W.H. Auden and Christopher Isherwood, The Ascent of F-6*: (1936), "a tragedy in two acts." Ritual manqué: a symbolic mountain journey ends in the failure of the climber to reach his goal. [NY, Random House, 1937]

   Ronald Duncan, This Way to the Tomb: (1946), a "masque and anti-masque," signifying the ironic juxtaposition of past ritual and modern vulgarization. [London, Faber & Faber, 1946]

   T.S. Eliot, Murder in the Cathedral: (1935); The later Eliot plays use the plot-patterns of Greek tragedies for their "myth patterns:" *The Cocktail Party*: (1949) after Euripides' *Alcestis*; *Family Reunion* (1939) after Aeschylus's *Oresteia; The Confidential Clerk*: (1954) after Euripides' *Ion*. They faintly echo the ironic juxtaposition of past and present in Joyce's *Ulysses*, in their use of these patterns, but they are used less for irony than for suggestive structures of parallel meaning. [in T.S. Eliot, *Complete Poems and Plays, 1909-1950*, NY, Harcourt, 1952.

21. *Kaiser, From Morn to Midnight:*(written 1912, publ. 1916), George Kaiser (1878-1945), in H.M. Bock and R.G. Shedd, eds, *Masters of ModernDrama*, NY, Random House, 1962,

22. *Murder in the Cathedral* (See Endnote, Ch. 6 #20.)

23. *Dionysus in 69: (1968),* Richard Schechner (1934-). [NY, Farrar, Strauss and Geroux, 1970.]

24. The charting of the "ladder-voyage" and the particular tasks and meanings assigned to each of the ladder's rungs along the way, are precisely diagrammed and articulated in the text of the play. Its concepts and vocabulary, derived from its multiple sources – the Kabala, the Tantric, the Hasidic, the I Ching – are carefully placed within the chart's structure. But what appears as lockstep in its editorial explanation, registered in performance, paradoxically, as the limit to which freedom can conceivably go in the accomplishment of ritual.

Living Theatre, Paradise Now: (1968), composed by the Collective: the Living Theatre, Julian Beck (1925-1985) and Judith Malina (1926-), NY, Random House, 1971.

25. *"Star Wars:"* (1977). [Directed by George Lucas, produced by 20th Century Fox, Lucas Films, Ltd, screenplay by Lucas.]

26. *Lucas, Joseph Campbell:* Bill Moyers' six-part PBS documentary, *The Power of Myth,* consisting of Campbell-Moyers interviews, was published, and the interviews expanded, in: Joseph Campbell and Bill Moyers, *The Power of Myth,* ed., B.S. Flowers, NY, Doubleday, 1988. Episode One in the documentary and Chapter Five of the book discuss Lucas' claim that Campbell's work directly influenced the creation of the *Star Wars* films. In 1999, in another PBS documentary, *The Mythology of Star Wars with George Lucas and Bill Moyers,* Lucas himself discusses the impact of Campbell's work on his films.

27. *Shaw's discussion plays:* "We now have plays that begin with discussion and end with action [naïve plays, in other words, that name their thesis and then tell a story to illustrate it], and others in which discussion interpenetrates the action from beginning to end. The action in such plays consists of a case to be argued." [*Major Critical Essays,* London, Constable, 1932, pp.37-39.] But the case to be argued must be done, he posits, in strictly dramatic [actually, conventionally dramatic] terms, with only the difference that *the action is in itself the arguing of the case,* but it must be embodied entirely in the actions of recognizable human beings: "An allegory is never quite consistent except when it is written by someone without dramatic faculty, in which case it is unreadable. There is only one way of dramatizing an idea: and that is by putting on the stage a human being possessed by that idea, yet none the less a human being with all the human impulses which make him akin and therefore interesting to us." [*Ibid.,* p.220.]

27. Granville Barker (1877-1946), Waste (1906), The Madras House (1909.)

28. Man and Superman (1905), [in Bernard Shaw, *Complete Plays with Prefaces,* NY and London, Dodd, Mead, 1962.]

29. Major Barbara (1905), [in Bernard Shaw, *Complete Plays with Prefaces,* NY and London, Dodd, Mead, 1962.]

30. *Right You Are If You Think You Are*: (1917), Luigi Pirandello (1867-1936), in *Three Plays by Pirandello*, [Kessinger, 2005.]

31. *Rashomon* (1950): [Directed by Akira Kurosawa, produced by Daiei Motion Picture Company, Ltd., screenplay by Kurosawa from stories by Ryunosuke Akutagawa.]

32. "*lehrstucke*": Bertolt Brecht (1898-1956).   The famous double-column comparison of "Culinary" Theatre with "Epic" (or Brecht's "Didactic") Theatre, appeared in English in the article, "Theatre for Learning," tr. Edith Anderson, in *Mainstream* (June 1958), (published by *Masses and Mainstream*.)

The essential thrust of Brecht's definition of Epic Theatre:

"The stage began to narrate. The narrator no longer vanished with the fourth wall.   Not only did the background make its own comment on stage happenings… lending tangible, concrete statistics to abstract discussions, providing facts and figures for happenings which were plastic but unclear in their meaning; the actors no longer threw themselves into their roles but maintained a certain distance from the character performed by them, even distinctly inviting criticism…..   As the [factual, historical] 'background' came to the fore…. The theatre entered the province of the philosophers – at any rate, the sort of philosophers who wanted not only to explain the world but also to change it."

The displaying of "background" facts and figures, though it played a role in early Epic Theatre theory, played a far less significant role in practice, and subsequently almost none at all. But the weight of historical and political context, even in Brechtian plays taking place in fanciful settings and in wholly invented geographies, stamp their presence – ironically, to be sure – but fundamentally and unmistakably as at the center of every drama's immediate subject matter.

The programmatic lehrstucke of the Twenties and early Thirties include: Man is Man (1924-5; revised 1964); The Baden Lehrstucke on Consent (1928-9); He Who Says Yes (1929); He Who Says No (1930); The Measures Taken (1930); The Exception and the Rule (1930-1.)

33. Shklovsky, See Endnote Ch. 9, #15, below.

34. *Piscator*: Edwin Piscator (1893 – 1966.)

35. *The Measures Taken* (1930) See Endnote Ch. 6, #32, above.

36: *Mother Courage* (1939): in Bertolt Brecht, *Collected Plays, Vol .Five,* A&C Black, 1995.

37.   The Round Heads and the Peaked Heads (1936): ibid, Vol. Four, ed John Willett, NY, Methuen, 2001.

38. *The Good Person of Setzuan* (1943): tr. and ed., Eric Bentley, U. of Minnesota Press, 1999.

39: Clifford Odets, *Waiting for Lefty*

40. *Everyman:* (c.1485-1495), Anonymous, in ed. A.C. Cawley, Everyman *and Medieval Miracle Plays,* London, Dent,

41. the *literal* (explicit meaning without figurative or metaphorical representation); the *tropological* (interpretation of meaning related to conduct or morals); the *allegorical* (the representation of one subject under the guise of another); and the *anagogical* (mystical or spiritual interpretation applying the literal sense to heavenly things, or applying matter of the Old Testament to the New "as when Peter [speaking of] the ark of Noah signifies baptism.") (From Mark Holtz, "Medieval Exegesis," *Catholic News,* n.d.)

42. *The Blue Bird:* (1909) Maurice Maeterlinck (1862-1949), *The Blue Bird,* Kessinger, 2004. The key to the doctrinal correspondences which Maeterlinck used is worked out in detail in Henry Rose, *Maeterlinck's Symbolism: The Blue Bird and other essays,* NY, Dodd Mead, 1911.

43. *Swedenborg:* Emanuel Swedenborg (1668-1772), scientist, philosopher and mystic, was rediscovered in the last years of the Nineteenth Century during the emergent popularity of esoteric doctrine and practice. He was, he wrote, "introduced by the Lord first into the rational sciences, and thus prepared,... Heaven was opened to him." What he discovered in dreams, illuminations, visions and mysterious conversations, was regularized in *A Hieroglyphic Key* (1741), which accounted for a doctrine of correspondences of the relations between body and soul, and between the natural and spiritual worlds.

Emanuel Swedenborg, A Hieroglyphic Key to Natural and Spiritual Mysteries by Way of Representations and Correspondences (1741), Kessinger, 2006.

44. *Jarry, Caesar-Antichrist.* (1895), tr. Antony Melville, annotated Alastair Brotchie, in *Collected Works of Alfred Jarry,* vol. 1, Atlas Press, London, 2001.

45. *"his fundamental operative term: instability:* "Since the writings are visionary they are subject to the alchemy of vision, to hallucination, to mutation, to transformation with little respect to form or substance. Things change. Base metals turn to gold, and stone becomes fluid. So it is that the three Christs forming the pillory do not remain jasper, but soon become green, white and yellow: bronze, silver and gold – the metals the idols mentioned in the Apocalypse…. One of the fantastic properties of this "theatre" [of the mind] is its remarkable ability to produce brilliant colors and to change them at will. Solids are fluids in these visions and characters and props can merely appear and fade away. They all have the physical properties of light. Throughout the play, animate and inanimate objects act alike. Both are equally capable of appearing on the stage; and furthermore, the visual transformations permit one to become the other." James H. Bierman, tr. and ed., "Introduction," to Alfred Jarry, *Caesar-Antichrist,* Tucson, AZ, Omen Press, 1971, pp. 26-27.

46. *Finnegans Wake* (1939) James Joyce, *Finnegans Wake,* Penguin, 1999.

7. CHARACTER

1. "Plato's moral judgmentalism:"

Plato's strictures on poetry and "representations" generally, which are on the face of it so inimical to our contemporary ideas of free expression, etc., are justified by a vision in itself frankly inimical to the very idea of democracy. The ideal of the State in Plato – more a vision than a conceivable reality – is one that is devoted first and foremost to the pursuit of the Good, and requires of its citizens to share that objective so completely as to be, in their pursuit of the ideal life, indistinguishable from the pursuit of that ideal State. It is with respect to the building *toward* such a state that the poet, the actor, the painter and so on are constrained to surrender those "representations" which do no honor, in their use and in their probable influence, to the building of the State.

As for the question of dramatic "representation" itself: the poet's "imitation" is at one remove from the Form or the Ideal of the object it attempts to imitate; therefore the actor's imitation of the poet is at two or three removes, and so constitutes a subversion of the Ideal and a lie, and therefore to be rejected.

In the light of these objections, the *Republic's* animadversions against poetic representation follows:

Its subversion of religious belief: [From *The Republic*, Bk. II:]

"... neither will we allow our young men to hear the words of Aeschylus, that God plants guilt among men when he desires utterly to destroy a house.... We must not permit [the poet] to say that these are the works of God... and that God is the author of their misery.... Such a fiction is suicidal, ruinous, impious.... Let this then be one of our rules and principles concerning the gods, to which our poets and reciters will be expected to conform."

Its encouragement of lax morals among the impressionable: [From *The Republic*, Bk. III:]

"... everybody will begin to excuse his own vices when he is convinced that similar wickednesses are always being perpetrated by the kindred of the gods.... And therefore let us put an end to such tales, lest they engender laxity of morals among the young."

From The Republic, Bk. X:

[Plato has already explained that God, the original artificer, has "made," so to speak, the model, or the Form, or the Idea, of the chair, and that the carpenter therefore makes only a necessarily imperfect imitation of it, and that the painter painting that chair is painting only the "appearance" of the chair. Applying this analogy to the tragedian, he concludes:]

"And so when we hear persons saying that the tragedians, and Homer who is at their head, knows all the arts and all things human, and divine things too, for the poet cannot compose well unless he knows his subject, we ought to consider whether here also there may not be a similar illusion.... They may not have remembered when they saw [the poet's] works that these were but imitations thrice removed from the truth, because they are appearances only, and not realities." [*The Republic and other works*, tr. Benjamin Jowett, NY, Anchor Books, 1960.]

2. *Iphigenia in Aulis: (406/05BC)* by Euripides (480-405BC.) The goddess Artemis demands the sacrifice of Iphigenia, Agamemnon's daughter, to bring fair winds to carry the troops over the sea to

Troy. But his change of heart, and the efforts of Clytemnestra and Achilles to spare her, count for nothing when the terrified Iphigenia undergoes a strange reversal of feeling, and offers herself willingly for sacrifice. What she recognizes in the face of death is the purpose to which her life might be dedicated – the Greek cause itself – rather than a life of personal gratification. She puts off the restraints of the soldiers and walks willingly to the altar to embrace her sacrifice. [in W.J. Oates and E. O'Neill, *The Complete Greek Drama,* NY, Random House, 1938.]

3.   *Ion:* (414BC) by Euripides. Exposed by his mother Creusa at birth to conceal the shame of her rape by the God Apollo, Ion was rescued and brought up as an attendant in the Delphic temple of Apollo. Later, Creusa, in childless marriage, with her husband Xuthus consults the Delphic oracle, from whom Xuthus understands that he is the father of "the first he meets," Ion. Creusa, supposing he was her husband's son by a former marriage, resolves to poison him. Ion detects her design in time, and would have killed her, but a priestess produces the cradle in which he was exposed, and so brings about, in the nick of time, recognition and reconciliation between mother and son. [*Ibid.*]

4:   *Fourth Century comedy:* Flourished from c.336BC. Its greatest master was Menander (342BC-292BC) whose first play was produced in 322BC, and is reputed to have subsequently written over a hundred plays. He was the student of Theophrastus, Aristotle's successor at his philosophic school. Theophrastus wrote the still-extant treatise on "Characters," very much reflected in Menander's portrayals, and the playwright was the friend from youth of the philosopher Epicurus. A summary of Menander's astonishing reputation in the Greek and Roman world: "There was only one opinion about his work. His principle merits were remarkable inventiveness, skillful arrangement of plots, life-lke painting of character, a clever and refined wit, elegant and graceful language, and a copious supply of maxims based on a profound knowledge of the world." These virtues appear only fitfully in the fragments and single complete play still extant, but during the Roman period, praise for Menander was universal. Even Euripides, commented Julius Caesar, was only "a half-Menander."

5.   *Hecuba:* In *The Trojan Women (*415BC) by Euripides, Queen Hecuba and her daughters are captives in the Greek camp. One by one, her daughters are either murdered or taken from her; she remains at the

end of the tragedy shrouding the body of her grandson, the last to be assassinated and the last hope of Troy's restoration, leaving her with only the solace that the sufferings of these enslaved women will be remembered as humanity's "song of sorrow."

At the conclusion of *The Trojan Women*, mad with grief, she is rescued from throwing herself into the flames of Troy. In Euripides' earlier tragedy, *Hecuba* (c425BC), so enraged is she by the indifference of the Trojans to her appeals to spare her daughter Polyxena from death, and then for justice for the murder of her son Polydorus by King Polymester, that she, with the help of the other Trojan captives, blinds the king and murders his sons. The blinded Polymestor prophecies that Hecuba, given the savagery of her hate, will one day turn into a dog. The nobly suffering queen, in enslavement, is ultimately reduced to bestiality. (In one myth, she was depicted as running along the seashore howling with grief, and being literally changed into a dog.)

6. *Tecmessa:* In Sophocles' (496-406BC) *Ajax* (pre-442BC) Tecmessa, daughter of a Phrygian king, has been captured by Ajax in one of his raids before the Troy expedition, and has borne a son to him in captivity. When Ajax runs mad and threatens suicide after his humiliating transgression (slaughtering livestock under the supposition that they were his enemies in the Grecian camp) Tecmessa – once a princess, now a slave and concubine – fears for her son and herself, since Ajax's death would mean their loss of shelter and protection among hostile Greeks. Her love for Ajax, her fear for herself and her son's safety and for her anomalous position should Ajax die, moves her pleas to Ajax to abandon his despair. She fails to prevent his suicide.

7. *Cassandra:* In Aeschylus' (526-456) *Agamemnon* (458BC) the Trojan princess, daughter of Priam the king of Troy, has been dragged by Ajax from the altar at which she had taken refuge during the sack of Troy. Rescued by Agamemnon and taken as his slave to Mycenae, she, with him, is murdered by Clytemnestra and her paramour, Aegisthus. Cassandra had won the gift of prophecy from Apollo in return for her love, but breaking her vow, he let her retain her gift, but deprived her of being believed. In *Agamemnon*, while she cries out her warning of the imminent murder of Agamemnon and herself, she is doomed to unintelligibility before the men of the city, who fail to believe or aid her.

8. *Medea:* In Euripides' *Medea* (431BC) after having betrayed her father and nation in her effort to aid Jason in winning the golden fleece, Medea is brought to Greece as his wife. But Jason wishes to marry the daughter of Creon, King of Corinth, and so is determined to divorce Medea. Not only her jealousy but her fear of being abandoned as a fugitive and beggar, leads to the revenge she executes against her betraying husband – the murder of their children.

9. *Electra:* In Euripides' *Electra* (413BC) Electra is wedded to a peasant-farmer by her father's murderers, her mother Clytemnestra and Aegisthus, so that her sons would be base born and therefore no future threat to their throne. Electra has lived for years in this enforced poverty and misery, hating her mother and the adulterer Aegisthus, and yearning for her brother Orestes' return to carry out their revenge. In Sophocles' Electra (420?-410?) she lives under the misery of the rule of her father's murderers and longs for the same revenge. Though her triumph at the end of Sophocles' play is absolute (whereas in Euripides, it is much tempered by Orestes' near madness at the guilt of his matricide), the years of misery and longing for vengeance are identical in both tragedies.

10. *Clytemnestra:* In Aeschylus' *Agamemnon,* Clytemnestra, after pretending hospitable welcome of her returning husband and his concubine Cassandra, murders them with the aid of her paramour Aegisthus. Clytemnestra's "manly valor" and "unscrupulous cleverness" are concealed throughout most of the play, but after their murder Clytemnestra, triumphant, proudly confesses her "manly cleverness" in having successfully concealed her aim, and confirms her "manly valor" by boasting of the double murder and of her ten years' plotting to accomplish it, while assuming the reins of government like a man. After her brash confession, she manages to control the horrified populace's response, and remains invulnerable to potential rebellion.

11. *"Hegel's monolithic characters:"* "The individuals subject to [these single ethical imperatives] are neither what, in the modern use of the term, we describe as characters, nor are they mere abstractions. They are rather placed in the vital midway sphere between both, standing there as figures of real stability, *which are simply that which they are,* without aught of collision in themselves… absolutely determinate characters, whose definition, however, discovers its content and basis in [one] particular ethical power." [Italics added.] Anne and

Henry Paolucci, eds., *Hegel on Tragedy,* NY, Anchor Books, 1962, p.64. (Excerpted from Hegel, *The Philosophy of Fine Art,* tr. F.P.B. Osmaston, London, Vol. IV, pp. 248-348.)

12. *Deianeira:* In Sophocles' *Women of Trachis* (date unknown.)

     Medea: (see Endnote Ch. 7, #8, above)

13. *Iphigenia:* (see Endnote Ch. 7, #2, above)

     Hecuba: (see Endnote Ch. 7, #5, above)

     Philoctetes: In Sophocles' Philoctetes (409BC.)

14. *"Athenian tragedy… fifth century"*: The first extant play is Aeschylus, *The Persians* (472BC); the last is Euripides, *The Bacchae* (406BC).

15. *"Pericles' awesome city-state…:"* The enormous pride of Athens in the victory of Marathon (490) and again at Salamis (480) over Persia's military might, and its development in the early Fifth Century of both a democratic city-state and a Mediterranean empire, was capped by Athens' prosperity and brilliant achievements under Pericles, the leader of the Democratic party. But its most prestigious days were in fact short-lived. Her attempts to dominate her enemies led to the long and at length debilitating Peloponnesian Wars which lasted for twenty-seven years from 431BC to 401BC.

It was during those years, worn down by siege, famine and even plague, that Athenian democracy gradually failed. "Her rule had ended in tyranny abroad and demagoguery at home. Abroad she subjugated her allies, looted them, and imposed on them, in the name of democracy…. At home the courts were a farce enlivened by capital punishment, while the assembly repeatedly refused to recognize unwelcome facts, make necessary sacrifices, and reward and punish justly. When the Spartans took the city, survivors and exiles joined in pulling down the long walls to the sound of flutes, 'believing that day was the beginning of freedom for Greece.'" [from J.A. Garraty and P. Gay, eds, *The Columbia History of the World,* NY, Harper and Row, 1981, pp.169-176.]

The Spartans' victory over Athens (in 404BC) was followed by a half-century of intermittent warfare with frequent and unstable realignments of power until Alexander's overrunning of Athens and his conquests in the East until his death in 331BC. It was during these intermittently calamitous, but also intermittently stable and prosperous years that the tragedies of Euripides, the satires of

Aristophanes, and subsequently the rise of Menander's New Comedy flourished.

16. *"Pollux's treatise on masks:"* Julius Pollux (180-238AD), an Alexandrian grammarian, who taught at Athens in the Academy (Plato's original school), compiled a dictionary, or thesaurus, in ten books called the *Onomasticon.* One of its lengthy entries is on "Masks," and describes the appearance of over one hundred theatrical masks worn by actors, presumably six centuries earlier, in 4th century theatre. Extrapolating from his original detailed list, it's possible to discern the *categories* of characterization his descriptions imply. How certain is the extrapolation? And how certain can we be that his descriptions define comprehensively Greek New Comedy character types? We can't. But Pollux's entry is the best evidence we have, though centuries removed, of masks worn. And comparing Pollux's masks with the characters in Menander's texts and in the Roman adaptations of Greek New Comedy, there's reason to suppose that Pollux's descriptions are reliable evidence of how Greek New Comedy thought of, and portrayed, "character."

Given that measure of certainty, here's a brief sampling of some of the evidence:

First, Pollux arranges categories by Genre: Comic Masks, Tragic Masks, Satyric Masks; and within the category of Comic Masks: Old Comedy and New Comedy Masks. Within each of these genres, he lists by Sex and Age, and some by Function, as: for New Comedy: Old Men, Young Men, Slaves, Old Women, Young Women. For Old Comedy Masks: "like the person they represented, only more ridiculous," (reflecting the individualized characterizations in Aristophanes, but no mention of the standard "types" in his comedies.) For Tragedy: Old Men, Young Men, Women, Slaves, Attendants (but "Attendants" are not Attendants, but actually mythological, allegorical, geographical, and architectural representations – an insight into representations in Fourth Century Tragedy, of which we have none extant – with "characters" such as Many-Eyed Argus, a River, an Anemone, a City, Titan, Giant, Mountain, Justice, Death, Deceit, Drunkenness, Idleness, etc.

It is in the breakdown of types within Genre, Age and Sex that we find highly particularized features in the masks that spell, with little difficulty in interpreting them, the precise "bent," whether moral or overtly behavioral, in the character being signified. The mask's features – hair, beard, complexion, position of eyebrows, ears – or more bluntly, the behavioral or moral description of the character – disagreeable, braggart, delicate, accomplished – are described. The list is long; a few illustrations will do:

Some "New Comedy" types particularized:

OLD MEN:

> First Grandfather – pleasant eyebrows, dim sight.
> Second Grandfather – morose, sharper-sighted.
> Governor – stooping, dimmer sight.
> Long-Bearded – "shaking" old man.
> Etc.

YOUNG MEN:

> Common – ruddy, athletic, swarthy.
> Delicate – youngest, educated in the nursery.
> Threatening – soldier, braggart, black complexion.
> Flatterer eyebrows disagreeably extended.
> Etc.

YOUNG WOMEN:

> Curled (i.e., hair) Virgin – false hair, pale white skin.
> Hoary Talkative – "the harlot left off trade."
> Concubine – resembles her, but full-haired.
> Beautiful Courtesan – has least finery, hair in fillet.
> Golden Harlot – much gold in hair.
> Etc.

OLD WOMEN:

> Prostitute – thin old woman, tall, many wrinkles.
> Domestic – (sedentary or active) two "axle teeth," flat-faced.
> Fat Old Woman – many wrinkles, plump skin.

[*Onomasticon*, English Extracts, London 1775 (Penn Library Web) Online version.]

17. *"Aristotle… comedy… below us, tragedy those above:"* [*Poetics*, Chapters. 5 and 15.] It is frequently argued that the recommendations of the *Poetics* are intended to be descriptive, not proscriptive, and that it was the Roman Horace who was responsible, in his *Art of Poetry*, for converting Aristotelian suggestion into later neo-classicism's "laws." But there appears to be a far deeper and more compelling sense of proscription in Aristotle's moralisms buried in his assumptions of universally understood opinion.   Aristotle's own

preferential judgments are tellingly   above the mean; his adjustments of the scales of "above" and "below" with respect to class status, tilt his "mean" decidedly toward the "above," and in addition, the association of character norms with the classes "above" and those "below," have so many objectionable features for us as to need no enumeration. But to pit our "men say" against his "men say" is to fall into the same insupportable mode of calibrating value systems. The difficulty lies precisely in the basic assumption of Aristotelian classification: each genus and each kind has a singularly dominant function of being and behaving. The moral value of human beings in their several conditions are also singularly definable: status = function = moral character. In effect, his "system" appears not too different from Plato's after all; his judgments may be more tempered and more variously stratified, but as a system of judgmental classification, it appears to be no less narrow and no less inescapably proscriptive.

But this is not merely an academic question; it has enormous bearing on the moral judgments still visited on dramatic fictions. That "*men say,*" and have continued to "say" what Aristotle said in the *Ethics* and the *Politics* and the *Poetics* concerning fitting and unfitting moral character has continued to cling to critical judgment of drama. So much is this so that there is a quaint divorce between the judgments we make in what we think of as real life, and the ones we make of a play or film, in the presence of which we continue to shake our heads and chuckle, or register shock and indignation, according to models of propriety attached still to that fantasy world.   It is unmistakable, the slippage in our ethical standards from the moment we leave the pages of the book or the theatre or the TV world, and drop back into the norms, the rights and wrongs, the appropriates and inappropriates, of the invasive world.

18. "*caractere*": Theophrastus (371BC-287BC), the author of *Characters,* was designated by Aristotle as his successor to the Peripatetic school, where Menander was his student. In Seventeenth Century France, the tutor of Louis XIV's son, Jean de la Bruyere (1645-16960,)   translated Theophrastus' *Characters,* and in his own "*caracteres,*" added to the ethical generalizations of Theophrastus his own sarcastic but brilliant characterizations of his contemporaries, for which he gained considerable fame and a considerable faction of enemies.   Both grew with each additional publication of his

portraits. It was La Bruyere's that became the model for the "*caracteres*" in the dialogue of the English Restoration playwrights.

19. *Petulant:* in William Congreve, (1670-1729), *The Way of the World,* (1700), Act I, sc.1. In G. Nettleton and A.E. Case, eds, *British Dramatists from Dryden to Sheridan,* NY, Houghton Mifflin, 1939.

20. "*from Baroque to Rococo*": The terms are hardly exact, and questioned both for their relevance and for their dating, but precise or not, they signify if only roughly the extraordinary difference between the extravagant, passionate, sensual and ecstatic art of the Seventeenth century – the great age in theatre of poetic discourse and imaginative opulence – and the succeeding time in much of the Eighteenth when the heroics and rhetoric of the Baroque were displaced by the daintiness of elegant etiquette and the gallantries of drawing room wit. In theatre, the terms signify well the difference between the soaring of Shakespeare, Corneille and Lope da Vega, and the charm and cleverness of Sheridan, Marivaux and Goldoni.

21. *Jane Austen* (1775-1817), whose novel, *Pride and Prejudice* (1813), illustrates her narrative of judgmental learning: Elizabeth Bennet begins her appraisal of Mr. D'Arcy with distinct prejudice, backed by unexamined scruple. The pride of Mr. D'Arcy is observed through Elizabeth Bennet's mistaken prejudice until characteristic instances of his behavior gradually reveal to her the true composite of his "natures." Her growing affection for him cannot be recognized as love until all the features of the man's character answer to her catalogue of ideal virtues. As each emerges, she gives it its right name; as they heap, the rewards become sufficiently plentiful for the approval of her sense and her feelings in one. [*Pride and Prejudice,* NY, Bantam, Classics Reissue, 1983.]

22. "*Seneca has been blamed for… what went wrong with Elizabethan tragedy*": Example of blame: "The oratorical and the horrible became the aim of serious drama in the hands of Seneca…. Seneca's aim was to produce a poem in dialogue form in which he could describe with an amazing flood of words and brilliancy of diction, scenes and deeds which he thought were tragic, but which, at most, gave one a creepy thrill…. But Senecan tragedy was the most artistic form of drama in the opinion of the men of the Renaissance, and contemporary ideals of dramatic technique were based upon these tragedies."

D.C. Stuart, *The Development of Dramatic Art,* NY Dover, 1960, p.242.

"T.S. Eliot first credited:" Eliot's essay on Seneca and the Elizabethans is judicious to a degree, scrupulous in neither praising nor faulting him more than his true deserving. He absolves Seneca from responsibility for Elizabethan Tragedies of Blood – it was Italian Renaissance example and native prurience – and praises him for what most have considered Seneca's primary sin against the Elizabethans: "Certainly Elizabethan bombast can be traced to Seneca.... Certainly it is all 'rhetorical,' but if it had not been rhetorical, would it have been anything?... Without bombast, we should not have had *King Lear*. The art of dramatic language, we must remember, is as near to oratory as to ordinary speech or to other poetry. If the Elizabethans distorted and travestied Seneca in some ways, if they learned from him tricks and devices which they applied with inexpert hands, they also learned from him the essentials of declaimed verse.... so that they were able to write plays which can still be viewed as plays, with any plays, and which can still be read as poetry, with any poetry." [*op. cit.*, pp.37-38.]

23. *Atreus*: in Seneca (4BC-65AD), *Thyestes*, (n.d.), tr., Ella Isabel Harris, Act II, sc.1, in Philip W. Harsh, ed., *An Anthology of Roman Drama*, NY, Rinehart, 1960.

24. *"Seneca, De Ira:"* Seneca writes: "There are certain things which at the start are under our control, but later hurry us away by their violence and leave us no retreat. As a victim hurled from the precipice has no control over his body, and once cast off can neither stop nor stay, but speeding on irrevocably, is cut off from all reconsideration or repentance and cannot now avoid arriving at the goal toward which he might once have avoided starting, so with the mind – if it plunges into anger, love or the other passions, it has no power to check its impetus; its very weight, and the downward tendency of vice needs must hurry it on, and drive it to the bottom." [*To Novatus on Anger*, Book I, ch. 7.]

25. *"Racine's Phedra:"* In her confession to her Nurse Oenone, Phedra recounts the fury with which she was seized by love, and then her hatred of its sin: "I hate my life," she cries, "and hold my love in horror. I die," and then begs Oenone not to "vainly try to snatch away from death/ The last faint sparks of life, yet lingering." Like Euripides' Phaedra, she recognizes that she is victimized by Venus and accuses her, but bears the "sin" as her own. [*op. cit.*, Act I, pp.258-258.]

26. "the burden of sin instantly rises:"

Barnwell: George Lillo (1693-1739), *The London Merchant* (1731), in G. Nettleton and A.E. Case, eds., *op. cit.,* Act III, sc.4, pp. 617-618.

Mistress Frankford: John Heywood (1574-1641), *A Woman Killed with Kindness* (1603), *op.cit.,* Act II, sc.3, p.160.

Bosola: John Webster (1580-1634), *The Duchess of Malfi* (1612-14), in ed, E.C. Dunn, *Eight Famous Elizabethan Plays,*NY, Random House, 1950, Act IV, sc.2, p.517.

Sarah Sampson: Gotthold Lessing (1729-1781), *Miss Sarah Sampson,*(1775): in *Sara; Minna von Barnhelm: Two Plays,* NY, Theatre Commnications Group, 1991.

Franz Moor: in Friedrich Schiller, (18759-1805), *The Robbers* (1782), in Schiller, *Five Plays,* Oberon Books, 1998.

Marguerite: Johann Wolfgang Goethe (1747-1832), tr., Peter Salm, *Faust Part One*(1808), tr., Peter Salm, NY, Bantam, 1962, pp.305-319.

Fagin: in Charles Dickens (1812-1870), *Oliver Twist,* London,. Toby Press, 2003, pp.497-506.

27. *Hroswitha, Paphnutius:* Hroswitha (c935-1001) *Paphnutius,* in *The Works of Hroswitha,* ed, Zoltalin Haraszti, Boston Public Library, 1945.

28. *"two contrary notions of the soul:"* "Previous investigators' [of English domestic tragedy] favorite descriptive terms are 'moral,' 'sentimental,' and 'realistic.' Their use of the first term is justified, but they have made no effort to discover the basis of this morality. In calling these dramas 'sentimental,' the critics appear to forget that *sentimentalism is based on a belief in the innate goodness of man, while these plays illustrate the innate viciousness of man – his certainty of turning to evil courses when he follows his nature rather than his faith."* [Henry Hitch Adams, *English Domestic or, Homiletic Tragedy 1575 to 1642,* NY, Benjamin Blom, 1943, 1965, p.186.]

A corollary to the second proposition is the belief that " no man except Christ ever lived without sin.... Man, left to his own devices, so the *Homilies* taught, runs headlong into sin, along the primrose path to the everlasting bonfire. He can escape Hell only through God's mercy.... It is not man's will but God's great love for mnkind that renders repentance efficacious." [*Ibid.,* p. 10.]

The helplessness of man and the efficaciousness of God alone is at the root of concurrent Jansenism in France.   Cornelius Jansen (1585-1638) in his *Augustinus*, "simply a digest of the teachings of St. Augustine," taught that if a man is born without the religious instinct, without, that is, the love of God, he can only gain it by going through a process of "conversion" – a conversion which is merely the beginning of seeking "justification" – a long and strenuous process that could take a lifetime.   "And whether God converts this man or that depends on his good pleasure.   Thus Jansen's theories of conversion melt into predestination; although in doing so, they somewhat modify its grimness."   Though Jansenism was in many ways close to the doctrines of the Protestant Calvin, it was strenuous in its insistence on its Roman Catholic orthodoxy, though the Church, disagreeing, suppressed and eventually persecuted the Jansenists. ["Cornelius Jansen" and "Jansenism," *Encyclopedia Britannica*, 14th ed., vol.12, pp.891-892.]

29:   *"the soul became the heart:"*   There's of course a long history in literature of the heart as the seat of love propelling love's psychological journeys.   The journeys were allegorized in the medieval Court of Love romances.   Later in France in the Seventeenth Century, the allegorical map of its terrain was revived for the multi-volume sagas of the love journeys in the romances of La Calpraneda.   But the heart in Sentimentality broadened its aegis, and became the seat of all feelings, just as feelings became the whole grounding of morality. The innate goodness of man was already divulged philosophically in the Eighteenth Century by Shaftesbury in England, and by Rousseau in France, but it was the English novelists and dramatists who truly sanctified the virtuous heart, its psychology, its physiology, and its moral supremacy, preeminently, Samuel Richardson in *Pamela, or Virtue Rewarded* (1750), and *Clarissa* (1748), and in theatre, Richard Steele in *The Conscious Lovers* (1722), George Lillo in *The London Merchant* (1731), Hugh Kelly in *False Delicacy* (1768)

30.   *Colley Cibber, The Careless Husband:*   ed. William Appleton, Licoln, Nebrasca, University of Nebraska Press, 1966, Act V, sc. 5, lines 45-56.

"How low a hypocrite:" ibid., Act V, sc.6, lines 131-144.

31.   Sir Francis Acton: *A Woman Killed with Kindness, op.cit.,* Act V, sc.1, pp.192-197.

32. *"Hartmann's 'unconscious'... before Freud's:"* Karl R.E. von Hartmann (1842-1906). His *Philosophy of the Unconscious*, originally published in 1869, went through eleven editions until 1904. Its popularity was emblematic not only of the Nineteenth Century's deepening sense of the "layers" of the soul, but also of its death-oriented pessimism, a vein that became increasingly popular and increasingly profound in the later century's major literature and thought. His pessimism initially came from Schopenhauer; the battle of the unconscious, as Hartmann imagined it, came from Hegel's "dialectics" of conflict. Though his model was displaced by Freud's, his version of the unconscious is at least as fanciful. At the Fall of Man, posited Hartmann, Will and Reason were separated, and Will became blind impulse, remaining in constant and melancholy strife against Reason. Its strife shares in the inevitable misery of human existence, but there is the hope, the anticipation, that when the Will is emancipated from this battle in the (conscious) Reason of the "enlightened pessimist," it will perceive the inevitability of that universal misery, and with a collective effort, *will* the world into nothingness, and the Unconscious into quiescence. The annulment of the will to live will signify the release of the Unconscious from its sufferings, and accomplish the end of civilization. Since that apocalyptic moment will not arrive for a long time, Hartmann urges that in the meantime, we affirm life provisionally, forego the pursuit of happiness which is a delusion anyhow, but also forego its opposite, suicide. And during that interim, we would discover that morality renders life at least less unhappy.

    As therapy, both Hartmann's and Freud's move in the same direction – toward adjustment to social morality – but Hartmann's remains more a recipe for brooding than food for therapeutic uplift. The spirit of European naturalism in the 70's to 90's, and the avant-gardism at the turn of the century, though, remained closer to Hartmann than to the less enervated Freud.

33. *"Below the castle... lies the dungeon:"* The hostage in the dungeon's chains is the buried secret, the villain's albatross. In Mathew Gregory Lewis's (1775-1815), *The Castle Spectre* (1797), the deadly secret is mobile and wanders, terrifying spasmodically. But in Schiller's *The Robbers* (1782), Franz Moor's father, whom he's put in chains, languishes in the dungeon, and waits for discovery until the denouement. [*The Castle Spectre*, Kessinger Publ., 2004. *The Robbers*, op cit., above.]

34. *"The mask of Dr. Jekyll*: Robert Louis Stevenson, *Dr. Jekyll and Mr. Hyde*, ed., J. Charyn, NY, Bantam Reissue, 1982.

35. *"Rousseau... development"*: Jean-Jacques Rousseau (1712-1778), was far from the first to recognize the developmental nature of human psychology, but the context in which he promoted it was overwhelmingly appealing first to Nineteenth Century romanticism, and then to the century's ongoing worries about the variables of "progress." He tracked "man's" progress from primitive simplicity to corrupt civilization, a progress that might have been toward "natural" community, but in its course became sophisticated and depraved. As for the individual's progress from childhood to adulthood, it was similarly a progress that might have been benign, but was corrupted by "education."

36. Rebecca West, see Ch. 10, #?, below.

37. Mrs. Alving, see Ch. 9, #?, below.

38. *"Zola's 'scientific' Naturalism*: Emile Zola (1840-1902), wrote in his "Preface to *Therese Racqin:"* "The movement was started by the new methods of science; thence, Naturalism revolutionized criticism and history, in submitting man and his works to a system of precise analysis, *taking into account all circumstances, environment and 'organic cases.'"* [Italics added.] The "science" lay in emulating the methods of Claude Bernard, who in his *Introduction to the Study of Experimental Medicine* (1865), applied experiments in chemistry and physics to physiology and medicine. By the same token, argued Zola, the "experimental" novel, using parallel methods for its own distinctive subject matter, could apply scientific method to "the two-fold life of the character and its environment." The experimental novelist could track his characters through his novel's or his drama's particular circumstances to show how (paying homage to positivism) a controlled ordering of events would demonstrate the 'determinism of phenomena.'" And so, he argued, "you possess... scientific knowledge of [the characters] in both [their] individual and social relations."

There are two important consequences to Zola's "experimental" novel concerning the description of "character:" (1) the "controlled ordering of events" is no longer understood to engage characters who are merely, and essentially, a chief motive threading through a plot, but encompasses the entire life of a character – his inherited characteristics, and the influence on his development of his environment. And all that is to be "experimentally" subjected to a series of events (the plot) to demonstrate the inevitability of the character's behavior and outcome, given the mix of those prior conditions. On the face of it, this seems little more than the old "apprenticeship" novel, but what has been added is the precise and detailed matching of each prior condition to current event and circumstance, as in Zola's own 20-volume series of novels of the Rougeon-Macquart family, in which characters' traits are tracked through generations to their ultimate behavioral consequences. (2) But probably its most important influence is this: a pattern was automatically introduced of multiple causative sequences. A character's single gesture, for example, could be shown to be the effect of a concatenation of causes, and consequently the drama itself could be shown to be governed by a mix of causative sequences that seem to function, on the face of it, as much like chance as by predictive certainties. Whatever these consequences meant for the credibility of Zola's "scientific" naturalism, they added to the possibilities of characterization, at least, a level of complexity that far exceeded those in the past. And in drama after Naturalism, Ibsen and Strindberg, far more than Zola and the other naturalists, demonstrated the extraordinary reach of those possibilities.

39. *"already noted... Wedekind's Lulu"*: (see Ch. 2, #14, above)

40. *in Stein's Three Lives:* (1906), NY, Knopf, 1936.

41. *"Meyerhold... staged Hedda Gabler:"* Vsevolod Meyerhold (1874-1940): "The walls and much of the furniture were blue-green; other furniture was white. One large chair covered in white fur served as a kind of throne for Hedda. Each character was costumed in a distinctive color and had a characteristic pose to which he or she always returned. In their most intimate scene, Hedda and Lovborg looked straight ahead at all times." [O. Brockett and R. Findlay, *A Century of Innovation*, 2nd. ed., NY, Allyn & Bacon, 1991, p.133.]

42. *Tzara's Manifestos:* Tristan Tzara (1896-1963), *Seven Dada Manifestos and Lampisteries,* (1916-1920), tr. Barbara Wright, Calder Publications (new edition), 1981.

43. *Mayakovsky's drama:* Vladimir Mayakovsky (1893-1930), *Vladimir Mayakovsky, A Tragedy* (1913), in *Mayakovsky: Plays,* tr. Guy Daniels, Evanston, IL, Northwestern UP, 1995.

"In 1913, when he was twenty, he wrote, produced and acted in his first dramatic work.   Characteristically, he called it *Vladimir Mayakovsky, A Tragedy*. He made no attempt to disguise the theme of the play, which was the celebration of his own poetic genius and apotheosis as the divine poet crowned with laurel leaves, ascending to heaven while intoning his own name…. He later extended the range of his exuberance and self-admiration until they encompassed vast unexplored regions of his ego…." [From introduction by Robert Payne, p.3.]

44.   Dada and surrealism…inanimate objects, parts of the body as characters:"

From the opening stage directions of Tristan Tzara's, *The Gas Heart* (1920): "Neck stands downstage, Nose opposite, confronting the audience…. The gas heart walks slowly around, circulating widely." The rest of the cast consists of Eye, Mouth, Ear and Eyebrow. [In M. Benedikt and G.E. Wellwarth, eds. And trs., *Modern French Theatre*,NY, Dutton, 1966, pp.132-133.]

In Rene Daumal's *en ggarrrde!*(1924), mingling with its human characters are a Toothbrush, a Cigar, a Pernot with Sugar and – close to inanimate – Some Snails. [ibid, p. 212.] Picasso, during the bleak days in World War II Paris, wrote *Desire Trapped by the Tail*, a surrealist drama with a cast of characters made up of food and the human parts involved in eating it.

Georg Grosz (1893-1959.) For the Erwin Piscator production of *The Good Soldier Schweik* (1928) in the Theatre am Nollendorfplatz in Berlin, Grosz designed cardboard cutouts for characters other than Schweik, who stood on a treadmill as though "marching," going from episode to episode as scenes and the cardboard characters passed in the opposite direction.

Bauhaus geometrical ballet figures: In Oskar Schlemmer's (1888-1943), *Triadic Ballet*, figures in three-dimensional costumes incorporated abstract geometrical forms. "He transformed into abstract terms of geometry or mechanics his observations of the human figure moving in space. " A student of Schlemmer's is quoted by Gropius: "Pace and gesture, figure and prop, color and sound, all had the quality of elementary form, demonstrating anew the problem of theater in Schlemmer's concept: man in space." [Walter Gropius, Íntroduction," in W. Gropius and A.S. Wensinger, eds, *The Theatre of the Bauhaus*,Middletown, CT, Wesleyan UP, 1961, p.8.]

45. *"Proust... Ibsen:"* The years of composition: Marcel Proust (1871-1922), *Remembrance of Things Past* (1913-1922); Gertrude Stein (1874-1946), *The Making of Americans* (1902-1911); James Joyce (1882-1941), *Finnegans Wake* (1922-1939); August Strindberg (1849-1912), *Dream Play* (1902); Henrik Ibsen (1877-1899), the last twelve play "cycle" (1877-1899)

Strindberg notes in his Dream Play, "The characters split, double, multiply, dissolve, condense, float apart, coalesce. But one mind stands over and above them all, *the mind of the dreamer*, and for him, there are no secrets, no inconsistencies, no scruples, no laws." [Italics added.] ["A Note from the Author," A Dream Play, in Evert Sprinchorn, ed. and tr., August Strindberg, Selected Plays, vol. 2, Minneapolis, U of Minn Press, 1986.

Brian Johnston on "the Ibsen cycle:" "The twelve plays from *Pillars of Society* to *When We Dead Awaken*, made up a single cyclical work, an odyssey of the human spirit directly paralleling that charted by Hegel in *The Phenomenology of Mind....* In Ibsen's own words, his plays formed a "cycle" with "mutual connections between the plays" one play being the dialectical development from its predecessor." [*Text and Supertext in Ibsen's Drama*, University Park and London, Penn State U Press, 1989, P.10.]

46. *"Schreidramen:"* The Expressionist's character's "speech... marks the boundaries of his individuality, setting him off from other individualities.... Horizontally, however, the Expressionist aims at a stylized uniformity of speech reminiscent of the classical drama. This sameness of idiom among the [other] characters... underlies the fact that the [other] characters appearing in it are fragments of a single mind." [Walter H. Sokel, *The Writer in Extremis*, Stanford, CA, Stanford UP, 1959. p.40.]

47. *Beckett's fragmentations:"* In Beckett's *The Unnamable* (1951), the multiple surrogates he had named in the trilogy that ended with *The Unnamable,* "named" in order to displace and fragment himself, are now recalled with regret that he had ever needed them: "All these Murphys, Molloys and Malones do not fool me. They have made me waste my time, suffer for nothing, speak of them when, in order to stop speaking, I should have spoken of me and me alone. But I just said I have spoken of me, am speaking of me. I don't care a curse what I just said. It is now I shall speak of me for the first time. I thought I was right in enlisting these sufferers of my pain. I

was wrong." [Samul Beckett, *The Unnamable,* in *Three Novels,* NY, Grove Press, 1955, p. 305.]

But even returning to the assurance of a singular self, he claims his victory through the old contending multiple voices.

48. *"Soul vs. Body"*: Allegorical battles between parts of the self was a popular medieval poetic genre: in Francois Villon's "The Dispute of the Heart and Body," the heart, already holding on by only "a slender string" upbraids the body for its thirty years of folly, which the body disputes, and answers in kind. [in H.W. Robbins and H.W. Coleman, *Western World Literature,* NY, Macmillan, 1938, p.399.]

The fifteenth century morality play, *Everyman, ibid.,* p.415.]

49. *"Plato's willful steeds"*: In *The Republic,* Plato defines Justice as the harmony of the three parts of the soul in the individual, reflecting the harmony of the three classes of citizens in the state. The idea is made graphic in one of the most famous passages in Plato, in which he describes, in the *Phaedrus,* the charioteer and his two steeds:

"I divided each soul into three – two horses and a charioteer, and one of the horses was good and the other bad…. The right hand horse is upright and clearly made…. He is a lover of honesty and modesty and temperance, and the follower of true glory; he needs no touch of the whip, but is guided by word and admonition only. The other is a crooked, bumbling animal, put together anyhow… the mate of insolence and pride, … hardly yielding to the whip and the spur.

"Now when the charioteer beholds the vision of love, and is full of the prickings and ticklings of desire, the obedient steed, then as always under the government of shame, refrains from leaping on the beloved; but the other, heedless of the pricks and the blows of the whip, plunges and runs away, giving all manner of trouble to his companion and the charioteer, whom he forces to approach the beloved and to remember the joys of love…. [But] the charioteer falls backwards… and by his fall is compelled to pull back the reins with such violence as to bring both steeds on their haunches. [The charioteer after overcoming the violence of the wild steed] from that time forward the soul of the lover follows the beloved with modesty and holy fear." [Plato, *Phaedrus,* in *Symposium and Phaedrus,* tr. Benjamin Jowett, Dover New ed., 1994.]

Plato's charioteer and his two steeds reemerge in the Seventeenth Century's French neoclassicist's struggle involving Reason, Passion and Will, in which Passion, like Plato's left-hand steed, is violently desiring, and the Will like the right-hand steed is allied to the judgment of Reason. The classic example of this in drama is Corneille's *Cinna,* in which the reason of the Emperor Augustus harnesses his will in a mighty, and at last successful, struggle to control the temptations of his passions to abandon ethical reason altogether. (See above, p.221-2.)

50. *"English four humours:"* Derived initially from the Sixth Century B.C., in the earliest period of Greek psychological investigation, when the doctrine of the temperaments first appeared. A temperament was regarded as a peculiar disposition which owed its character to the ratio in which the "humours" were mixed in the body. These humours were four in substance which, by analogy with the four elements of earth, air, fire and water, were regarded as composing the body. In the Medieval period, an Arab physician introduced the terms for the different temperaments, sanguine, phlegmatic, melancholic and choleric, and were so adopted in Western Medieval medical theory and practice. It was Ben Jonson among Elizabethan playwrights who most prominently adopted – and adapted – the concept to serve characterization in his comedy, in which human folly deserves to be "scourged" when "the confluxions all run one way." The "tribe of Ben," his followers among English playwrights, subscribed moderately to this notion of satiric characterization, but remained more true to the tradition of Theophrastus' "Characters," i.e., emblematic social rather than psychological/moral types, less interested in their correction than in their detailed comic depiction.

51. *"id-ego-superego infighting"*: In 1923, Freud in *The Ego and the Id* substituted these terms for his original tripartite division of personality into *conscious, preconscious,* and *unconscious.* In the transformation, the three elements of personality became more conscientiously interactive and bellicose. In dealing with one another, the superego represses and punishes the transgressions of the id, the id yearns unrepentantly, and the ego copes as best it can with the anxieties and tensions of the id as well as the demands of the superego for it to reach beyond the mere "reality principle" to emulate the ideals and values of the superego's demanding legislation. What had been merely descriptive terms transformed into volitionally aggressive terms. [Sigmund Freud, *The Ego and the*

Id, in *Complete Psychological Works of Sigmund Freud,*   ed. James
Strachey, NY, Norton, 1962.]

8. THE ACTOR AS PLAYWRIGHT

1.   *four character attributes:* see Ch. 7, #16, above

2.   Aristotle   "characters   must   be   consistent…   consistently
inconsistent:" [Passage quoted on Ch. 8 1ˢᵗ 2 pgs before #1, above]

3.   *Hamlet in Saxo-Grammaticus:"* Shakespeare's tragedy is derived from
the story of Amleth in Saxo-Grammaticus' *The History of Denmark*
(c.1200AD).   The Hamlet we know obviously traveled a
considerable distance from hls source, but a residue of the "single-
minded" savagery of Amleth, and his ploy of "madness," remains.
Amleth's return from England – where, unlike Hamlet, he actually
lived for a number of years – is for the unrelenting purpose of
effecting his revenge and claiming his throne.   The Hamlet who
returns to Denmark is a mature, a somewhat tempered courtier, as
though the ambivalence of his motives has been – perhaps uneasily
– resolved.   Compare Amleth's motive, and his accomplishments,
on his return:

"On reaching Jutland [i.e., Denmark] he exchanged his present
attire for his ancient demeanor, which he had adopted for righteous
ends, purposely assuming the aspect of absurdity.   Covered with
filth, he entered the banquet-room where his own obsequies were
being held, and struck all men utterly aghast, rumour having falsely
noised abroad his death.   At last terror melted into mirth, and the
guests jeered and taunted one another, that he whose last rites they
were celebrating as though he were dead, should appear in the
flesh….   Thereupon, wishing to bring the company into a gayer
mood, he jollied the cupbearers, and diligently did the office of
plying the drink….   Then, to smooth the way more safely to his
plot, he went to the lords and plied them heavily with draught upon
draught, and drenched them all so deep in wine, that their feet
were made feeble with drunkenness….   Then he saw they were in a
fit state for his plots, and thought that here was a chance to do his
purpose.   So he took out of his bosom the stakes he had so long
prepared, and went into the building where the ground was covered
with the bodies of the nobles wheezing off their sleep and their
debauch.   Then, cutting away its support, he brought down the
hanging his mother had knitted, which covered the inner as well as
the outer walls of the hall.   This he flung upon the snorers, and

then applying the crooked stakes, he knotted and bound them up in such insoluble intricacy, that not one of the men beneath, however hard he might struggle, could contrive to rise. After this he set fire to the palace. The flames spread, scattering the conflagration far and wide until it enveloped the whole dwelling... and burned them all while they were either buried in deep sleep or vainly trying to arise.... Then awakening his uncle, he told him that his nobles were perishing in the flames, and that Amleth was here, armed with his crooks to help him, and thirsting to exact the vengeance, now long overdue, for his father's murder. Feng, on hearing this, leapt from his couch, but was cut down while deprived of his own sword.... O valiant Amleth, and worthy of immortal fame, who being shrewdly armed with a feint of folly, covered a wisdom too high for human wit under a marvelous disguise of silliness! And not only found in his subtlety means to protect his own safety, but also by its guidance found opportunity to avenge his father." [*The History of Denmark*, Book III]

4. *Nero Wolfe:* the fictional detective in the novels of Rex Stout (1934-75).

5. *Arsenic and Old Lace:* (1944), by Joseph Kesselring, (1902-1967), NY, Dramatists Play Service, 1995.

6. *Phantom of the Opera:* (1910), the novel by Gaston Le Roux;

   Hunchback of Notre Dame: (1831), the novel by Victor Hugo (1802-1885);

   The Flying Dutchman: (1841), the opera by Richard Wagner (1813-1883);

   The Wandering Jew: (1844), the novel by Eugene Sue.

7. *"The Baron, Nastya's pimp:" in The Lower Depths,* Act 4, tr. Alexander Bakshy, eds., Block and Shedd, *op. cit.*, p.242.

8. *"Stanislavsky... Gaev:"* Constantin Stanislavky (1863-1938), in the first (1904) production of *The Cherry Orchard*, (about which Chekhov complained because of its "heavy-handed, tragic" quality, the opposite of his own notion that it was a comedy and a farce.)

   Henry Irving: (1838-1903), in his role as Matthias in *The Bells,* by Leopold Lewis, adapted from Erchmann-Chatrian's novel, *The Polish Jew*, (the role that overnight established Irving as England's leading actor.)

Olivier: Laurence Olivier (1907-1989), in his role as Richard III, stage production, 1944; film, 1954 (the makeup for which, "long dark dank hair, crooked nose, twisted body, spindly legs, one shorter than the other, stunted hand," was reputed to require four hours of assembly before each performance.)

His performance in *Othello*, 1964, at the National Theatre of Great Britain, a similarly laborious makeup and costume (but was somehow modeled on the appearance of a contemporary African-American, rather than a Renaissance Moor) was nevertheless lauded as "the greatest performance of the greatest actor of our time."

9.   Hamlets:

John Gielgud, his first performance of the role at the London Old Vic in 1930;

Lawrence Olivier, in the film *Hamlet,* 1948, directed by Olivier, produced by Two Cities Films, Ltd, (uncredited) screen adaptation by Olivier;

Smotunovsky, Innokenti Smotunovsky, in the Russian film, 1963, *Gamlet,* directed by Grigori Kozintsev and Josif Shapiro, screenplay adaptation by Kozintzev from the translation by Boris Pasternak.

Mel Gibson, in the film *Hamlet,* 1990, directed by Franco Zefirelli, produced by Canal and Warner Brothers, screenplay adaptation by Christopher de Vore.

10.   *"Duse's deep flush:"* "Before long, there came a stroke of acting that will probably never be forgotten by those who saw it.... In the third act of the play, she is on the stage when [her former lover] is announced as a visitor. The moment she read the card handed her by the servant, you realized what it was to have to face a meeting with the man.... He paid his compliments and offered his flowers; they sat down; and she evidently felt that she had got it safely over and might allow herself to think at her ease, and to look at him to see how much he had altered. Then a terrible thing happened to her. She began to blush; and in another moment was conscious of it, and the blush was slowly spreading and deepening until, after a few vain efforts to avert her face or to obstruct his view of it without seeming to do so, she gave up and hid the blush in her hands.... I could detect no trick in it: it seemed to me a perfectly genuine effect of the dramatic imagination.... And I must confess

to an intense professional curiosity as to whether it always comes off so spontaneously."

[Bernard Shaw, *Our Theatres in the Nineties*, vol. 1, pp. 153-154.]

"Nazimova's Hedda Gabler:" Alla Nazimova (1879-1945) took extraordinary liberties in her acting with which some in her audiences were overwhelmingly in accord, while others, like the "method" director and critic Harold Clurman, condemned for their flagrant wanderings from "naturalism." In the role of Hedda (her fourth production of the play in 1936, under her own direction, in an intensely restudied role she had already performed in 1906, 1907, and 1918), she moved with the extravagant freedom of a dancer – her movement resembling no one's so much as the greatest of modern dancer's, Martha Graham – and her voice was far closer to operatic delivery than to ordinary speech: her voice could rise and fall as much as three octaves in a single sentence. The expressivity of her acting had little relation to "naturalism." It was closer to what one might imagine was the performance range of actors in the amphitheatres of Fifth Century Athens, and consequently touched on moments in modern dramas – especially when she was performing Ibsen, Chekhov or O'Neill – that left one as overwhelmed and grateful as Bernard Shaw so memorably was after performances by Eleanora Duse.

11. *"Olivier's Oedipus… Astrov:"* *Oedipus the King* in Yeats' translation and Chekhov's *Uncle Vanya* in Constance Garnett's translation, were performed in repertory in the Old Vic productions brought to the U.S. in early 1946.

12. *Andre Serban,* directed the production of *The Cherry Orchard*, 1977, at the Lincoln Center, NY.

13. "Stanislavsky's… spine of the action:" "The conclusion to be drawn from this is: "Above all preserve your super-objective and through line of action. Be wary of all extraneous tendencies and purposes foreign to the main theme…. Everything that we have undertaken in this first course has been directed toward enabling you to obtain control over three most important features in our creative process: (1) Inner grasp; (2) The through line of action; (3) The super-objective…. We have covered all these points in general terms. Now you know what we mean by our 'system.'" [An Actor Prepares, tr., E.R. Hapgood, NY, Routledge, 1964, pp. 278-279.]

The underlying belief and major difficulty in Stanislavsky's teaching is his supposition of a rigidly logical structure in every play and of every character in it. For an actor or director to follow his teaching, it's necessary to contort the actuality of a play or a role into this straight line, this "spine," even in plays which march to no such lockstep. It's had its effect on playwrights too, who, taking his lessons seriously, have adhered to the same Nineteenth Century well-made play model, to which Stanislavsky's suppositions about plays' "spines" remained anachronistically loyal.

14. *"Strasberg's production:"* Lee Strasberg (1901-1982). Director, *Three Sisters'* Actor's Studio production, NY, 1964.

9. DIALOGUE

1. The Poetics on dialogue: in The Poetics, Chapter 19.

2. Plato, *Protagoras,* (380BC) in *op.cit.*

3. *"Nora's macaroons:"* In Act I, Nora conceals the macaroons she has been eating when Torvald enters: a "white lie" for her husband. [*A Doll House,* in *Ibsen's Major Prose Plays,* Act One, p.126.]

4. Miller's All My Sons (1947); A View from the Bridge (1955): in Collected Plays.

5. *"Shaw's Mrs. Warren:"* Bernard Shaw, *Mrs. Warren's Profession,* (written 1893; produced 1902), in Sandie Byrne, ed., *George Bernard Shaw's Plays,* NY, Norton, 2002.

6. Eugene O'Neill, Touch of the Poet (written 1942;produced1958), in Touch of the Poet and More Stately Mansions, ed., M.G. Bower, Yale UP, 2004.

7. *Chekhov's The Sea Gull:* (1896) in *Chekhov: The Major Plays,* NY, New American Library, 1964, p.108.

8. *"Yerushalmi in Israel:"* The Three Sisters, directed by Rina Yerushalmi, ITIM Theatre Ensemble, Cameri Theatre, Tel-Aviv, 2005.

9. *Pulp Fiction:* (1994), directed by Quentin Tarantino, produced by Miramax Films, Jersey Films, A Band Apart, screenplay by Tarantino from stories by Tarantino and Roger Avery.

10. *"football saga":* *Knut Rockne, All American:* (1940), directed by Robert Buckner, produced by Warner Brothers Pictures, screenplay by

Buckner. (The dying character whose lines are quoted was played by Ronald Regan.)

11. *Clifford Odets* (1906-1963), *Paradise Lost,* (1935), NY Random House, 1936.

12. *"leadenly uniform first-level... dialogue:* from "Lost Son," *CSI: Miami*, directed by Duane Clark, teleplay by Ann Donahue & Elizabeth Devine, aired CBS, 9/20/04.

13. *Webster, Duchess of Malfi:* John Webster (1580-1634), *Duchess of Malfi* (1612-1614), *op.cit.,* Act IV, sc.2, page 514.

14. *"subtext in Stanislavsky's sense:"* (See Endnote for Ch. 8, #8, above.)

15. "Shklovsky... the familiar unfamiliar": "The purpose of art, according to Shklovsky, is to force us to notice. Since perception is usually too automatic, art develops a variety of techniques to impede perception, or, at least, to call attention to themselves.... The chief technique for promoting such perception is 'defamiliarization.' It is not so much a device as a result obtainable by any number of devices. A novel point of view, as Shklovsky points out, can make a reader perceive by making the familiar seem strange."

     L.T. Lemon and M.J. Reis, trs, and eds, in Introduction to Victor Shklovsky, "Art as Technique," in *Russian Formalist Criticism: Four Essays,* Univ. of Nebraska Press, Lincoln, NB, pp. 3,4.

16. The Unfamiliar Made Familiar: ibid.

17. *Edmund in Lear: King Lear,* Act I, sc.2, lines 1-22: "Thou, nature, art my goddess...."

18. *Aaron in Titus Andronicus:* Act II, sc.1., lines 1-24: "Now climbeth Tamora Olympus' top...."

19. *Hamm in Endgame: ibid,* The soliloquy that begins: "It's finished," p.50-54.

20. Franz in *The Robbers* (1782) by Friedrich von Schiller (1759-1805)

21. *"Harper's airborne reflection:"* Tony Kushner (1956-), *Angels in America, Part two: Perestroika* (1992), NY, Theatre Communications Group, 1994, p,144.

22. Harold Pinter,(1930 –) The Homecoming: (1965), in Complete Works, vol. 3, 1978, p. 46.

23. *Pulp Fiction:* see Endnote Ch. 9, #9, above

24. *Mamet's Spartan:* (2004), David Mamet (1947-   ), directed by David Mamet, produced by Apollo Media, screenplay by Mamet.

25. Pinter's The Birthday Party: (1958), in Harold Pinter, The Birthday Party and The Room, NY, Grove Press, 1961, pp.77-78.

26. *A Slight Ache,* (1959), in *Complete Works,* vol. 1, pp. 191-193.

27. Sexual Perversity in Chicago: (1974); in Sexual Perversity in Chicago and The Duck Variations, NY, Random House, 1978.

    American Buffalo, Arion Press, 1992.

28. *Mamet's A Life in the Theatre* (1977). [NY, Grove Press, 1977, pp.191-193.]

29. *Watchman's speech:"* in Aeschylus, *Agamemnon,* (458BC) lines 1-37.

30. Chorus of old men: Agamemnon, lines 38-257.

31. Oscar Wilde's Lady Windermere's Fan: (1892), op.cit., Act I.

32. *Augustus in Cinna:* Pierre Corneille (1606-1684), *Cinna* (1640), Act II, Sc.1, in *Six Plays by Corneille and Racine,* tr. Paul Landis, NY, Modern Library, 1931.

33. "second speech of justification:" ibid, Act IV, sc.2.

34. *Rodrigue's speech:* Corneille, *Le Cid* (1633), in *Six Plays,* Act I, sc.6.

35. *Medea's speech:* Euripides, *Medea,* lines 1031-1074.

36. *Danton's speech:* Georg Buchner (1813-1837), *Danton's Death,* (1835), Act IV, sc.1, in *Complete Plays and Prose,* tr. Carl R. Mueller, Hill and Wang, 1963.

37. "Hermione defends herself:" Winter's Tale, Act II, sc.1, lines 33-125.

38. Agrippina's speech: Jean Racine, Britannicus, , in Six Plays, Act III, sc.2.

39. Hippolytus's speech: Euripides, Hippolytus, lines 986-1039.

40. "Mark Antony's speech of persuasion:" Julius Caesar, Act III, sc.2, lines 79-266.

41. "Lear's denunciation of his daughters:" Act III, sc.1, lines 267-288.

42. *Oedipus' denunciation:* Sophocles, *Oedipus at Colonus,* (406BC) tr. Robert Fitzgerald, in D. Grene and R. Lattimore, *The Complete Greek Tragedies, Sophocles,* Vol.1, U. of Chicago Press, lines 1354-1396.

43. *Philoctetes' speech:* Sophocles, *Philoctetes,* (409BC), tr. David Grene, in *Sophocles,* Vol.2, lines 927-963.

44. Rojas' Celestina: Rojas, *Celestina,* in Eric Bentley, ed, *The Classic Theatre, Vol. Three: Six Spanish Plays,* NY, Doubleday, 1960.

45. Anne Frankford: in A Woman Killed with Kindness, op.cit., Act IV, sc.5, p.188.

46. *Guess Who's Coming to Dinner?:*(1967), directed by Stanley Kramer, produced by Stanley Kramer Productions, screenplay by William Rose.

47. Final chorus, Oedipus at Colonus: op.cit., lines 1777-1779:

48. *Samson Agonistes:* John Milton (1608-1674), *Samson Agonistes* (1671):

> "Nothing is here for tears, nothing to wail
> Or knock the breast, no weakness, no contempt,
> Dispraise, or blame, nothing but well and fair,
> And what may quiet us in a death so noble....
> And calm of mind all passion spent."

[F.T. Prince, ed., *Sampson Agonistes,* Oxford UP, 1970.]

49. "exodus of... Prospero: The Tempest, "Epilogue," lines 1-20.

50. "[Lear's] howling at the storm:" Act III, sc.2, lines 1-25.

51. *"interrupted double sonnet:" Romeo and Juliet,* Act I, sc.5. The completed first sonnet, lines 94-108; the first four lines of the second, lines 109-112, is interrupted by the Nurse's call.

52. *"Henry's harangue to his soldiers:"* There are two harangues: the first begins, "Once more into the breach, dear friends," in Act III, sc.1, lines 1-34; and the second begins, "What's he that wishes so..." in Act III, sc.3, lines 18-67.

53. Blanche recounting the suicide: A Streetcar Named Desire, in The Theatre of Tennessee Williams,NY, New Directions, 1971, vol.1., pp. 354-355.

54. Amanda Wingate soliciting: The Glass Menagerie, ibid., sc.3, ibid, vol. 1, p.160.

55. Catherine's account: Summer and Smoke, sc.4, ibid, vol.3, pp. 411-422.

56. *Big Daddy telling: Cat on a Hot Tin Roof,* Act III (Broadway version), *ibid,* vol.3, pp.205-206.

57. Hannah's recitation: Night of the Iguana, Act III,   ibid, vol.4, pp.361-363.

58. Levene's speech beginning "Bruce, Harriet..." David Mamet, Glengarry Glen Ross, NY, Grove Press, 1983, pp. 72-73.

59. Crow's speech: Sam Shepard (1943-) Tooth of Crime, in Tooth of Crime and Geography of a Horse Dreamer,   NY, Grove Press, 1974, pp.44;52-53.

60. *Levee's speech: Ma Rayney's Black Bottom,* NY, New American Library, 1985. pp. 99-100.

61. Harper's speech: op,cit, p.144.

10. "PACKAGING" MEANING

1. *"Nietzsche... reassures us... about thought:"* Nietzsche, *The Will to Power,* tr. A.M. Ludovici, in *The Complete Works of Friedrich Nietzsche,* ed. Oscar Levy, vol. 15, NY, Russell and Russell, 1964, p. 105.

2. *"Shklovsky:"* Victor Shklovsky (1893-   ), "Art as Technique," in *Russian Formalist Criticism: Four Essays,* tr. & ed., L.T. Lemon and M.J. Reis, Lincoln, NB, University of Nebraska, pp.3-24.

3. *"Chomsky:"* Noam Chomsky (1928-). The principle that an innate knowledge of basic grammatical structure is common to all languages, is "modeled" entirely within the structures of sentences.

4: *"early Wittgenstein:"* Ludwig Wittgenstein (1889-19521), in *Tractatus-Logico-Philosophicus* (1921), "early" Wittgenstein's "picture theory of meaning" represented every "atomic" sentence as forming a logical picture in which exactly the same formal structure as the atomic sentence itself is mirrored. Hans Sluga, "Ludwig Wittgenstein," *Cambridge Dictionary of Philosophy,* 1945.

5. *"Einstein once said...:"* Benedict Carey, "Analyze These," The NY Times, April 25, 2006, an article reporting on a May 11, 2006 exhibition of Freud's drawings at the NY Academy of Medicine.

6: *"Eyes turn in:"* Gertrude Stein (1874-1946), Notebook N-1, in *The Notebooks of Gertrude Stein* (unpublished.)

7. *"That world history repeats…:"* Bertrand Russell, *A History of Western Philosophy,* NY, Simon and Schuster, 1945, p.735.

8. *"Herbert Spencer:"* (1820-1903). "His synthetic philosophy, expanded in books written over many years, assumes (both in biology and psychology) the existence of Lamarchian evolution…. The human condition is perfectible… implying that evil and immorality will eventually disappear."

    R.E. Butts, "Herbert Spencer," *Cambridge Dictionary.*

9. *"Wittgenstein's 'language games:'"* "Middle" Wittgenstein, in a revision of his earlier "picture theory of language:" "Language was not strictly held together by logical structure, but consisted in fact of a multiplicity of simpler substructures or *language games.* Sentences could not be taken to be logical pictures of facts and the simple components of sentences did not all function as names of simple objects." H. Sluga, *op cit.*

10. *"Do you know, do you know:"* Gertrude Stein, *The Mother of Us All,* in Carl Van Vechten, ed., *Last Operas and Plays,* NY, Rinehart, 1949, p.88.

11. *"Freud's Rosmersholm:"* Sigmund Freud, "Those Wrecked by Success," in James Strachey *et al* ., eds., *Complete Works of Sigmund Freud,* vol.14, London, Hogarth Press, 1957, pp.316-331.

12. "imperiled the effect of the drama:" ibid, p.329.

13. *"Shaw's Rosmersholm:"* George Bernard Shaw, "The Plays: Rosmersholm," in The Quintessence of Ibsenism* (1890), NY Dover reprint of NY, Brentano's 1904 edition, pp.51-55.

14. "What, during all these overthrowings…:" "The Two Pioneers," ibid., pp. 8-9.

15. "What I have sinned…:" "The Plays: Rosmersholm," op.cit., p.55.

16. *"Johnston's Rosmersholm:"* Brian Johnston (1932-   ), "The Dialectic of *Rosmersholm,"* *The Ibsen Cycle* (revised ed.), University Park, PA, Pennsylvania State UP, 1992, pp.237-288.

17. "While watching an Ibsen play…:" ibid. p.244.

18. "The psychology of Rosmersholm:" ibid, p.244.

19. *"Hegel's Phenomenology of Spirit:"* (1807), The introduction to Hegel's comprehensive philosophy, one of the major texts in Western

philosophy. G.W.F. Hegel, A.V. Miller and Findlay, tr.&ed., Oxford UP, 1977.

20. "The grave closing moments…:" Johnston op.cit, pp. 285f.

21. *"some pages back:"* see Ch. 8 (p. 224) after #14, above.

AFTERWORD

1. "There is a story:" "[H]e said every now and then there is one like that.   He said when the rest of the pigs were all in the slaughterhouse, they would have to come back and take this one alone, section by section of movable fence. Franz and I went away excited and happy to have seen a hero among the pigs…" Elia Katz, Armed Love, NY, Bantam Books, 1971, p.100

Made in the USA
Lexington, KY
19 November 2012